One Billion Dollars of Influence
The Direct Marketing of Politics

R. KENNETH GODWIN

University of Arizona

CHATHAM HOUSE PUBLISHERS, INC.
Chatham, New Jersey

CHATHAM HOUSE SERIES ON CHANGE IN AMERICAN POLITICS

SERIES EDITOR: Aaron Wildavsky
University of California, Berkeley

ONE BILLION DOLLARS OF INFLUENCE
The Direct Marketing of Politics

CHATHAM HOUSE PUBLISHERS, INC.
Post Office Box One
Chatham, New Jersey 07928

Copyright © 1988 by Chatham House Publishers, Inc.

PUBLISHER: Edward Artinian
ILLUSTRATIONS: Adrienne Shubert
COVER DESIGN: Antler & Baldwin, Inc.
COMPOSITION: Chatham Composer
PRINTING AND BINDING: Port City Press

LIBRARY OF CONGRESS CATALOGING-IN-PUBLICATION DATA

Godwin, R. Kenneth
    One billion dollars of influence.

    (Chatham House series on change in American politics)
    Bibliography: p.
    Includes index.
    1. Pressure groups--United States--Finance.
2. Political action committees--United States--Finance.
3. Direct marketing--United States. I. Title.
II. Series.
JK1118.G63   1988   324'.4'0973   88-28540
ISBN 0-934540-68-3

Manufactured in the United States of America
10 9 8 7 6 5 4 3 2 1

Contents

Acknowledgments

I owe a debt to many persons who helped in the preparation of this book. Four graduate students at the University of Arizona—Irini Kariallious-Kutoroff, Mohammed Bramazadeh, Silvia Pinal, and Uri Maimon—provided research, coding, and computer assistance. My colleagues in the department of political science brought in political direct mailings that they received and without which the book would have been far less interesting. John Schwarz, Jeanne Clarke, and John Crow, colleagues within my department, not only provided mailings but read earlier drafts of the manuscript and made extensive comments.

I owe special thanks to Robert C. Mitchell for making his National Environmental Membership study data available to me, and to Dr. Margaret Latus Nugent of Marquette University who provided me with her interviews with political party fund raisers and direct-mail specialists.

Because this book is intended to be read by persons who are not social scientists, I relied on my wife, Karen Sato Godwin, and my mother, Ethel Godwin, to keep jargon to a minimum and to ensure that bright, educated persons would find the manuscript readable. Although I did not always appreciate their suggestions, I inevitably benefited from them. I owe a special debt to my friend and colleague Jim Clarke for his extensive editorial suggestions and his incisive and useful comments. He gave far more time than I had any right to expect. I would like to thank the series editor, Aaron Wildavsky, for his prompt evaluation of the manuscript and the Chatham House publisher and editor for their helpful suggestions.

Much of the funding that allowed the preparation of this manuscript came from the National Science Foundation and the Social and Behavioral Science Research Institute of the University of Arizona.

For my son
ERIK KINJI

Introduction

Just When You Thought Your Children Were Safe from Homosexual Advances, Congress Introduces House Resolution #427: "The Gay Bill of Rights."
—Mailing from Murray Norris,
president of Christian Family Renewal

The first time I went out to the pack ice and saw the seal hunt, I was with a British veterinarian . . . *the very first baby seal. It was being skinned alive by a Canadian fisherman.*

I rushed over to save the little creature from torture, but it died before I could intervene.
—Mailing from Brian Davies, executive director of
the International Fund for Animal Welfare

I am writing you today to alert you to a radical Big Labor takeover in the schools of your community.

The National Education Association (NEA)—a union second only to the Teamsters in size and power—is about to seize total control of public education in America. . . .

Here are just a few of the NEA's official goals:

☐ permitting avowed homosexuals to teach children;
☐ legalizing marijuana;
☐ and indoctrinating teenagers in agitating for a nuclear freeze.
—Mailing from Senator Steve Symms
for the Heritage Foundation

The excerpts above are from letters I received, inviting me to participate in surveys to be sent to members of Congress and to contribute funds to the organizations sending the letters. They are typical of more than 200 million direct mailings sent to generate resources for political action. And they are representative of the most effective approach for involving people in politics: direct marketing.

To understand how effective direct marketing has become as a political tool we need only compare the fund-raising results of the Republican party in the 1972 and 1984 elections. With legal and illegal maneuvering and arm twisting, Richard Nixon's Committee to Re-Elect the President in 1972 generated less than half as much money as the Republican national committees raised through direct-mail programs for the 1984 election. The direct marketing of politics induced 14 million persons to give money to political candidates and causes, raised almost $1 billion, and generated over 20 million letters to Congress during the 1983-84 election cycle.[1] The success that direct marketing demonstrated, not only in political fund raising, but also in mobilizing the masses to action, has changed dramatically how political resources are generated and utilized in American politics. This book examines how this new technology works and what its impact on the American political system has been in the past and is likely to be in the future.

Americans are increasingly worried about money in politics.[2] Organizations such as Common Cause, which complains that we have "the best Congress money can buy," have devoted a large percentage of their political resources lobbying for laws that would reduce the amount of money involved in political campaigns. Congress has responded by passing piecemeal "reforms" designed to limit the impact of money, but most of these efforts have been aimed at reducing the contributions of large donors and have done little to address the megadollars that direct marketing has produced. In fact, the 1971 Federal Campaign Finance Act and its 1974 amendments were major forces in encouraging direct marketing's expansion. Rather than have "fat cats" contribute tens of thousands of dollars as individuals, political consultants like Richard Viguerie on the right and Roger Craver on the left now use direct mail to raise hundreds of thousands or even millions. And, as the quotes that opened this book suggest, these messages appeal not to reasoned thought and opinion, but to fear and outrage.

To investigate the political uses and impact of direct marketing this book addresses several important "hows": How does the direct marketing of politics work? How have the users of the new technologies attempted to change politics and political participation in the United States? How much success have these efforts had? And how has direct marketing altered public policy and the way that public officials make their decisions? To explore these issues, this volume looks at the many criticisms of political direct marketing and examines the opportunities that these new technologies provide to improve democratic government. Direct mail is the most important of these because it far surpasses all other marketing innovations in both use and effectiveness. To a large degree, the other direct-marketing techniques, such as cable television, low-cost long-distance telephone communication, and interactive computer hookups, depend on direct mail to get started and to stay funded. Direct mail is the meat and potatoes of computer-based politics; all other direct-marketing and communication innovations are merely sauces and desserts.

The Rapid Development of Direct Mail

Direct mail emerged as an important political weapon as early as 1952 when Dwight Eisenhower ran as the Republican candidate for President.[3] Eisenhower entered the race unsure of which issues he should emphasize. An innovative staff member, one who probably had a good background in new product promotions, suggested that the best way to choose among issues would be to try several topics or themes at the same time. To do this, the campaign sent a different fund-raising letter to ten groups of 10,000 persons—each letter stressing a different issue. The letter that discussed the Korean war received the biggest response, raised the most money, and indicated to Eisenhower that this was the issue he should use to become the next President of the United States.

By 1962, members of the House and Senate had discovered direct mail and the value of their franking privilege.[4] Elected representatives spent $4.9 million dollars on "free" political mailings to constituents in that year alone. By 1980, the figure had risen to well over $100 million and by the mid-1980s *Congressional Quarterly* estimated that more than a billion pieces of franked mail would be sent, for which the Postal Service would bill Congress close to $150 million.[5] These costs do not include the staff time required to write and print the mailings.[6] Studies of congressional campaigns have shown that the franking privilege represents the single most important perquisite of office in a congressperson's reelection campaign.[7]

Today, with low-cost computers and quality computer printing techniques, direct mail is an important political weapon, not only in campaigns, but also in lobbying Congress, mobilizing the public to political action, and obtaining members for citizen action groups.

Direct mail may be unsurpassed as a campaign fund raiser. In the first four months of 1984, the Reagan reelection campaign raised over $12 million through direct mail, and the Republican party raised over $200 million for all 1984 races.[8] In 1980 and 1982, ideological political action committees (PACs) such as the National Conservative Political Action Committee (NCPAC), used direct marketing to raise over $100 million. Direct mail has changed the meaning of "expensive election" in races for Congress. Jesse Helms, the "$7 million dollar man" in his 1978 election, spent $12 million in his 1984 race, the majority of which came from responses to direct-mail solicitations.

Direct mail also offers lobbyists exceptional opportunities to pressure elected officials. In 1976, Richard Viguerie, the chief organizer and the direct-mail specialist for the New Right, mobilized 720,000 letters to President Gerald Ford demanding that he veto labor's common situs picketing bill;[9] and, during the 1977-78 debate over the Panama Canal Treaty, the New Right sent out between 7 and 9 million letters as part of a mobilization drive to defeat the treaty.[10]

3

This same mailing list received much of the credit for getting Ronald Reagan's 1981 budget cuts through a Democratic House of Representatives. Still other beneficiaries of direct-marketing's selling capabilities have been citizen action groups such as Common Cause, the National Organization for Women, the National Rifle Association, the American Civil Liberties Union, and the Moral Majority. Many of these associations depend almost entirely on direct mail to recruit members and contributors.

At the same time that low-cost, high-speed computers were making direct mail available to almost any existing (or potential) association or interest group, two changes in the social and political systems greatly enhanced the impact of direct mail. First, citizen participation in social movements became increasingly common as civil rights, antiwar, women's, antiabortion, and environmental movements spawned citizen action groups such as the National Organization for Women, Friends of the Earth, and Right to Life. Direct mail often provided the communication channel that allowed the national leadership of these groups to mobilize members for action.

The second factor enhancing the impact of direct mail was a change in federal laws governing campaign contributions. The 1971 Federal Election Campaign Act and its 1974 amendments, legislation designed to reduce the abuses of past elections by minimizing the advantages of organized political interests, made small contributions from many individuals increasingly important to political success and encouraged the phenomenal rise of a new kind of political organization: the political action committee. This combination of computer innovation, a rise in social movements, and new legislation has made direct mail a major political tool and has created a new kind of politician: the direct-mail expert.[11]

Criticisms of Direct Marketing

The emergence of direct mail for recruiting and mobilizing the public into national citizen action groups and for generating political contributions creates substantial alarm among academicians, journalists, and politicians. David Broder writes that direct mail and the single-issue political action groups it spawns lead to political extremism among the public and "gutless government" by political elites.[12] Daniel Bell and Robert Teeter agree that direct mail and its associated citizen action groups and political action committees are further fragmenting an already dangerously fragmented political party structure.[13] According to Mary Topolsky, large, direct-mail-based citizen action groups such as Common Cause are a symptom of a sick society in which individual citizens choose to abandon true democratic political participation where persons meet and debate face to face. Instead, they select ersatz political participation in which the electorate responds only to a national elite that communicates through direct mail.[14] Perhaps the strongest condemnation of direct-mail and direct-mail-based citizen action groups comes from Michael Hayes. He argues that these forces are creating a "mass society" in which intolerance triumphs over tolerance, and national elites, not held accountable by the ballot box, manipulate the public.[15] Such criticisms indicate the importance of understanding direct mail and other computer-based political innovations. Are these new technologies endangering the American political system? If so, how can they be prevented from doing so?

Not all comments concerning the direct marketing of political ideas and candidates are negative. A minority sees this new technology as a positive innovation that allows greater democratic participation and a more equitable access to political information than currently exists. These writers view the direct connection between national elites and the public as a breakthrough in democracy. They believe that new direct communication technologies, particularly two-way cable television, make it possible for a large, heterogeneous country to achieve a truly national consensus.[16] This book examines the extent to which the new technologies have brought new people into politics, whether these new activists come from social strata not previously represented, and what possibilities these innovations may present in the future. Will direct marketing make America more democratic by bringing in citizens whose views have not previously been heard in the political process, or will these technologies make America less democratic by encouraging intolerance and creating a political elite that is not accountable to democratic institutions?

To learn how direct mail actually works we look at why people respond to direct-marketing appeals. How is communication structured and what messages does it contain? Do the political orientations of the new recruits really differ from those of persons who respond to traditional recruiting and mobilization techniques? To what extent do direct-mail-based campaign contributions actually affect electoral outcomes? To what extent do political leaders respond to lobbying and electoral activities mobilized through direct mail, cable television, and WATS lines?

Political organizations use direct mail in four important ways: (1) to advertise issues, programs, and candidates; (2) to mobilize public pressure on political decision makers; (3) to raise money for electoral campaigns and organizational maintenance; and (4) to recruit new members for citizen action groups. Before the use of direct mail and inexpensive long-distance telephone lines, elites who wanted to accomplish these tasks had to rely on radio and television or regionally organized institutions such as political parties and voluntary associations.

Radio and television have generally proven both expensive and ineffective for long-term organizational recruitment and maintenance; as a result, national elites have depended on local institutions and leaders to get their message to persons at the local level. Thus, local leaders provided a buffer between the national elite and the public. They minimized the exploitation and manipulation of the masses by the national elites and siphoned away the direct pressure the masses could exert on the elites.[17]

The National Farmer's Alliance (Populists) in the 1880s provides one example. Although the alliance had national leaders such as William Jennings Bryan and national symbols like "the cross of gold," the movement depended on local leaders and newspapers to give local meaning to national symbols, to keep followers mobilized, and to make the movement work.[18] The temperance and abolition movements are other examples of situations where local leadership played an important part in translating the elites' message to the public and relaying the public's demands to national elites.

Most contemporary movements also used existing communication networks built on local chapters and leaders. For example, the civil rights movement used the network of black colleges and black churches in the South; the New Left and student movements used the sit-in network established by the civil rights movement and college campuses; the women's movement employed existing New Left structures, the University of Wisconsin Extension Division, and the United Auto Workers' Women's Committee; and the prolife movement built on the organization and leadership of the Catholic church.[19] With the development of direct mail, these networks of local chapters and leaders are no longer necessary. Mass political mailings allow a political entrepreneur such as Terry Dolan, former director of NCPAC, or John Gardner, former director of Common Cause, to mobilize sets of individuals who may never have heard of or have met one another, but who share common political concerns.[20] All that is necessary are a list of persons who are likely to share the values the entrepreneur wishes to mobilize, the marketing expertise to write a good direct-mail letter, and the monetary resources (or financial credit) necessary to prepare and send it.

As the figures cited earlier for the Republican party and ideological PACs demonstrate, direct mail is an excellent fund-raising mechanism. What is often forgotten is that for every ten or twenty letters sent, only one person responds with a contribution. But the other letters are not wasted. Each is an effective advertisement for a candidate, an issue, or a political position. Richard Viguerie argues that the major function of direct mail is to advertise, not to raise money; mailers who forget this will not be successful in their political endeavors.[21]

Direct mail and low-cost telephone lines allow elites to communicate directly with the public that shares their values. A small group of individuals in

Washington or New York can send a message to thousands of persons through-out the country; it is a message neither censored, moderated, nor translated by local political leaders, station managers, or newspaper publishers and editors. Such messages can mobilize a letter-writing campaign to a congressperson or a street demonstration in his district. This use of direct mail, along with WATS lines and cable television, has made elected officials vulnerable to pressure and manipulation by the public, which in turn is manipulated by an elite not sub-ject to electoral defeat. This new political elite—one that often generates its resources using fear-filled and emotional messages such as those quoted at the beginning of this chapter, and one that realistically is not held politically ac-countable for its actions—presents a significant problem for democratic theory and practice.

The Approach of This Book

I utilize three major data sets to examine how interest groups, political action committees, and political parties use direct-marketing techniques to achieve political goals and objectives: a sample of 150 political direct mailings; over 3000 mail questionnaire responses received from members of citizen action groups; and interviews with leaders of political parties, PACs, and interest groups. Chapters 1 and 2 look at the special technical advantages direct mail and other direct-marketing techniques provide and examine how those who use these new techniques utilize them to political advantage. Chapter 1 includes an analysis of the content of direct mailings to discover what messages are sent and which materials create the best response rates in terms of money raised or actions taken by recipients. Chapter 2 examines other direct-marketing tech-niques, including closed-circuit cable television, telephone appeals, and direct voting through cable and telephone hookups. Chapter 3 examines question-naire responses from members of citizen action groups to find out who joins these groups, and it compares members who joined in response to direct mar-keting with those who joined in more traditional ways. These comparisons help answer the question whether the direct marketing of politics leads to participa-tion by persons who are more extreme than most citizens in their opinions and actions and more intolerant of opinions other than their own. The question-naire data also help determine whether supporters of direct marketing are cor-rect in their expectation that it encourages political equality by increasing par-ticipation among persons previously excluded from political activities.

Chapters 4 and 5 present interviews with leaders of interest groups, PACs, and political parties. These interviews indicate how elites actually use direct mail to raise money, lobby, and campaign. The interviews also show how direct marketing affects political strategies, issue choices, and objectives of the various political institutions. Chapter 6 examines the actual impact of direct marketing on who wins and who loses elections, and on public policy. It includes a statistical analysis of congressional voting and compares votes during the period before the rapid increases in campaign resources provided by direct marketing with votes on similar issues after those increases. This analysis yields a number of surprising findings. Perhaps the most startling is that the critics of direct marketing have missed its most pernicious effect. Chapter 7 summarizes the costs and benefits to American politics and examines how the detrimental effects of direct marketing might be alleviated without jeopardizing the benefits it has created.

Notes

1. The $1 billion figure is conservative in that it omits local groups such as one gay rights activist group in New York City which raised over $5 million through direct mailings. The figure for letters generated is also quite conservative in that the banking lobby alone generated over 16 million pieces of mail to Congress urging it to reverse the withholding tax on savings (*Business Week*, 28 March 1983, 40).

2. Herbert Alexander, *Financing Politics: Money, Elections, and Political Reform,* 3d ed. (Washington, D.C.: CQ Press, 1984), 1-5.

3. The use of political direct mail actually predates the Eisenhower campaign. Woodrow Wilson used direct mail to campaign for President, and other candidates used it sporadically.

4. The franking privilege allows members of Congress to mail information to their constituents free of charge.

5. Richard S. Hodgson, *Direct Mail and Mail Order Handbook,* 2d ed. (Chicago: Dartnell, 1977).

6. "Frankly Outrageous," *Tucson Citizen,* 5 November 1985, A14.

7. Gary Jacobson, *Money in Congressional Elections* (New Haven: Yale University Press, 1980); and Gary Jacobson, "Congressional Elections: The Case of the Vanishing Challengers," in *Congressional Elections,* ed. Louis Maisel and Joseph Cooper (Beverly Hills, Calif.: Sage, 1981), 228-29.

8. This figure was obtained by adding the totals reported to me by the direct-response departments of the Republican National Committee, the National Republican Senatorial Committee, and the National Republican Congressional Committee.

9. Larry J. Sabato, *PAC Power: Inside the World of Political Action Committees* (New York: Norton, 1984), 14.

10. This bill would have allowed labor unions not directly involved in a strike to picket the employer being picketed by another union. If the legislation had passed, it would have made it substantially more likely that members of one union would support members of other unions and not cross picket lines.

11. Pamela Conover and Virginia Gray, *Feminism and the New Right: Conflict Over the American Family* (New York: Praeger, 1983); and Richard Viguerie, *The New Right: We're Ready to Lead* (Falls Church, Va.: Viguerie Co., 1981), 65-70.

12. David Broder, "One Issue Groups: The New Force in Politics," *Boston Globe,* 13 September 1978.

13. The opinion of Teeter was published in *Newsweek,* 6 November 1978; for Bell's and Viguerie's comments see Daniel Bell, "The End of American Exceptionalism," *Public Interest* 41 (1975): 193-224.

14. Mary Topolsky, "Common Cause?" *Worldview* 17 (1974): 35-39.

15. Michael Hayes, "Interest Groups: Pluralism or Mass Society," in *Interest Group Politics,* ed. Allan Cigler and Burdett Loomis (Washington, D.C.: CQ Press, 1983).

16. See, for example, Benjamin Barber, "Voting Is Not Enough: How Modern Communications Can Enhance the Ideal of Citizenship," *Atlantic* 253 (June 1984): 45-53.

17. William Kornhauser, *The Politics of the Mass Society* (New York: Free Press, 1959); and Amitai Etzioni, *An Immodest Agenda: Rebuilding America Before the 21st Century* (New York: McGraw-Hill, 1983).

18. Robert Caro, *The Years of Lyndon Johnson* (New York: Vintage, 1981); and Jo Freeman, *Social Movements of the Sixties and Seventies* (New York: Longman, 1983).

19. Freeman, *Social Movements.*

20. John McCarthy, "Social Infrastructure Deficits and New Technologies: Mobilizing Unstructured Sentiment Pools" (paper presented at the 1982 meetings of the American Sociological Association).

21. Viguerie, *New Right,* 82.

1. How Direct Mail Works

Direct mail is a powerful political tool because it provides politicians with technical advantages no other political communication can match: market pretesting, personalization, concentration, and immediacy. Because politicians can send several alternative appeals to samples of their audience and then statistically compare response rates, market pretesting informs politicians which appeals work best. Personalization means that each communication can address a particular person or family and cite their special characteristics. This indicates to recipients that the sender of the letter sees them as individuals and shares their values and concerns. Concentration permits the sender to reach particular audiences, such as registered voters in his district. Money is not wasted contacting people who cannot help his cause. Immediacy is the characteristic of direct mail that precipitates action by recipients. Direct mail accomplishes this not only by inspiring the desire to act but also by supplying all the reply materials the addressee needs to take action.[1]

Beyond these advantages, direct mail can create a product (a person, idea, or issue) to meet existing desires instead of having to change those desires to sell an existing commodity. It can locate a position or issue in the political spectrum where there is currently an unmet desire and can design an appeal to fill that gap. Finally, as we see in a content analysis of direct mailings, this medium makes more effective use of threats, fear, and appeals to personal efficacy than other forms of political communication.

Direct mail's many advantages provide its users with a significant political edge over their opponents; because of this, successful politicians and prosperous political consultants have labored to learn how direct mail works and how they can best use it.

Market Pretesting

Every political direct mailing contains a postcard or reply envelope that allows the recipient to order a product, contribute money, or take some other action desired by the mailer. On this reply form is a number key identifying to whom the mailing was addressed. If a mailer is testing the effectiveness of several different letters, the number key on the reply informs him which message generated that reply. This information permits the sponsor to compare statistically the relative success of each appeal and choose the best for future mailings to similar audiences. The set of mailings for Dwight Eisenhower's first presidential bid, cited in the introductory chapter, demonstrates the importance of these comparisons. The numbers on the return envelopes told Eisenhower that among the ten issues tested, the Korea mailing elicited the greatest response and largest contributions.

The advantages of the number key are not limited to market testing. The computer-readable numbers on the reply card identify who has responded. This enormously facilitates the ever-increasing levels of recordkeeping required by state and federal campaign finance legislation. In addition, the number key allows the organization doing the mailing to keep a history of each donor and estimate the frequency of his responses. This permits the mailer to time future requests appropriately.

Before political mailers can utilize market pretesting and the other advantages provided by the number key, they must first determine to whom they should mail. And it is an axiom of direct mail that a poorly prepared mailing to a good list of names can be profitable, while the best mailing, no matter how well conceived, to a poor list will lose money.[2] Direct mail begins with "target" or "prospect" lists of carefully chosen audiences. Lists are selected on the basis of whether or not the people on them have "purchased" a product similar to the one offered in the current appeal. The first mailing to a list is known as *prospecting*. For example, the National Conservative Political Action Committee (NCPAC) may obtain a list of persons from outside North Carolina who contributed to Senator Jesse Helms's 1984 reelection campaign. These people have proven that they are willing to donate to conservative candidates outside their own state. Because NCPAC's political program shows a strong affinity to positions taken by Senator Helms, a NCPAC appeal to them would probably be quite successful. Similarly, the Wilderness Society prospects with names of Sierra Club members, and Environmental Action mails to members of the Environmental Defense Fund. The important thing is the kinship between the item of idea that the prospects previously purchased and the product the direct mailer wishes to sell. The persons on the list have demonstrated that they will buy a commodity similar to what the prospector is providing—if they are properly motivated to do so.

This first mailing is the most expensive and difficult task in starting a direct-mail program. The organization must construct or purchase the necessary list of potential contributors and then pay the costs of preparing and sending the mailing. Typically, only 1 or 2 percent of prospects respond and the cost of each letter ranges from $.30 cents to $3. For this reason, prospecting usually loses money.[3] The organization sponsoring the mailing is willing to incur these costs to obtain its "house list"—the list of persons who actually respond to the prospecting letters. These names constitute the single most precious asset of a direct mailer. While the average response rate to a prospect mailing is only 1 or 2 percent, the typical response rate for appeals to the house list is over 10 percent and may range as high as 20 percent.[4] Equally important, the direct mailer can solicit the house list again and again and again.

Richard Viguerie writes that repetition in direct mail is not only possible but absolutely necessary. "If you see three ads for Coca-Cola in one day, you don't get upset or think the Coke people are wasting their money. . . . It's the same with direct mail."[5] Roger Craver, John Anderson's direct-mail consultant for his 1980 presidential bid, mailed to his house list every eight days, and the percentage of persons responding never fell during the entire campaign.[6]

Compared with the traditional method of soliciting political contributions, the ability of direct mail to make repeated appeals constitutes a major breakthrough. Selling, whether it means selling industrial solvents or a political candidate, typically requires several calls before a sale is made. Political volunteers, however, do not like to make repeated requests of the same people; and it is particularly hard to go back two weeks after a person has made a donation and ask for more. Yet previous givers are the persons most likely to respond to a new appeal. Direct mail allows the fund raiser to return repeatedly and without embarrassment. In George McGovern's 1972 campaign, the 15,000 givers who responded to the first prospect mailing provided the most reliable set of future givers. Thirteen percent of the persons on this list gave every month during the campaign![7]

Personalization

One reason house lists are so profitable is that the organization mailing to them is able to establish a seemingly personal relationship by using information provided in responses to past appeals. This ability of senders to personalize their message provides an important clue in understanding the success of direct mail.

With direct mail, the organization or individual sending the communication need not direct it to an entire radio or television audience. Instead, he can address the letter's salutation to a particular person.[8] The appeal can be personalized still further by citing special attributes of the recipient. For example, if the addressee has contributed previously to the cause, the mailing can refer to that donation and tell the donor how much it was appreciated and what it accomplished. Or, where a prospect list has been chosen because the members of the list live in a particular area, the mailing can utilize an opening guaranteed to be of interest to the reader. A recent successful challenger for a county commission seat in Tucson, Arizona, opened her letter to all registered voters in a particular precinct with, "_____, the current County Commissioner from your district, voted to run a freeway right through your neighborhood. Wouldn't you like to let her know how much you appreciate it?"

A particularly effective personalized letter was sent by a member of the House of Representatives who kept track of births in his district as they were reported in the vital statistics section of hometown newspapers. Using his franking perquisite—congresspersons do not pay postage on mail sent to constituents unless it relates directly to their reelection—the congressman sent a letter to new parents congratulating them on the birth of their child. Included with the letter was a booklet on new baby care prepared by the National Institute of Child Health and Human Development. Albert Cover and Bruce Brumberg found that recipients of this "nonpolitical" mailing were significantly more likely to have a positive impression of the congressman after they received his letter.[9]

When mailing to the house list, the degree of personalization in a direct mailing can be substantial. Previous mailings and responses to them answer such vital questions as "Does the respondent know personally a member of Congress?" "Has the respondent written or contacted a public official?" "What is the respondent's past history of giving and what type of appeal has been most effective?" For example, a letter to someone who has previously identified herself as a friend of Congressman Morris Udall might begin:

Dear Ms. Clarke:

Next week the final vote on the MX missile system comes up. We know that your neighbor and congressman, Morris Udall, greatly respects your opinion on national defense issues and that you have contacted him before on issues of such vital concern to our nation.

Won't you please. . . .

Personalization touches recipients. They are far more likely to feel that the person or organization requesting something from them knows how they feel and what they value. Personalization makes people feel important and helps them perceive their contributions as significant. Witness a Sierra Club mailing from its president to past contributors:

Your support in the past, Mr. and Mrs. Cortner, has been crucial to our success. I sincerely thank you for your generosity. We can be proud of the Sierra Club's accomplishments. . . .

> Our unparalleled record over the past 91 years would not have been possible without your financial support. We are counting on you to help us continue.

By showing that the president of the Sierra Club is aware of the Cortners' past contributions, the letter generates a feeling of efficacy on the part of the addressee. And, as we see below, that is essential in making people want to contribute and work on behalf of the group.

Even the envelope and the paper used in preparing the letter can increase personalization. With modern printing and computer laser techniques, a mailing can have the look of an "engraved" invitation from the President of the United States, such as the one shown in figure 1.1. This expensively produced appeal is an effective tool when asking for $500 contributions to the Republican National Committee, but it would not be helpful in appeals from other groups, such as Environmental Action, a radical environmental group. Environmental Action receives most of its contributions from young professionals with moderate incomes and left-wing politics. To reach this audience, the group prints its letters on inexpensive recycled paper. By doing this, Environmental Action stresses that it spends as little as possible on mailings, does not require any new trees to be cut, and uses contributions to influence public policy and not to impress its donors.

Personalization is not easy to achieve. Writers of direct mail are unanimous in their opinion that the best way to accomplish this goal is to think of a friend who knows little about the organization or cause sponsoring the letter. Write that friend a personal letter appealing for funds or action. Then, put another friend's name in the salutation and see if the letter remains appropriate. If so, address the letter to still other friends and acquaintances. If the letter is appropriate for twenty persons whom the writer knows, it is a good personalized letter.[10] (I invite the reader to try and write such a letter. It is an instructive exercise in understanding how personalization works and how hard it is to realize.)

Concentration

A closely related advantage to direct mail's ability to personalize communication is its success in concentrating on particular audiences, audiences that share an attribute that makes them likely respondents to a particular appeal. Concentration allows the candidate or organization doing the mailing to send different letters to special target groups. A candidate can send one message to the Veterans of Foreign Wars, indicating support for defense spending and higher government benefits for veterans. The same candidate can send a different letter

President Ronald Wilson Reagan,
Senator Paul Laxalt, General Chairman,
and
Frank Fahrenkopf, National Chairman,
on behalf of the
Republican National Committee
cordially invite you to become a member of
the 500 Club
and to attend a private briefing
with Administration officials and
Republican Congressional leaders

FIGURE 1.1
AN ENGRAVED INVITATION TO JOIN THE
REPUBLICAN NATIONAL COMMITTEE'S 500 CLUB

to members of the National Organization for Women, showing backing for women's rights.

The prolife movement's Voter Identification Project supplies an impressive example of how concentration can be used to political advantage. The project takes advantage of the fact that when candidates take public stands on the abortion issue, they are likely to lose a vote on one side of the issue for every vote they gain on the other side. Therefore, candidates want to make their position on abortion known only to supporters of that stand. The Voter Identification Project allows prolife candidates to do this. Using voter registration lists, prolife volunteers call registered voters and ask them six questions concerning when they believe abortion should be permitted. Those respondents who give strongly prolife responses become part of the Voter Identification house list; their names are coded onto computerized lists by party identification, voting precinct, and congressional district. Candidates who support the prolife position can purchase these lists for their districts at very low rates and send prolife appeals only to households containing registered voters who agree with their stand. To a registered voter in the party opposite that of his own, the candidate might send a letter like this:

> Dear Mrs. Roe:
>
> I write this letter to you knowing that you are a registered Democrat and I am a Republican candidate. Yet, you and I share a common belief, THE RIGHT TO LIFE OF THE UNBORN! I believe this is the most important issue in the upcoming election and if you vote for me on election day I promise you that I will do everything possible to make sure that no more innocent babies die. . . .

Interest groups utilize concentration to mobilize their members to political action efficiently. Many groups organize their membership and activists lists by congressional district. When a major vote is coming in Congress or a crucial decision is being made in committee, the group mobilizes only those members who reside in the districts of representatives whose votes are undecided or are critical to the decision. By so doing, the interest group does not waste money on people who cannot affect the decision; it concentrates only on those whose input might have an impact. This saves time and money, and is a more effective lobbying technique than mobilizing members in every congressional district.[11]

Immediacy

The ability to request or even demand an immediate action represents still another advantage of direct mail. Conventional messages in newspapers and on radio and television may establish a desire to act, but they do not encourage the immediate fulfillment of that desire.[12] Direct mail, telephone marketing, and telethons provide avenues for an instantaneous response to a political appeal. Direct marketing techniques ask for action NOW and provide the necessary return envelope, postcard, or telephone number for the person moved by the message to respond at that moment.

Good direct-mail messages stress immediacy. This is true whether the mailing is selling soap or a new public-interest group. The message emphasizes that you must act now, before it's too late! The abridged letter below illustrates this:

Dear Mr. and Mrs. Godwin:

I am writing you today to alert you to a radical Big Labor takeover in the schools in your community.

The National Education Association (NEA) — a union second only to the Teamsters in size and power — is about to seize total control of public education in America.

Unless you and I take IMMEDIATE ACTION on this EMERGENCY situation, the NEA will succeed in pushing legislation through Congress that will force compulsory unionization on every public school in the country.

The threat to America's public schools and to our children is so serious and SO IMMEDIATE that I am determined to do everything I can to fight the NEA's radical agenda.

That is why I am asking you to support STOP THE NEA, a special project of The Heritage Foundation. As part of this project, several other senators and I have asked Heritage to prepare a National Survey on Big Labor and Education. . . .

I must ask you TODAY to send $25, $50, $75, or even $100 to STOP THE NEA TODAY. . . . I've already enclosed a special reply envelope for your use. So please send your answered survey TODAY.

It's URGENT THAT I HEAR FROM YOU AS SOON AS POSSIBLE. BELIEVE ME YOUR HELP IS NEEDED MORE THAN EVER.

Sincerely,

Steve Symms
U.S. Senator

This letter, part of a several-page mailing from a conservative fund-raising group, accentuates the imminent threat to conservative values. It also provides two ways for the recipient to respond. The first is a survey designed to elicit a particular response from the individual while making him feel efficacious by suggesting that his views will become part of an important survey that will go to high-level public officials. An envelope accompanies the survey to encourage its easy return. A second response tool, the contribution pledge card, is attached to the survey, encouraging the individual to mark his pledge to the Heritage Foundation. Respondents do not have to provide a stamp, address an envelope, or even make out a check; they need only to mark the appropriate answers on the survey and promise a future contribution.

Another letter uses a different technique to encourage rapid responses. It promises prestige goods to individuals who answer by a particular date:

> Dear Mr. and Mrs. Rusk:
>
> We are writing you today to personally invite you to join with us in the SELECT United States Congressional Advisory Board that is now being organized. As a charter member you will advise and support the members of congress who belong to the coalition for Peace Through Strength. . . .
>
> This could be AMERICA'S LAST CHANCE. PLEASE ACT TODAY and join us and other opinion leaders as a distinguished member of the Advisory Board. If you act by September 15, 1983, you will be considered a charter member and will receive a special identification tag to wear at Congressional receptions as well as an impressive 9 × 12 embossed and sealed Membership Certificate.
>
> We look forward to hearing from you. Simply mail the enclosed letter in its envelope and indicate the contribution that you are making to this important cause. . . .

A far more urgent request came in a letter from the Defenders of Wildlife. The outside envelope showed a picture of a grizzly bear with a red slash across it. Bold letters in the slash stated, "NORTH AMERICAN WILDLIFE EMERGENCY." Above the name and address of the recipient, bold red letters called out, "IMMEDIATE RESPONSE REQUESTED." The top of the first page contained still another red slash, reading, "PRIORITY MESSAGE * PRIORITY MESSAGE * PRIORITY MESSAGE." Finally, above the salutation were two paragraphs emphasizing that if immediate action was not taken, "this unique symbol of strength and courage may soon disappear from the lower 48 states." As always, the mailing contained the appropriate contribution pledge card and reply envelope stressing the importance of immediate action.

Position

Successful direct mailers must differentiate their interest group, political action committee, or candidate from similar appeals. This process, known as *positioning*, has been identified by a leading direct marketer, Edward Nash, as "the single most important creative decision in the making of a successful ad or mailing piece."[13] If the message is an invitation to join a citizen action group such as the Wilderness Society, the mailing must show the prospect why he should join the Wilderness Society rather than the National Wildlife Federation or the Sierra Club. A letter from the World Wildlife Fund tells its prospects that it has achieved so much "because The World Wildlife Fund works by setting up projects that are based on solid scientific research." This sentence is underlined in red ink to ensure that the reader does not miss the point: The World Wildlife Fund does not try to lobby for all projects regardless of their scientific merit, as, presumably, some other environmental groups do.

The Nature Conservancy, another environmental citizen action group, sends an envelope with the eye-catching American sandhill crane on the front (see figure 1.2 on page 20). The letter contained within tells the reader that a gift of just $10 will provide a place for the bird to nest so that its eggs can incubate.

It then centers three lines in the letter:

How will we reserve that incubator with your $10?
Not by campaigning or picketing or suing.

We'll just BUY the nesting ground.

In this way, Nature Conservancy locates its own nesting place, differentiating itself from other environmental associations that work through lobbying and court cases.

All direct-marketing appeals use a combination of incentives, price, and policy issues to position their product. The Wilderness Society, a direct competitor of the better-known Sierra Club, positions itself by offering membership at a lower price and placing greater emphasis on the problems of wilderness and open space. The National Wildlife Federation (NWF) locates its niche by emphasizing its beautiful magazines and other material benefits. Instead of stressing a particular policy issue or lobbying technique, NWF mailings point out that membership in NWF would make a thoughtful gift to an environmentally concerned friend.

The important point the direct mailer must remember is that he and his organization are in a competitive business and that the recipient of his mailing will receive other mailings with similar appeals. The victorious mailer is the one who does a better job of building the product package that sparks the desire to act politically.

Motivating with Fear

Market pretesting, personalization, concentration, immediacy, and positioning are five technical advantages of direct mail. They offer a combination of attributes that cannot be matched by any other medium. But these advantages, in and of themselves, would not be sufficient to generate the tremendous criticism that direct mail and direct-mail-based organizations have created. What accounts for these reactions from the press, academicians, and politicians?

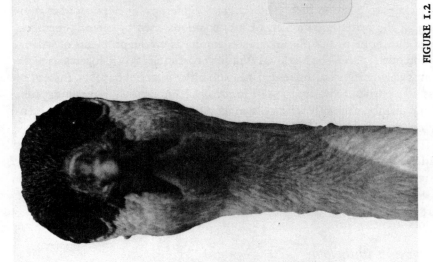

RELAX!

Both of you.

150401

MR. KENNETH GODWIN
1447 W MAXIMILLION PL
TUCSON, AZ 85704

(A $10 nest egg will do it.)

Nonprofit Org.
U.S. POSTAGE
PAID
PERMIT 5226

RIVERDALE
MD.

(Do not fold. Bumper sticker enclosed.)

The Nature Conservancy 1800 North Kent Street, Arlington, Va. 22209

FIGURE 1.2

A PROSPECTING ENVELOPE FROM THE NATURE CONSERVANCY

Critics argue that the paramount factor is direct mail's use of fear as the basic motivating force. Negative and fear-filled messages are blamed for increasing alienation, reducing voter turnout, "balkanizing" politics, generating government by distraction, and creating gutless government and ideological bullies.[14]

Does direct mail make greater use of negative information and fear than other kinds of political messages? Yes! The use of fear in direct marketing is based on an important psychological axiom: Persons are willing to pay more and to do more to prevent the loss of something they already have than to achieve something that they might obtain in the future.[15] The earlier letters concerning the unionization of public schools, the coalition of Peace through Strength, and the destruction of the grizzly bear provide examples of direct mailers utilizing this axiom. If you do not act now, your children will become controlled by radical unions; the Soviet Union will destroy us; defenseless animals will be destroyed by evil people. In a similar way, a 1983 mailing requesting contributions to the Republican National Committee and signed by President Reagan threatens still another disaster:

> If we fail to stop the Democrats from winning in 1984 they could overturn and destroy all the progress we have made in pulling our nation back from the brink of catastrophe.
>
> And if the Democrats and their liberal special interest group allies regain power, then I am convinced they will force our nation right back down the disastrous road to more spending and higher income taxes.

The National Audubon Society writes its membership requesting additional contributions and requesting them to write their congresspersons:

> Dear Mr. and Mrs. Godwin:
>
> Today a new breed of plume hunters, as short-sighted and self-seeking as ever, has declared war on environmental protection. Under the pretense of eliminating government waste and ending inflation, the Reagan Administration, led by Secretary of the Interior James Watt, is attempting to reverse two decades of progress in protecting our birds and other wild animals and the air, land, water, and forests on which all life depends.

The letter goes on to list eleven specific actions by the Reagan Administration and Secretary Watt that are threatening wildlife.

An antinuclear group, SANE, threatens nuclear war if you do not respond:

> President Reagan and his military advisers have embarked on the most dangerous course of action in the history of nuclear arms — and we must speak out against it. The Administration is preparing to fight and "win" a nuclear war!

Common Cause uses a similar fear-based appeal:

Your signature on the enclosed petition is needed to help stem the flood of Political Action Committee (PAC) money which is threatening our representative form of government.

Alarming. Outrageous. Downright dangerous. That's the only way to begin to describe the threat posed by the torrents of special interest campaign cash being offered up to our Representatives and Senators by the special interest political action committees.

Perhaps the most extreme example of this appeal introduced this book. Written over the signature of Murray Norris, president of Christian Family Renewal, that letter began:

Just When You Thought Your Children Were Safe From Homosexual Advances, Congress Introduces House Resolution #427: The "Gay Bill of Rights."

The letter goes on to state that the bill is currently under debate in the House Judiciary Committee and in the Civil and Constitutional Rights Subcommittee, committees chaired by liberal Democrats from California and New York, "the most ultra-liberal homosexual centers in the nation"; and that the bill would allow the prosecution of churches and schools that refuse to hire homosexuals "for any reason."

Critics of direct mail argue that using fear as the primary motivation for political action brings out the worst in politics and people. It reduces the common ground that makes compromise possible and replaces reason with emotion. They see letters indicating dire threats as efforts to manipulate the public and mislead them into believing that they are far more threatened than they actually are. The letter suggesting that the NEA has sufficient power to pass a bill requiring the unionization of all local public schools and the mailing indicating churches could be prosecuted for refusing to hire homosexuals provide obvious examples of such manipulation. Such bills would never become law; even if they miraculously passed both houses of Congress, the President would certainly veto them. And if they overcame these obstacles, they would undoubtedly be declared unconstitutional by the courts. Nevertheless, the letters suggest that the threats are real and immediate.

Examples of this obvious exaggeration of threats can be found in almost every direct mailing. The American Civil Liberties Union sends several letters each year to its members citing obscure court cases that, if they were successful, would lead to substantial curtailments of civil liberties in America. The letters do not indicate that the probability of the cases being successful is probably less than one in a thousand.

Direct mailings are accused of stressing the darker side of politics and portraying the opposition in the worst possible way. For example, many mailings repeatedly use words with strong negative connotations, such as "radicals," "bureaucrats," "left-wing hippies," "destroyers," and "so-called minorities." Mailings combine these aspersions with personal names to form epithets such as "Ted Kennedy liberals," "Nadarites," and "Watt's destroyers and exploiters." Perhaps the most frequent use of negative language is the use of "enemies" rather than "opposition" or another less provocative word. At the same time, of course, the writers identify themselves, their organizations, and their readers with such flattering symbols as "the majority," "Americans," "Christians," "decent," and so forth. Jerry Falwell of the Moral Majority sends prospects a letter of powerful descriptors with a membership card:

Here is your official Moral Majority Membership Card.
I have issued this card to you because I believe that you are the kind of American who would like to see our nation returned to moral sanity . . .
. . . And because I need dedicated Americans like you on my team. . . .
The liberals are continuing to launch their campaigns to pass the anti-morality legislation that failed in the last session of Congress.
So as I write you today, the battle lines are already drawn up. And the fight is on!
So now, we are locked in a raging battle with the proabortionists, homosexuals, pornographers, atheists, secular humanists, and others.
And, my enemies have vowed to stop us!

Similarly, the Washington Legal Foundation writes:

Are you fed up, and I mean fed up, with liberals, progressives, and so-called minorities and their lawyers using the courts for their own selfish ends?
Are you tired of seeing the courts ignoring you and the majority of Americans?
. . . I was tired of seeing radicals use our courts to try to disarm America.
I was tired of watching government bureaucrats handcuff businessmen, strangle free enterprise, and then ignore the law themselves. . . .

The quotes from Common Cause and SANE cited earlier in this chapter demonstrate that conservatives and the New Right are not alone in their use of such language. Archibald Cox, chairman of Common Cause, calls for funds to help pass legislation to limit contributions from political action committees and writes, "Congress is For Sale" and PACs will fight Common Cause by a "massively financed campaign . . . to distort the issue and to intimidate Congress."

When letters were matched according to their use of fear, guilt, and name-calling, the letter that most closely approximated the Moral Majority letter above was a letter from Greenpeace, a radical environmental group. Direct mail from Alan Cranston, one of the most liberal senators, provided the closest match to a letter from Senator Helms, one of the most conservative.

Various wildlife and environmental groups use photographs of the killing of baby seals and the butchering of dogs for food in much the same way as prolife groups have used photographs of mangled fetuses and bloody operating rooms to attract attention and obtain contributions. Liberal groups and environmental organizations accuse President Reagan of encouraging nuclear war and selling our nation's birthright. In short, provocative and acrimonious language pervades all direct mailings, not just one "side" or the other.

A Content Analysis of Direct Mailings

To determine the extent to which direct mail employs fear, negativism, sensationalism, and other propaganda techniques, I collected 150 political mailings and analyzed their content. The letters came from two sources: Forty-one were from responses to a request sent to the campaign organizations of persons running for President in 1984, major political parties, and large ideological political action committees. Each organization was asked to send the house and/or prospect letter from the previous twelve months that received the highest response or contribution rate.[16] Colleagues at the University of Arizona brought in an additional 109 political mailings. Of the 150 mailings, 33 were sent by environmental citizen action groups, 30 were sponsored by Republican party organizations or candidates, 28 were from conservative groups such as the National Conservative Political Action Committee and the Moral Majority, 21 came from Democratic party organizations or candidates, 25 were mailed by liberal political action committees or causes, and 13 were mailed by unclassified causes such as the MIA/POW mailings and the American Friends of Israel. Although the total sample is not random, it provides a broad cross-section of political mailings and includes many of the most productive political mailings from the 1983-84 election cycle.

The content analysis of the mailings compared the extent to which each paragraph emphasized conflict, threats, enemies, and the darker side of politics. Each paragraph was coded either *yes* or *no* on whether or not it contained information about the organization and its cause. Did it appeal to fear and guilt? Did it stress citizen duty and personal efficacy?[17] After the paragraph-by-paragraph analysis, the entire mailing was rated on five categories: (1) the extent to which the letter stressed saving a threatened value; (2) the extent to which it emphasized the pursuit of a future value; (3) the overall negativism of the letter; (4) the amount of "card stacking" involved, where all good characteristics

TABLE I.I

ANALYSIS OF DIRECT MAILINGS

(IN PERCENT)

Attribute	Conservative	Liberal	Republican	Democrat	Environmental	Other	Total
				Source of Mailing			
Paragraphs[a]							
Information	68	69	58	58	66	75	67
Fear and guilt	31	38	26	31	32	25	30
Duty/efficacy	31	28	46	31	31	31	34
Entire mailing[b]							
Threatened value	42	43	37	36	46	27	28
Future value	19	10	28	23	10	34	18
Negativism	47	47	46	45	40	25	40
Card stacking	67	59	31	35	47	64	47
Glittering generality	87	65	33	39	56	58	51

a. Percentage of paragraphs containing this element.
b. Percentage of entire messages that scored *high* or *very high* on this characteristic.

were attributed to one side and all bad characteristics attributed to the other; and (5) its use of glittering generalities. Each category received a score from 1 (very low) to 5 (very high) from each coder. Table 1.1 shows results of this analysis.

SIMILARITIES AMONG MAILINGS

Perhaps the most interesting aspect of table 1.1 is that the various mailings are so much alike. Regardless of the source of the mailing, 60 to 70 percent of paragraphs contain information concerning the organization and its political goals; between 30 and 40 percent appeal to citizen duty or personal efficacy; and approximately 35 percent of the paragraphs motivate through fear or guilt. It is interesting to note that despite all the negative press the New Right receives concerning its use of fear and guilt, Democrats and liberal mailers use these appeals more frequently than do Republicans and conservatives.

There are some important differences among the mailings if liberal and conservative causes are combined to form one category, and Republican and Democratic party mailings are placed in another. As table 1.2 shows, political parties are significantly more likely to stress citizen duty and the pursuit of future values. In contrast, ideological mailings emphasize information about their organization, fear and guilt, and currently threatened values, and they are approximately twice as likely to receive high scores on card stacking and glittering generalities.

TABLE 1.2

COMPARISONS OF POLITICAL PARTY AND IDEOLOGICAL MAILINGS
(IN PERCENT)

Attribute	Source of Mailing	
	Political Party	Ideological
Paragraphs[a]		
Information	58	68
Fear and guilt	28	34
Duty/efficacy	42	30
Entire mailings[b]		
Threatened value	36	42
Future value	26	15
Negativism	46	47
Card stacking	33	63
Glittering generality	36	76

a. Percentage of paragraphs containing this element.
b. Percentage of entire messages that scored *high* or *very high* on this characteristic.

To illustrate these differences, compare a letter written over President Reagan's signature for the National Republican Congressional Committee (NRCC) with the earlier letter from Senator Symms written for the Heritage Foundation. In the NRCC letter, President Reagan does cite a threat, the possible domination of the House of Representatives by liberal Democrats that would lead to the end of the President's economic recovery program; but the letter devotes far more space to the rewards that will be gained by the NRCC if it has sufficient funds for the 1984 electoral campaign. These rewards include attracting outstanding Republican candidates, providing these candidates with training and cash support so that they can combat labor-supported Democrats, and tracking the voting records of Democratic incumbents so that the Republican candidates can call attention to those votes by Democrats that their constituents would oppose.

In sharp contrast to Reagan's letter on behalf of the NRCC, the letter from Senator Symms motivates through the fear of labor unions taking over the public schools; homosexual schoolteachers; and the provision of drugs to, and indoctrination of, children. The only promised goods are the stopping of this takeover and the development of "backgrounders," research papers on how to teach math and science in the public schools. Mailings on behalf of the Democratic party differ in similar ways from those of liberal causes. Party appeals dwell less on the powerful emotions of fear and use instead the ideals of citizen duty, loyalty to the party, and promises of future goods.

How to Structure a Direct Mailing

The above content analysis tells which emotions various categories of direct mail tap, but it does not indicate the ordering of these appeals within the letters. This ordering provides a more accurate assessment of how direct mail touches its targets. Every one of the forty-one letters in the sample of most effective mailings begins with a short line or paragraph designed to grab the reader's attention and threaten his values. Simultaneously, the letter asks for the reader's help. A mailing from the National Audubon Society opens, "Audubon urgently needs your help to protect the wildlife and wilderness you love, the air you breathe, the water you drink." A letter from General John Singlaub for the Council for Inter-American Security begins, "As a retired major general in the United States Army, I am earnestly asking you to sign my national petition to stop the Ted Kennedy liberals from blocking President Reagan's vital MX Missile program." Greenpeace tells us that the international decision to phase out all commercial whaling is "under attack from those who profit from the slaughter," and "that you and thousands of other Greenpeace supporters" convinced Iceland not to challenge the phaseout and a similar effort will convince Japan, Russia, Norway, and Peru. A letter from Jerry Falwell for the Moral Majority asking persons to boycott 7-Eleven stores and display a bumper sticker telling people to "Drive on by 7-Eleven" stores asks, "Do you have the courage to take a stand against pornography?" Finally, a mailing from the American Legislative Exchange Council starts:

> I am writing to you because I need your help! Without *you,* our ability to defend our great nation will vanish.
> The *Soviet Union* has once again shown the world their barbaric nature by MURDERING 269 civilians, including U.S. Congressman Larry McDonald, aboard Korean Air Lines Flight 007.

This kind of opening—a threat and a call for help—characterizes over 85 percent of all direct mailings. After these initial paragraphs, direct mailings take advantage of their ability to send the addressee almost unlimited amounts of information. The letter's middle section provides an extended picture of the cause, the organization, and what actions the addressee can take to alleviate the threat. The typical mailing also includes a lengthy section explaining how the organization got started on this issue or threat. A Greenpeace letter soliciting funds to stop the killing of baby seals in Canada begins with the usual grotesque description of how the seals are slaughtered and the message that the recipient can help stop the killing by helping Greenpeace. Then, the fourth paragraph initiates a thirteen-paragraph description of Greenpeace's past accomplishments in reducing these atrocities and how seal hunters and national governments responded to Greenpeace's actions.

A six-page letter from the Sierra Club spends four entire pages describing the organization and the benefits of membership. The mailing includes an additional four-page folder describing the organization, its past victories on environmental issues, and the benefits the addressee will receive by joining the Club. Similarly, the Moral Majority letter urging the boycott of 7-Eleven stores describes the achievements of past efforts with other retail chains and the culpability of 7-Eleven stores in spreading pornography.

These middle portions of direct mailings are not designed to inform the reader of the seriousness of the threat, although they may do this, but to sell the organization. This is the positioning portion of the letter, the part that differentiates this cause, group, or organization from others like it. This section describes any material or social benefits a prospective donor or new member will receive by responding positively to the mailing.

To assist this positioning process, many mailings insert folders or fliers. The Sierra Club's folder explains that a member will receive *Sierra,* the club's

Task Force Membership Benefits

1. MEDAL OF MERIT

President Reagan's specially commissioned Medal of Merit. This unique, golden Medal of Merit is awarded only to Presidential Task Force Members, ensuring that its rarity and meaning will increase with the years. Your personal Medal of Merit will be presented to you in a handsome case. Displayed in home or office, the President's Medal of Merit is a beautiful and positive way to show you're working to make a better America.

2. LAPEL PIN

The Medal of Merit Lapel Pin—this beautifully detailed reproduction of the Medal of Merit is as beautiful and unique as the Medal itself.

Wear this golden pin proudly to signify your special relationship with President Reagan.

3. CEREMONIAL FLAG

A unique, full-size American Flag, President Reagan has commissioned Senator Richard Lugar to dedicate this beautiful symbol of your special love for America at an official ceremony in the rotunda of our nation's Capitol Building.

4. MEMBERSHIP CARD

Your embossed Presidential Task Force Membership Card.

This card reveals your toll-free, members-only, Washington hotline number—your direct line to important developments in the United States Senate.

Your card and toll-free telephone number brings you to the doorstep of action in Washington—your super-fast way to contact President Reagan and every Republican in the United States Senate. And when you visit Washington, your personal membership identification number will allow you to call ahead on the hotline for your special United States Senate Gallery Pass. It's all part of membership in President Reagan's Task Force.

5. HONOR ROLL

Your name will be inscribed on the President's Honor Roll and be kept forever with his permanent Presidential Papers.

Perhaps someday your grandchildren or great-grandchildren will see your name linked historically with President Reagan himself on this rare document.

6. "THE NEW FORCE"

You'll receive "THE NEW FORCE"—a special insider's briefing on the real stories behind what's happening at the White House, on Capitol Hill and around the world.

"THE NEW FORCE" goes only to Task Force members and will help you tell friends and neighbors the truth about major events.

Also, special personal letters from Task Force Chairman Senator Richard Lugar, to keep you informed about the issues the Task Force should be taking immediate action on—issues of particular importance to you.

FIGURE I.3

REPUBLICAN TASK FORCE FLIER DESCRIBING THE BENEFITS OF MEMBERSHIP

bimonthly magazine, chapter newsletters from the local branch of the club, discounts on Sierra Club publications, opportunities to join other Sierra Club members in a worldwide outing program, and a voice in setting local and national policy priorities for the club's lobbying efforts. The Republican Task Force flier shown in figure 1.3 illustrates this important sales device. It offers the prospective donor six material incentives including a permanent place in President Reagan's Presidential Papers that the donor's grandchildren will be able to see and that will link the member historically with President Reagan himself.

The last section of the text goes back to the opening themes: There is a serious threat, and you can help overcome it. In the final section of a Republican Task Force letter, President Reagan uses eight short paragraphs to bring home two points: The threat is serious and he needs the recipient's help:

> Right now we Republicans control the Senate by only a slim four-vote margin.
> It took us 26 long years to elect 54 Republican Senators to get that narrow majority, and two years of hard work to maintain it. But the Democrats need only gain four seats in the '84 Senate elections to win it back from us.
> Frankly, the odds are against us. And we'll never be able to continue on the road to prosperity unless you and others say, "O.K., count me in."
> By joining the Republican Presidential Task Force, you'll be doing the single most important act a person can do to help ensure Republican control of the Senate for the next twenty years.
> Let me say it again.
> America's future for the next twenty years rests on who controls the U.S. Senate in 1984.
> I hope and pray that Senator Dick Lugar and I can count on your Task Force membership. Serious work needs to be done now to preserve our Senate majority.
> Please join today. Your membership will help make the difference.

In a similar vein, a request from Mothers Against Drunk Drivers (MADD) ends its mailing with the following three paragraphs:

> *I'm asking for your help to deal with this national crime* that kills and injures so many innocent victims every year. Will you stand with us?
> We urgently need your gift of $20, $100, $25, $50 or whatever you can send. I need to hear you say you're behind us—that you're willing to do what you can to help change the laws of this country.
> Drunk drivers kill. They maim. They seriously injure. *And they get away with it.* Please help us fight back.

Enclosed with every direct mailing is the all-important reply card or envelope. Figure 1.4 shows the reply card for the Task Force letter. The response card contains the key number (upper right-hand corner just to the right of

REPUBLICAN PRESIDENTIAL TASK FORCE
Acceptance Certificate 004500

𝕹𝖆𝖓𝖊𝖙𝖙𝖊 𝖂𝖆𝖗𝖓𝖊𝖗

Dear President Reagan:

☐ YES, I accept your personal invitation to join the Republican Presidential Task Force, and I'll work with you to help ensure a continuing Republican majority in the U.S. Senate.

I'm excited that together we're seizing this once in a lifetime opportunity to maintain Republican control of the U.S. Senate.

☐ I pledge $120.00 for Charter Membership.

☐ Enclosed is my $120.00 payment in full.

☐ Enclosed is my first payment of $10.00. And I promise to pay the balance over the next eleven months.

I also understand my name will be added to your special "Honor Roll" and that this historic document will be kept forever with your permanent papers.

_____
Signature

Nanette Warner

Tucson, Arizona 85705

278T (over please)

Please make your check payable to **Republican Presidential Task Force.**

Nanette Warner, please detach and keep for your records.

REPUBLICAN PRESIDENTIAL
TASK FORCE

Your specially dedicated American Flag symbolizes the pride Task Force members take in supporting President Reagan.

Check Number_____Amount_____

Date_____

FIGURE 1.4
**A REPLY CARD FROM THE REPUBLICAN PRESIDENTIAL TASK FORCE
SHOWING THE USE OF KEY NUMBERS**

"Certificate"); a second number shows the congressional district (lower right-hand corner). This reply card illustrates many of the structural advantages of direct mailings—personalization (the engraved name and the message "YES, I accept your personal invitation"), immediacy (the recipient checks a box, writes a check, and mails the enclosed reply card in the stamped reply envelope provided), and positioning (setting a moderately high price of $120 and offering a number of prestige benefits such as your name on a special "Honor Roll" that will become a historic document to be kept forever).

Many reply forms allow the recipient to act in support of the cause without monetary cost. The purpose of these devices is to involve the respondent in the solicitation. On the Task Force form, the action is a simple one, checking a box. A more effective technique is providing a stamp for the recipient to remove from one part of the letter and place on the reply card. Political direct mailers have found that this simple action dramatically improves response rates. The most common way of doing this is to place two stamps of different colors at the end of the letter. One stamp says "Yes," the other, "No." The letter tells the recipient to remove one stamp and place it in the appropriate box on the reply card, where there are two options:

Count me in! I pledge _ $20, _ $30, _ $50 to help stop . . .

I don't think this problem is important to Americans.

Mail experts believe that stamps work well because they are colorful, visible, and easy to do; and a respondent who places the "Yes" stamp has made a commitment. Instructions from the Republican National Committee to 1984 candidates for Congress concerning how to prepare their mailings suggest that candidates should make use of such stamps in both their prospecting and house list letters.

A third device for getting the addressee started toward responding is the inclusion of a questionnaire on the issue to which the mailing is addressed. Usually the organization sponsoring the mailing promises that results of the survey will be sent to all members of Congress or to the President. These simple instruments—the box to check, the stamp to transfer, or the questionnaire to answer—involve the recipient in the mailing and get him started toward writing what the organization really wants: the contribution check.

Summary

Direct mail has several technical advantages over traditional techniques of recruiting and mobilizing citizens into political activity. The most significant are the ability to pretest political messages and to personalize, concentrate, and encourage an immediate response from the target audience. In addition, direct-mail messages can be as long as necessary to explain fully a cause or a candidate. In terms of content, direct mailings make greater use of threat and fear than other political communication and present these threats in a carefully structured three-part appeal. The first section of the mailings emphasizes threats to existing values and tells recipients that they can do something important that will reduce these dangers. The middle portion of the letter deals largely with information about the organization sponsoring the mailing and the cause for which the solicited resources will be used. This section also describes any special material and social benefits recipients will receive should they respond. The final part of the mailing returns to the themes of threat and personal efficacy and utilizes devices such as stamp transfers and questionnaires to involve the addressee in the mailing and get him started toward responding.

While political direct mail is providing significant advantages to its users, it may be creating substantial harms for the American political system. Our content analysis of mailings showed that they stress fear and threat, and portray issues in extreme black-and-white alternatives. Opponents are "enemies" who want to destroy values that the recipient holds dear. Propaganda techniques pervade direct mailings, tapping emotions designed to generate an immediate response, not to help think through a complex issue. Although all effective direct mailings make use of fear to motivate potential respondents, ideological mailings from groups such as the Moral Majority, the Heritage Foundation, Common Cause, and the American Civil Liberties Union do so to a much greater degree than mailings from the major political parties. In addition, ideological mailings are more provocative and conflict oriented than are appeals from the major political parties.

Notes

1. Edward L. Nash, *Direct Marketing: Strategy, Planning and Execution* (New York: McGraw-Hill, 1982), 1-2.

2. Ibid., 86-87.

3. Margaret Latus, "Ideological PACs and Political Action," in *The New Christian Right*, ed. Robert Liebman and Robert Wuthnow (Hawthorne, N.Y.: Aldine, 1983).

4. Ibid. Just how valuable a house list can be is demonstrated by the sale of Barry Goldwater's contributor list to a political consulting firm for $300,000. *Arizona Daily Star*, 16 February 1986, A7.

5. Richard Viguerie, *The New Right: We're Ready to Lead* (Falls Church, Va.: Viguerie Co., 1981), 94.

6. Ibid.

7. Richard Hodgson, *Direct Mail and Mail Order Handbook,* 2d ed. (Chicago: Dartnell, 1977), 397.

8. Personalized salutations are used far less frequently in prospecting letters. Ron Shaiko in a sample of 90 such letters found that only 20 personalized the saluation.

9. Albert Cover and Bruce Brumberg, "Baby Books and Ballots: The Impact of Congressional Mail on Constituent Opinion," *American Political Science Review* 76 (June 1982): 347-59.

10. Hodgson, *Direct Mail,* 91.

11. Andrew S. McFarland, *Common Cause* (Chatham, N.J.: Chatham House, 1984), 62-67.

12. Nash, *Direct Marketing,* 4.

13. Ibid., 215.

14. Margaret Latus, "Assessing Ideological PACs: From Outrage to Understanding," in *Money and Politics in the United States,* ed. Michael Malbin (Chatham, N.J.: Chatham House), 166.

15. See Amos Tversky and Daniel Kahneman, "The Framing of Decisions and the Psychology of Choice," *Science* 211 (January 1981): 453-58; and Pamela Conover and Virginia Gray, *Feminism and the New Right: Conflict over the American Family* (New York: Praeger, 1983).

16. I sent 73 requests and 34 organizations responded positively. Seven of them sent two mailings, one to a house list and the other to a prospect list.

17. The content analysis also examined the incentives used by the various mailings to encourage persons to join citizen action groups and contribute to political parties and political action committees. These analyses are reported in chapter 3.

2. Direct Marketing by Television and Telephone

Although direct mail is the most productive direct-marketing technique, it is not the only option available to political entrepreneurs. Television, particularly cable television, and long-distance telephone services provide alternatives to direct mail for fund raising, recruiting, and mobilizing citizens to direct political action. Cable television presents opportunities for achieving the immediacy of direct mail and adds the visual appeal that makes television such a special medium. Through weekly syndicated shows, a politician or organization can develop a consistent audience at a much lower price than would be available through the major networks. Two-way, closed-circuit broadcasts permit individuals to see and talk directly with one another and thereby provide unmatched personalization capabilities. Closed-circuit television can also increase political participation through "electronic town meetings." Using new technologies, citizens can watch and participate in public debates and then cast their votes for the alternative that appeals to them.

Telephone direct marketing also has advantages. First, it allows the "seller" to speak directly with the prospective "buyer." As we saw in chapter 1, this personalization is critical to motivating people to political action. Telephone communication encourages immediacy and concentration as well. One of the telephone's most important advantages is the speed with which it can reach a target audience. When there is insufficient time to develop and send a mass mailing or to arrange a special television program, long-distance telephone lines allow groups to mobilize their activists to pressure governmental officials.

Direct Marketing through Television

Political direct marketing through cable television and syndicated television shows to independent stations presents an interesting option to direct mail. Currently, fundamentalist ministers including Jerry Falwell, Pat Robertson, and Charles Stanley are the major users of this medium. These ministers use religious broadcasts to prospect for new members, to raise funds for political purposes, and to mobilize their followers to political action.

Jerry Falwell's broadcasts provide an example of how these programs can combine with direct mail to provide an effective prospecting mechanism. Each Sunday evening, Reverend Falwell's program offers free materials and services to his television audience. These include audio cassettes, books, and special prayers for a viewer or his friend or relative. Viewers obtain these goods and services by calling a toll-free 800 telephone number or by writing to the "Old Time Gospel Hour."[1] Persons making these requests become part of the Moral Majority's next prospecting list. They have shown through their request that they share many of the values and beliefs of the Moral Majority and that they can be motivated to respond. In addition, the material they request provides the Moral Majority with valuable information that can be used to personalize the prospecting letter.

The political content of most broadcasts of the Christian Right is limited, however, because politics must be interspersed with religion; and, by and large, religion gets first billing. Whereas direct mailings begin with the powerful combination of threat and appeal to personal efficacy, the Christian Right's television solicitations commence with a prayer and a hymn. The necessary threats and calls for help are placed within the context of a sermon. This format, in combination with television's inability to concentrate on a particular target audience, forces preaching politicians to moderate their political messages. The "enemies" named are not usually "liberals" or any other group that might have a significant number of self-identifiers watching the broadcast. Instead, foes are limited to more clearly defined and despised groups, such as pornographers and communists.

To compare the Christian Right's television appeals with their direct mailings, Christian Right programs broadcast during the thirty days before the 1984 elections were videotaped and transcribed. They were then content analyzed in the same fashion as the direct mailings reported in chapter 1. Even after hymns, prayers, and other preliminary religious messages were omitted, televised appeals used threat and fear far less frequently than the mailings did, and the propaganda ratings of the televised messages were much lower than those of the direct mailings.

Analyses of Reverend Falwell's Sunday evening broadcasts the month before the 1984 elections found that his most aggressive message aired on 28 October 1984. This program, titled "A Time for Anger," attacked persons advocating abortion rights and homosexuality, and candidates who were soft on communism. An additional characteristic of that broadcast was its clearly partisan nature. Reverend Falwell strongly endorsed President Reagan and candidates who were running as conservatives on social issues and had taken strong and aggressive stands against the Soviet Union. Despite its clearly political nature and the fact that it was televised just nine days before the national election, the program's content was not nearly as extreme as the Moral Majority's mailings during the same period.[2]

Although they are the most frequent users of cable television for the direct marketing of politics, the preaching politicians of the Christian Right are not the only users of this medium. The National Chamber of Commerce carries a syndicated television program, "It's Your Business," to publicize political issues and the chamber's positions on those issues. The chamber also owns a subscription-based, two-way, closed-circuit television network, Biznet. This network, which has its own studios, technical staff, and satellite access, permits the chamber to mobilize members in cities with Biznet facilities in a matter of hours.[3] The chamber need not wait to schedule its programs through other networks or independent stations; it simply alerts its local chapters that a program will be aired, and the local chambers call their members. Biznet's facilities make it possible not only for persons in the Washington studio to talk to listeners in other cities but persons at those locations can talk back and ask questions of people in the D.C. studio and in other Biznet locations.

Biznet carries personalization, concentration, and immediacy to their apex. Unfortunately for the chamber, Biznet also reaches the summit in costs. When originally developed, the Chamber of Commerce hoped that local chapters throughout the country would buy into the network and purchase the necessary equipment to participate in the two-way broadcasts. This has not occurred. Despite being one of the most expensive and innovative uses of television by a political interest group, Biznet has not proven as successful as the chamber had hoped. After five years, the two-way, closed-circuit network remains limited largely to major metropolitan areas in the East and Midwest. The chamber has been able to overcome this partially by utilizing the television facilities of the Holiday Inns of America and local university and public broadcasting stations. The use of these nonchamber facilities, however, reduces the ability of Biznet to schedule programs on short notice.

Despite its limitations, Biznet, in combination with "It's Your Business" and the chamber's national radio show, "What's the Issue," have proven quite useful in recruiting new members for the chamber and in mobilizing the business community to lobby Congress on issues such as revisions in the Clean Air Act and major labor legislation. One of Biznet's more effective and innovative uses was a 1984 Republican series of broadcasts in which Lyn Nofziger and other high-level Reagan advisers raised money for the Republican party and President Reagan. This series reached chamber members in Orlando, Atlanta, and Cleveland and allowed them to interact directly with important White House officials and to receive immediate responses to questions they had concerning President Reagan's positions. This technique proved effective in generating funds for Republicans and enthusiasm for the Biznet network. Since this fund-raising series, the network has received far more requests for closed-circuit broadcasts, and Biznet has been able to convince cabinet members in the Reagan administration to provide question-and-answer sessions for several cities considering joining the network.[4]

TELEDEMOCRACY

In addition to its role as a direct marketing tool, the two-way cable networks offer extensive new opportunities for citizen participation and direct democracy. Through this technology, persons can participate in political debates and make their opinions known without leaving their homes. These opportunities allow instant votes or referenda on issues and can provide valuable feedback to government officials. Given sufficient funding, this technology makes it possible to have national referenda on issues.

Among the more vocal proponents of direct democracy through electronic media are Ted Becker and Benjamin Barber. In an article in the *Futurist,* Becker contends that with the help of closed-circuit television, public opinion will become the law of the land as persons express their opinions from their own homes.

Using as his technological model the Warner-Amex QUBE system with which people use their television to shop and choose among consumer products, Becker argues that citizens should be able to watch a public debate and then decide the issue. No representatives are necessary; instead we achieve direct democracy and government by the "general will" advocated by Rousseau.[5] The QUBE system uses a module that attaches to the television set in much the same manner as current cable television hookups. With this system, individuals are not limited to a single yes-or-no decision, but can choose from among as many as five options. Combined with telephone hookups, these systems permit citizens to communicate with officials in television studios and with one another. Several experiments in less technologically sophisticated television/telephone town meetings have been evaluated quite positively.[6]

Benjamin Barber's book *Strong Democracy: Participatory Politics for a New Age* provides a more complex portrayal of how direct-marketing techniques might work to encourage greater political activity by the less advantaged sectors of society. Barber advocates the use of technologies such as QUBE in combination with direct-marketing tools including direct mail, a civic videotext service for home computers, and heavily subsidized postal rates for newspapers, magazines, and political journals and books.[7] Through a multimedia approach, Barber hopes to increase the levels of political knowledge and interest among the citizenry by making information more readily available. In addition, Barber believes the visual presentations that television provides are more attractive than other methods to the less advantaged sectors of society and will therefore encourage their participation in politics.

Underlying the Becker and Barber proposals is the assumption that current imbalances in patterns of participation are caused by an unequal access to political information coupled with a strong and growing preference in the society for video rather than printed communication. Becker, for example, writes that where QUBE is in place, "folks truly enjoy using this teledemocratic system: they express an avid interest in participating in feedback; they find the use of the system rewarding. And they are willing to pay for the service."[8] Barber cites the example of a Reading, Pennsylvania, video communication network among senior citizens in shut-in environments. The closed-circuit video system mobilized that population and eventually led to regular video town meetings for the entire community.[9]

The optimism of Becker and Barber concerning the benefits of teledemocracy are not shared by all who have observed it. Michael Malbin writes in *Public Opinion* that the value of representative democracy, as opposed to direct democracy, is that the need to form majorities from multiple factions forces representatives to modify and compromise proposals before adopting or rejecting them. This forces representatives to deliberate and to consider the needs of others. But, Malbin argues, political deliberation cannot be a solitary activity carried out in one's home. Opinions become refined through give and take with people whose backgrounds and opinions differ from one's own. And discussion presupposes reasonably well informed citizens. With teledemocracy these conditions are not met, and discussion is replaced by exhortation. Advocates of the various positions on an issue would be encouraged to take the same fear-filled and extreme positions found in direct mailings.[10]

An additional problem with electronic town meetings where citizens vote among prepared alternatives is that such systems place tremendous power in the hands of those who frame the questions.[11] Persons who know how to manipulate political symbols effectively can predetermine how votes will be cast in much the same way that persons who prepare questions for surveys can dictate the answers that a respondent will likely give.

Whether television is used to market political ideas, candidates, and causes or whether it is used to facilitate direct democracy, certain aspects of cable and syndicated television are clear. First, televised political messages must be supported by some other fund-raising activity. The Christian Right's broadcasts are funded by donations to religious causes as well as to political efforts. The National Chamber of Commerce subsidizes Biznet through membership dues and by renting Biznet's facilities to other organizations. And teledemocracy must be funded by the public sector or through advertising. Second, if televised direct marketing is to be effective, its messages must be preceded by other communication. Television appeals mainly to persons who are already convinced of the virtue of the cause or candidate. Rather than recruit new converts, television mobilizes those who already agree with the goals of the organization but need some special incentive or appeal to spur them into action.[12] Finally, network television—even cable networks—because it is not sufficiently concentrated, costs too much for sustained use by citizen action groups or political action committees. Closed-circuit television, while concentrated, costs far more per viewer and requires a level of capital investment beyond the means of all but a few institutions.

Direct Marketing by Phone

Like direct mail, telephone contacting allows for substantial personalization, concentration, and immediacy. But, like television, telephone direct marketing works better for mobilizing persons already committed than for prospecting new donors. Telephone contacts cannot prospect effectively because there is insufficient time to make a sale. Mailings can include long letters, photographs, and multiple inserts; prospecting phone calls are limited to less than two minutes.[13] In addition, the cost of staff time in telephone prospecting is prohibitive. If the typical staff member makes fifteen calls per hour and the response rate is 2 percent, the average number of "sales" will be less than three per day.

Although not a practical prospecting tool, long-distance telephone services are effective in mobilizing an organization's activists to political action. If a group has a list of enthusiasts on a particular issue and there is insufficient time to mobilize them through a mailing, long-distance services such as WATS lines and MCI allow the national leadership to mobilize their grass-roots supporters in a matter of hours. Many organizations use "telephone alert" or "telephone tree" systems where each member of the national staff calls one or two activists in each congressional district. These people, in turn, call three persons assigned to them and pass along the mobilization message. Each of these persons calls another three, and this progression continues in the mode of a chain letter until the entire network has been contacted.

The advantages of these telephone chains are that they are relatively inexpensive, encourage member involvement, and can be effective lobbying techniques when time is short. In less than forty-eight hours a group such as the Sierra Club or the National Right to Life can generate 10,000 letters, phone calls, and telegrams to members of Congress. The disadvantage of telephone chains is that members of the chain do not always do what they are supposed to. The greater the number of steps in the chain, the more likely it is that either the message delivered becomes altered or that persons fail to make the required calls. To the extent that the communication changes as it moves from one activist to the next, the organization doing the lobbying has lost control of its message.

Summary

In chapter 1 we found five important advantages of direct mail: market pretesting, personalization, concentration, immediacy, and message length. Other direct-marketing techniques share the advantage of immediacy; but with the exception of the expensive two-way, closed-circuit television, they fail to offer all of the remaining benefits. Cable television, particularly syndicated shows such as the "Old Time Gospel Hour" and "It's Your Business," offers sufficient length and greater visual appeal than direct mail, but lacks pretesting, concentration, and personalization. Telephone marketing offers concentration, personalization, and pretesting; but it lacks visual appeal and is extremely limited in message length. Both cable television and telephone direct marketing are more expensive than direct mail and have more difficulty in reaching first-time donors.

Cable television—particularly two-way, closed-circuit television—provides an enticing opportunity to expand democratic participation and encourage direct rather than representative democracy. Past experiments with electronic referenda have proven successful in allowing the elderly and others who have difficulty leaving their homes to participate in politics; and the visual appeal and immediate feedback of these experiments may prove capable of enticing the poor and other underrepresented sectors of society into the political arena. Whether this would actually occur if the opportunities were offered is yet to be determined. Certainly, if the Democratic party telethons are indicators of who would turn their televisions to political shows, closed-circuit broadcasts would increase the current socioeconomic bias in participation. In addition, there are dangers to direct democracy that could outweigh its benefits. Most of these dangers center on whether or not reasonable and informed discussion and decisions are possible in the absence of face-to-face discussion, and the question of who will decide the wording of final alternatives on which viewers will vote and the order in which the alternatives will be voted on.

The next chapter provides some evidence on these issues as it analyzes the changes that direct marketing has made in who participates in American politics. The chapter also addresses the issue of whether or not persons recruited through direct marketing have less knowledge and tolerance than more traditional participants in the political process.

Notes

1. Reverend Falwell has had to stop offering a number of these free services as members of organizations opposed to the Liberty Foundation (the new name of the Moral Majority) have requested so many free services that the Liberty Foundation was pushed into debt.

2. A different program aired on the same evening, "Life and Liberty for All Who Believe." This program was almost as extreme as the ideological direct mailings. Sponsored by the liberal political action committee People for the American Way, the broadcast attacked the intolerance of the Moral Majority and other organizations of the Christian Right and scored as highly on its use of fear and threat as all but a few direct mailings.

3. Burdett Loomis, "A New Era: Groups and the Grass Roots," in *Interest Group Politics,* ed. Allan Cigler and Burdett Loomis (Washington, D.C.: CQ Press, 1983), 175-86.

4. Biznet officials were kind enough to allow me to watch one of these sessions in which Labor Secretary Brock answered businesspersons' questions concerning the administration's position on business-labor legislation.

5. Jean Jacques Rousseau, *The Social Contract and Discourse on Inequality* (New York: Washington Square Press, 1967).

6. For discussions of these experiments see Ted Becker, "Teledemocracy," *Futurist,* December 1981; Ted Becker et al., *Report on "New Zealand Televote"* (Wellington, New Zealand: Victoria University, 1981); and Ted Becker et al., "Hawaii Televote: Measuring Public Opinion on Complex Policy Issues," *Political Science* 33 (July 1981).

7. Benjamin Barber, *Strong Democracy: Participatory Politics for a New Age* (Berkeley, Calif.: University of California Press, 1984). A condensed version of Barber's proposals can be found in "Voting Is Not Enough: A Plan for Strengthening Democracy," *Atlantic* 252 (June 1984): 45-53.

8. Cited in Michael Malbin, "Teledemocracy and Its Discontents," *Public Opinion,* June/July 1982, 58.

9. Barber, *Strong Democracy,* 276.

10. Malbin, "Teledemocracy," 58-59.

11. Ibid. An even more perplexing issue is presented by "Arrow's paradox." The economist Kenneth Arrow has shown that given three or more alternatives and the absence of a clear majority preference for any one of the three, it is quite possible that the alternative finally chosen will be a product, not of majority rule, but of the order in which alternatives are voted on. This means that in an electronic town meeting the individual who chooses the order of voting on the various alternatives can dictate the outcome he prefers, not the outcome that would be favored by a plurality of the citizens voting.

12. This point was stressed in interviews with both the directors of Biznet and fundraisers of the Christian Right.

13. The 2-minute limit is somewhat longer than most direct marketing experts advocate. Interviews with political and private direct market specialists found that most believe 60 seconds is the best message length. For a call to continue beyond that, the caller needs the permission of the person called. To receive this, prospects must already have been convinced in the first 60 seconds that the product or idea being sold is important to them.

3. Mobilizing the Public

The previous chapters examined the advantages that direct mail and other direct-marketing techniques provide to politicians; this chapter reveals how these techniques have changed political participation in America. It answers the questions Why do people join citizen action groups and contribute to political action committees? Do direct-marketing recruits participate in political associations for reasons other than those of persons who join in more traditional ways? Does direct marketing increase political participation by persons who normally are not active in American politics? Are direct-marketing recruits different in their political attitudes and behaviors from individuals who come into the political process through more traditional means? Are critics correct in their expectation that direct-marketing recruits are less tolerant and more aggressive than others, or are supporters right in believing that direct marketing will assist democratic government by making people better informed and by reducing the current participation imbalances among socioeconomic groups?

Participation in traditional partisan political activities such as voting and taking part in electoral campaigns has declined in the past two decades. Yet overall participation in politics has increased. Today neighborhoods organize to prevent the location of nuclear plants or toxic-waste facilities; citizens contest local planning decisions and change zoning regulations; more people than ever before write to their senators and congressional representatives; and increasing numbers of individuals contribute to political action committees and become members of public-interest groups.[1]

The Growth of Citizen Action Groups[2]
We need merely to look at the tremendous membership increases in organizations such as Common Cause, the National Right to Life, Committee for the Survival of a Free Congress, and the National Organization for Women to see that citizens are interested in politics and are willing to organize around a cause, an idea, or an ideology. Fully one-half of the citizen action groups that exist today formed after 1960. And during a period of increasing interest-group activity of all kinds, these organizations have increased from 15 to 21 percent of all reg-

istered lobbies represented in Washington.[3] Direct marketing, particularly direct mail, has played a major role in assisting this growth. To appreciate this role, we must first understand what motivates persons to join citizen action groups.

The seemingly self-evident answer to the question why people join interest groups is "to pursue shared political goals." Through 1965, political science and sociology accepted this obvious answer, and it provided a major underlying assumption of the pluralist theory of politics.[4] The leading proponent of this view, David Truman, saw both economic and noneconomic interest groups as products of the increasing division of labor and specialization in society. This increasing social complexity created many distinct interests, each valued intensely by a minority of the population. Truman believed that when threats to interests occurred, individuals who valued the threatened goods formed a political group to protect themselves.[5] For example, when the railroads made it possible for farmers to transport their excess produce to distant markets, large farms with specialized crops developed. Later, railroad trusts threatened the relatively cheap transportation of these goods, and farmers organized to lobby the government and force a reduction in rates. The railroads formed their own lobby, and the competition between the competing groups resulted in the Interstate Commerce Commission.

Just as pluralist theorists expect individuals to create and join political interest groups to protect their values, these theorists see social movements emerging by attracting people who share a common grievance against society. Movements provide new and appealing images of society, of right and wrong, and of justice and injustice.[6] If enough persons share a grievance, have similar beliefs about its cause, and agree on the appropriate remedies, a social movement will appear.[7] This view of social movements argues that the civil rights, antiwar, and women's movements appeared because a sufficient number of people shared common beliefs concerning what was wrong and what steps should be taken to change the situation. Groups within the movements, such as the National Association for the Advancement of Colored People (NAACP), the Weathermen, and the Women's Equity Action League attracted members by appealing to shared grievances and convincing potential members that their group was the one most likely to achieve the desired political results.

The publication of Mancur Olson's *The Logic of Collective Action* challenged the pluralist assumption that rational people join interest groups or social movements to pursue shared values. Olson's refutation centers on the theoretical concept of *collective goods,* such as national defense, clean air and water, public parks, and an absence of discrimination. These goods, if available to one person, will be available to all.[8] If your neighbor has clean air or national defense, you too will have it.

Olson asks, "Why would a rational person voluntarily commit money to the national defense?" One person's contribution to a $200 billion defense budget will not make an appreciable difference in the level of national defense provided. The individual who avoids paying a share in the provision of this collective good has other uses for the money that will yield much greater benefits *to him*. For this reason, contributions to the national defense cannot be voluntary. Neither are other taxes that the government uses to supply collective goods such as highways, police protection, and clean air.

Olson argues that most political goals sought by interest groups are really no different from national defense; they are collective goods. And, just as rational persons will not voluntarily pay taxes for national defense, neither will they join an interest group or participate in social movements to help achieve the political goals of the organization. If, for example, you want the government to spend more on environmental protection, why should you join an environmental interest group? There are already more than 2 million dues-paying members of such groups, and their budgets total over $50 million a year. Your $25 contribution will not affect the amount of environmental protection you enjoy.

In Olson's theory, people join political interest groups, not to achieve collective goods, but to obtain private, material goods available *only to members*. Medical doctors join the American Medical Association to receive the association's medical journal and obtain less expensive malpractice insurance; they do not join to influence public policies. Recruits to the National Retired Teachers Association (NRTA) do not seek to further the collective goals of retired teachers (although they may be happy if their contributions help to do this); they join to obtain medical insurance and lower prices on other products that are available only to NRTA members. Finally, persons do not join the National Wildlife Federation (NWF) to help preserve wildlife and wilderness areas; they join to receive the NWF magazine and discounts on outdoor recreation products. Olson calls these private, material goods "selective incentives" and argues that, without them, there would be few political interest groups.

Although Olson's analysis explains why those who want a particular collective good do not join political interest groups or join only when the selective incentives are worth the price of membership, his theory does not enlighten us concerning the motivations of the millions of individuals who join citizen action groups despite the absence of selective incentives. Why would a rational person join Common Cause, the League of Women Voters, Zero Population Growth, or the Conservative Caucus? These groups provide few selective incentives.

James Q. Wilson suggests that people join political interest groups for three reasons: (1) to obtain the selective incentives described by Olson; (2) to receive social benefits, such as friendship ties and the satisfactions obtained through associating with others who share their values; and (3) to further the pursuit of the collective goods. Wilson labels these three benefits "material," "solidary," and "purposive."[9] Empirical examinations of why people join voluntary associations found that each inducement described by Wilson is important and that three other factors also encourage membership: a sense of civic duty, a feeling of personal efficacy, and the utility persons receive from knowing that others are enjoying a collective good that they helped supply.[10] For example, a woman might join the National Organization for Women (NOW) because (1) she enjoys the local NOW meetings where she has the opportunity of meeting persons who share her interests (a solidary benefit); (2) she enjoys the organization's bimonthly magazine or expects to become part of a women's network that will aid her in getting a job (material benefits); (3) she feels that by joining the group she can make a difference and that acting alone she cannot (personal efficacy); (4) she believes that it is her duty to do "her part" in forwarding the cause of women's rights (civic duty); (5) she hopes to make life better for her female friends and her daughters (interpersonal utility benefit); and (6) she desires the collective good for herself (purposive benefit).

Perhaps the three most important of these many incentives are purposive incentives, civic duty, and personal efficacy.[11] The motivation to join because of civic duty is an incentive with which most of us are familiar. Every four years, millions of persons vote in the presidential election, even though they know that their vote will not make "the difference" in the outcome. They simply fulfill their civic duty to vote.[12] This desire to "do our part" is an important attribute in understanding Americans' participation and has been a notable characteristic of our culture from as early as 1835 when Alexis de Tocqueville first observed it in his book *Democracy in America*.

Personal efficacy refers to the psychological benefit a person receives from believing that his or her contribution can make a difference. Despite the objective reality that this is not the case, interviews with persons concerning why they joined a citizen action group indicate that many joiners *believe* their individual contributions are important.[13] Even when persons know that a single contribution will not materially affect the outcome, they surmise that the most effective way to work for the achievement of the collective goal is to join with others.[14]

Direct mailers are aware of the importance of purposive incentives, civic duty, and personal efficacy. As we saw in chapter 1 (table 1.1), two-thirds of all paragraphs in direct mailings contain appeals to these three motivations. Either the writers of direct mail are unconvinced of Olson's analysis or they rely on irrationality and altruism, rather than narrowly defined rational self-interest, to motivate prospective donors and members. In sharp contrast to the space devoted to purposive incentives, duty, and efficacy, only 5 percent of all direct-mail paragraphs appeal to either solidary or material incentives.[15]

Disincentives to Participation

While there are multiple incentives for joining a citizen action group, there are also disincentives. Before paying the obvious cost of the membership dues, people must spend the time and effort necessary to identify those organizations pursuing the collective goals that interest them. Then they must choose among the competing groups and discover how to join the one selected. Persons interested in conservation can join any of more than a dozen environmental groups, including the Sierra Club, Environmental Action, the Wilderness Society, and the Environmental Defense Fund. After spending the resources necessary to decide which group to join and paying the required membership dues, new members may face additional obligations. They may be asked to attend local chapter meetings, take part in a telephone alert system where members call other members to mobilize them for action, and contact their political representatives when Congress is voting on environmental issues. In short, membership in citizen action groups may require more than a simple contribution; it can entail substantial time and effort as well.

Direct marketing dramatically reduces the above costs. A mailing from a citizen action group informs prospects of the causes the group pursues, the actions the group takes to achieve its goals, the material and solidary benefits members receive, and the money and time costs members are expected to bear.

Many direct mailings lower participation costs in a more pernicious way: They discourage any activity beyond the writing of a contribution check. For example, the National Right to Work Legal Defense Foundation writes potential contributors:

> Will you go to the Supreme Court with me to fight the corrupt ways the big union bosses are now spending compulsory union dues on their own pet political campaigns and candidates?
>
> I don't mean actually appear in court, of course; I mean support the one organization that has the courage to stand up to the bosses—the National Right to Work Legal Defense Foundation. . . .
>
> Will you accept this nomination to join more than 320,000 men and women who fight the abuses of compulsory unionism by supporting the National Right to Work Legal Defense Foundation by sending a tax-deductible check for $21—or more—today?

The implication of this message is that all the "participant" needs to do is send money. The foundation will take care of everything else.

Two groups, the Moral Majority and Greenpeace, use an interesting variation of the above message. Their direct mail informs recipients that the leaders of the Moral Majority and Greenpeace place themselves in personally dangerous situations. Reverend Falwell describes threats on his life and the verbal abuses he and his family receive from enemies of the Christian Right. Greenpeace chronicles the arrests that the group's activists have undergone and the dangers to them that their radical actions in behalf of wildlife and the environment create.[16] Then both groups tell the readers that they will not be asked to subject themselves to these dangers. All they need do is send money; the leaders will take the risks.

This "participation through contribution" is the ersatz participation that alarms many of the critics of direct marketing. Direct mail, instead of encouraging active participation through meetings and discussion, often encourages the prospective "member" to do nothing beyond writing the contribution checks necessary to keep the leaders solvent. Mailings may soften this message by including a questionnaire for respondents to fill out so that their opinions "will be heard in Washington," but there can be little doubt that, for many groups, the objective is a quiescent contributor, not an active member.

The Potential Impact of Direct Marketing

Why is it important whether a person joins a citizen action group in response to a direct-marketing solicitation or in response to social and occupational network ties? Direct marketing's critics suggest that how persons join groups affects their tolerance of opposing views. Persons who join voluntary associations because of occupational and social ties often end up in organizations with substantially different political ideologies and purposes. For example, a woman may belong to the League of Women Voters, the Association of Business and Professional Women, the Lady Jaycees, and the United Way. Her spouse may belong to the Jaycees, a trade association, and a local fishing club. Together they may be members of a local outdoor recreation association and a local church. The dominant political persuasion in each of these voluntary associations is likely to be somewhat different. Because of this, our hypothetical couple encounters several sets of political ideas, which encourages tolerance of differing political views.[17]

Contrast this membership pattern with that encouraged by direct marketing. In place of memberships in different kinds of voluntary associations, the direct-mail recruit typically belongs to several organizations with similar ideologies and goals. The cause of this is the mailing list. Once an individual responds to an appeal from one group, that association will trade or sell his name to other organizations with similar purposes. For example, persons responding to a direct mailing from the Wilderness Society will soon receive prospect mailings from Environmental Action, the Audubon Society, and the Sierra Club. Each of these solicitations shows the same persons and groups as the "good guys" and another set of individuals and organizations as "the enemy." If people who respond to these mailings are not involved in other associations where conflicting ideas are presented and debated, then their knowledge of an environmental issue depends on information supplied in mailings from environmental groups. And, as we saw in chapter 1, this information is not noted for its restraint and encouragement of balanced opinions and compromise.[18]

How might this move from active membership in multiple organizations with differing political objectives to membership in associations with similar goals and objectives affect American politics? Critics of direct marketing charge that such changes in membership and participation patterns will decrease political tolerance and reduce the likelihood that political officials can achieve meaningful compromises. When participation is limited to writing a check in response to an emotional, fear-filled mailing, there is no opportunity to listen to the other side. Whereas multiple active memberships in organizations with different political orientations encourage persons to hear conflicting opinions, multiple passive memberships in groups with similar objectives encourage individuals to see only one point of view. The result is intolerance.

Critics of direct mail believe the pattern of overlapping, passive memberships leads people to see the political opposition as totally greedy, selfish, and mean. Given this perception, when political leaders seek compromises, supporters on both sides will see the politician as having sold out and the government's decision as illegitimate. Because of this, direct-mail recruits become alienated from government, and nonelected elites are able to manipulate them into aggressive and undemocratic political behaviors.

Not all writers who evaluate direct marketing's impact on the political system see its results as harmful. A minority argues that it can lead to a more democratic society. These more supportive assessments stem largely from the view that because political knowledge among the American public is so superficial, any increase in it will improve rather than harm the system.[19] The low level of political awareness among American citizens is well documented. A 1976 survey conducted immediately after the national election found that less than one-half of American adults could correctly identify which political party controlled the House of Representatives before and after the election. Similarly, only a small minority of the adult population can both name their congressional representative and how he voted on just one issue during the most recent session of Congress.[20] If political mail, even with its purported faults, can motivate the public to pay attention to important issues and the actions of their representatives, then it may strengthen democracy.

Supporters also believe that direct marketing will increase political equality by providing opportunities for participation to sets of individuals who were previously unlikely to participate. Numerous studies have shown that persons from the upper and upper-middle classes have much higher rates of political participation than other sectors of the population. Greatest participation in voluntary associations comes from persons who have high incomes and are college educated, long-term residents of their communities, married, middle-aged, white, and male.[21] These persons are far more likely to join social, civic, and political organizations than are persons who did not go to college and whose income and business activities do not put them into contact with persons who are active in politics. This bias becomes still greater if religious or racial barriers are present.

Direct marketing may overcome these biases because it need not rely on existing social network ties to recruit participants. If individuals have telephones, televisions, and postal addresses, direct-marketing techniques can reach them. Direct mail has proven quite successful in motivating these persons to purchase private goods and services; the question is, Can direct marketing encourage greater public action as well?

As we saw in chapter 2, television, particularly cable television and the two-way, closed-circuit hookups such as the National Chamber of Commerce's Biznet or Warner-Amex's QUBE, offer extensive opportunities for citizen participation. If Reverend Falwell can mobilize rural, fundamentalist Baptists to participate, and closed-circuit hookups can encourage the elderly and shut-ins to become active, it seems reasonable to expect that a broad array of direct-marketing techniques can achieve greater participation by previously inactive persons.

The Actual Impact of Direct Marketing

Are the critics or the supporters correct in their expectations of direct marketing's impact on citizen attitudes and behavior? To answer this, let us test three hypotheses: (1) Direct marketing encourages political equality by recruiting persons who have different demographic and socioeconomic characteristics from persons who became active through traditional social network channels; (2) direct marketing encourages alienated, distrustful, and aggressive political attitudes and behaviors; and (3) persons recruited through direct-marketing techniques know less, care less, and do less for their citizen action groups than persons who joined in response to social network invitations. Findings concerning these hypotheses can start us on the road to discovering how direct marketing actually affects the American political system.

To test the hypotheses, we compared members of citizen action groups who joined in response to a direct-marketing solicitation with members recruited through social networks. Samples of the two kinds of recruits were obtained through a mail survey that requested information concerning respondents' socio-economic and demographic attributes; their political attitudes and behaviors; and their motivations for joining the group, orientations toward it, and participation in it.[22]

The survey was sent to a national sample of 5000 persons, 1000 members in each of five environmental citizen action groups. Three of the groups—the Wilderness Society, Environmental Action, and the Environmental Defense Fund—recruit most of their members using direct mail. Two groups—the Sierra Club and the National Wildlife Federation—obtain the majority of their members through social network ties. Over 3500 persons responded to the questionnaire of which 3128 were complete and usable.

So that generalizations concerning the impact of direct marketing are not limited to environmental group members, two additional surveys of political action committee and political party contributors supplement the environmental group poll. One survey, conducted by James Guth and John Green, contains 2864 donors to political action committees; the other, performed by the Center for Political Studies at the University of Michigan, includes 2938 respondents to a national probability sample.[23]

METHODS AND MEASURES
Respondents to the environmental group survey are classified as either "social network" or "direct marketing" recruits by their responses to the question "How did you originally come to join [the name of the group]?" Persons who joined because of friends or who were given a membership were classified as social network recruits. Individuals who responded to a direct-mail solicitation or other advertisement were placed in the direct marketing category. To test the hypothesis that direct marketing brings new kinds of participants into the political process, the survey included questions concerning respondents' age, race, gender, education, income, occupation, employment, length of residence, size of community, marital status, and whether or not they were students.[24]

DEMOGRAPHIC COMPARISONS
Previous studies of direct-mail-based political action committees and citizen

action groups have indicated that direct marketing does not change the socio-economic and demographic characteristics of political participants. John Green and James Guth, in their studies of donors to political parties and ideological PACs—political action committees that are most dependent on direct marketing —found these donors to have even higher incomes than the more traditional contributors to politics. Sixty-nine percent of PAC contributors had family incomes over $75,000 per year. Even among contributors to religious PACs and groups of the Christian Right, 63 percent had incomes over $50,000 and 75 percent were college graduates.[25] Studies of Common Cause and other direct-mail-based citizen action groups have found that participants in these groups have similar demographic and higher socioeconomic characteristics than participants recruited through more traditional ways.[26]

In contrast to expectations that more visual direct marketing would lead to greater participation by the less advantaged sectors in society, comparison of television and social network recruits yields similar results to those found in direct-mail studies. In a study comparing contributors to three Democratic party national telethons with other donors to the party, John Ellwood and Robert Spitzer discovered that, contrary to what Benjamin Barber and Ted Becker would have predicted, the video appeals did not encourage participation by persons with lower levels of education and income. Instead, as table 3.1 clearly demonstrates, telethon donors had substantially higher socioeconomic status than other contributors to the party. The results in table 3.1 are not limited to donors. Even among persons who only watched the telethons, the socioeconomic characteristics of watchers were significantly higher than those of the voting population.[27]

TABLE 3.1

DEMOGRAPHIC AND SOCIOECONOMIC COMPARISONS BETWEEN
TELETHON CONTRIBUTORS AND OTHER DONORS TO THE DEMOCRATIC PARTY
(IN PERCENT)

Characteristic	Telethon Contributors	Other Party Donors
Attended college	63	56
Yearly incomes over $20,000	26	19
Professional or managerial	54	38

Analysis of the survey of environmental group members supports the finding that direct-marketing participants have as high or higher socioeconomic characteristics than traditional political activists. Direct-marketing recruits and social network joiners do not differ substantially in age, education, income, occupation, gender, marital status, or length of residence in the community.

All correlations between being a direct-marketing recruit and a given socio-economic or demographic variable had an absolute value of less than .20, and most were less than .10. The substantively significant variations that did occur indicated that persons who were recruited through the use of direct marketing had higher incomes (R = .17), were better integrated into community networks (R = .15), and came from more urban areas (R = .15) than individuals recruited via social networks.[28]

What about teledemocracy? If persons were electronically voting on policy issues instead of being asked for money, would this increase their participation? Certainly the Reading, Pennsylvania, experiment demonstrates that such two-way television communication can encourage the elderly and shut-ins to participate. The experiments cited by Becker and Barber in chapter 2 (see notes 5 and 6) do not indicate, however, that individuals with lower levels of education and income will participate more. One would suspect that, as was the case with the national telethons, persons who are willing to spend time watching political programs are far more likely to come from the upper and upper-middle classes. And if participatory tools such as Barber's civic videotext network using home computers were introduced, the probability is high that the participatory differences between the upper and lower classes would increase rather than decrease.

Why has direct marketing not encouraged greater participation by the previously underrepresented sectors of society? As we saw in chapter 1, the key to direct mail is the mailing list. To obtain names, voluntary associations and political action committees turn to sources such as membership lists of related organizations and subscribers to magazines with similar messages as the political interest group (e.g., the National Conservative Political Action Committee would use the subscription list of the *National Review*). The underrepresented in our society rarely appear on these lists because they lack the discretionary income and political interest to subscribe to news magazines or donate to causes that would place them on prospecting lists. Larry Sabato found the same phenomenon in campaign financing. Direct mail seeks out those who are already committed or who share the same socioeconomic characteristics of those who are already participating.[29]

This does not mean that direct marketing cannot reach the poor, the elderly, or the less educated in our society. The National Retired Teachers Association and the American Association of Retired Persons (AARP) have certainly mobilized the elderly, and the Moral Majority has made significant inroads into organizing fundamentalist Christians. In each instance, however, the organizing was made possible by a previously existing social network. The AARP built its membership using existing senior citizen centers. In addition, labor unions, particularly the United Auto Workers, developed programs for retired workers.[30] Finally, the National Retired Teachers Association and the AARP made significant progress in mobilizing only after they followed Mancur Olson's advice and offered the selective incentive that most appealed to the elderly: insurance coverage for the portion of the medical expenses not paid for by Medicare.

The Moral Majority recruits through the Baptist Bible Fellowship — a network of independent fundamentalist churches and clergymen who are graduates of the Baptist Bible College and are proven religious entrepreneurs — and through lists of contributors to Falwell's weekly television broadcast.[31] Even within the Christian Right, however, television has not attracted Moral Majority members from the ranks of the less educated and less affluent, but from those persons within the Christian Right who have substantially above-average educations and incomes.

If direct-marketing techniques are to reach the politically disadvantaged and underrepresented in our society, significant changes must occur in the development of prospecting lists. In addition, direct-marketing experts must discover ways to increase levels of political interest among the underrepresented sectors of society. Numerous studies of political participation in the United States and other Western democracies have demonstrated clearly that a key predictor of political participation is perceived personal efficacy.[32] While direct mail works to tap this feeling, it does not appear to create it. Direct marketing reaches persons who already perceive themselves as efficacious and moves them to political action. The levels of political efficacy among the poor and less educated in our society have not been changed.

POLITICAL COMPARISONS

Most critics of direct marketing believe that it injures the American political process through its impact on the public's political attitudes and behaviors. These writers hypothesize that because direct marketing utilizes extremism, fear, and threat, it encourages political alienation and ideological extremism. Because it makes participation fairly easy, direct marketing leads to participation by persons who are less knowledgeable about politics, less involved in traditional political parties, and less active in democratic forms of political participation such as voting and campaigning. In addition, because direct mail encourages overlapping rather than cross-cutting voluntary association memberships, its recruits are more dependent on the leadership of their citizen action group for information and direction. Critics contend that this combination of effects leads direct-mail recruits to be more accepting than others of political violence and to be more likely to engage in aggressive and illegal actions themselves.[33]

To test the hypothesis that direct mail leads to issue extremism, intolerance, alienation, and aggressive political attitudes and behaviors, the environmental group survey included a variety of questions concerning environmental issues and respondents' attitudes and behaviors toward the political system and public officials. For example, the first question pertaining to environmental extremism asked, "Overall, how serious are the nation's environmental problems today?" Possible answers ranged from "they are not very serious" to "we are rapidly approaching disaster."

Two scales, or combinations of questions, gauged the respondent's support for the basic values of the environmental movement. The first, a postmaterialism scale, asked respondents to rank competing values, such as maintaining a high level of economic growth and protecting nature from being spoiled and polluted.[34] The second scale measured a respondent's opposition to technology. Past studies have found that these two scales best differentiate environmentalists from the general population and provide an accurate indication of extremism in environmental concerns.[35] Whereas traditional American values include support of continued economic growth and the expectation that it will occur through technological improvements, orientations in favor of postmaterialism and in opposition to technological improvements run directly counter to those traditions.

Of course, behavior, not professed attitudes, is often the better indicator of how strongly an individual values particular goods. To compare the extent to which direct-marketing and social network recruits are willing to behave in ways that challenge opposing orientations, the survey investigated both public and private actions aimed at environmental preservation. Public activities included how often the respondent contacted public officials on environmental matters and whether or not he had been involved in protests against private corporations' polluting activities. Private actions were measured by the respondent's reported energy conservation, recycling, and avoidance of environmentally damaging products.

To test the proposition that direct marketing leads to generalized political alienation and political extremism, the survey included questions pertaining to (1) alienation from the current political system; (2) political ideology; (3) political interest; (4) perceived political efficacy; (5) participation through voting, campaigning, and other traditionally democratic behaviors; and (6) participation in and approval of illegal protests, occupying buildings and factories, destroying property, and other aggressive political acts.

Previous studies of direct-mail-based groups indicate that some of the critics' fears have an empirical basis. Constance Cook, in her 1983 study of four citizen groups—the League of Women Voters, the American Civil Liberties Union,

Common Cause, and the Conservative Caucus—found that only one-third of the members of these groups could name a single substantive issue that their group had worked on that year! While this is not surprising for members of the League of Women Voters, given its service and nonpartisan orientations, it is astonishing that members of the three ideologically based groups knew so little of their organizations' activities.[36] Similarly, in their study of contributors to political action committees, Ruth Jones and Warren Miller found that persons who respond to a direct-mail solicitation had substantially less political knowledge than other political activists and contributors.[37] These findings give credence to the criticism that direct-mail recruits have lower levels of political knowledge than other activists, and because members know so little, the leadership of direct-mail-based groups is not held accountable by those who provide the political resources.[38]

A serious issue concerning direct marketing is its impact on political tolerance. Regrettably, little previous research exists on the levels of tolerance among direct-marketing recruits. The studies that bear most directly on this question are those of political scientists Green and Guth.[39] Their comparison of political tolerance among contributors to ideological political action committees and political parties discovered that contributors to PACs are less tolerant of opposition groups than are contributors to political parties. Donors to PACs are more tolerant, however, than the general public. Unfortunately, these studies did not control for income and education when making the comparisons. And, as we saw earlier, persons who respond to direct-mail solicitations have far-above-average educations and income, characteristics that typically lead to above-average levels of political tolerance. For this reason, although we may take comfort in the fact that the tolerance level of the average contributor to an ideological political action committee is higher than that of the average citizen, we do not know whether this tolerance is higher than that of other kinds of political activists or of persons with similar levels of education and income.

The Green and Guth studies did discover that persons who belong to a large number of ideological PACs have lower levels of tolerance than persons who belong to fewer of these organizations. And persons who belong to political organizations that cut across political issues and ideologies are more tolerant than persons who belong only to organizations with similar purposes. These findings suggest that critics of direct marketing are correct in their expectation that the overlapping memberships typical of direct-mail recruits encourage intolerance, while the cross-cutting memberships more typical of social network recruits encourage tolerance.

Indirect evidence that direct marketing may lead to lower tolerance comes from comparisons of party and economic PAC donors with ideological and issue-oriented PAC donors.[40] If we can assume that a much larger percentage of ideological PAC donors are recruited by direct marketing than traditional party donors or economic PAC donors, the differences between the donor categories become important.[41] Issue and ideological PAC donors feel more strongly about their issues than either economic PAC donors or party donors. For example, Green and Guth report that 78 percent of Right to Life donors "strongly" want government to limit abortions, but only 11 percent of Republican donors do. Similarly, issue-oriented and ideological PAC donors are far more willing to classify themselves as "extremely liberal" or "extremely conservative." Only 15 percent of Democratic party donors and 30 percent of Republican donors are willing to accept these labels, while more than 34 percent of ideological PAC givers on the left and 58 percent on the right accept them.[42]

Critics' concern over potential political extremism and aggressive political behaviors finds further support in the study of telethon contributors by Ell-

TABLE 3.2

COMPARISONS BETWEEN POLITICAL ATTITUDES OF TELETHON CONTRIBUTORS
AND ATTITUDES OF THE GENERAL PUBLIC AND OTHER DONORS TO THE
DEMOCRATIC PARTY (IN PERCENT)

Question	Total 1974 Voting-Age Population	All 1974 Contributors to Democrats	1974 Telethon Contributors
1. Generally do you think of yourself as a conservative, moderate, liberal?			
Liberal	28.3	43.9	47.8
Moderate	36.1	29.6	42.2
Conservative	35.6	24.3	9.9
2. Some people think the federal government should see to it that every person has a job and a decent standard of living; others think the government should let each person get ahead on his or her own. What is your opinion?			
Government see to it	30.2	36.7	46.4
Neutral on issue	24.6	27.6	23.6
Each person on own	45.2	35.7	30.0
3. How do you feel about people expressing their disapproval of the government by taking part in protest meetings or marches permitted by local authorities?			
Approve	16.2	40.4	70.3
Neutral, depends	43.0	34.6	14.5
Disapprove	40.8	25.0	15.2
$N =$	2476	104	558

SOURCE: John Ellwood and Robert Spitzer, "The Democratic National Telethons: Their Successes and Failures," *Journal of Politics* 41 (1979): 854, table 6.

wood and Spitzer. In their comparisons of telethon contributors and more traditional donors to the party, the authors found substantially greater ideological
extremism among persons who responded to the television appeals. In addition, telethon contributors were far more approving of protest meetings and
marches. Table 3.2 on page 57 compares telethon contributors with the general
population and Democratic party contributors. As can be seen, the telethon
contributors are more liberal in both their ideology and in their position on
a government-guaranteed job. But the question that most clearly differentiates
them from the other three groups is approval of protest activity. Instead of only a few percentage points difference between the other groups and telethon
contributors, the latter group was almost twice as likely to approve of protest
activities as the next-closest group![43]

Briefly summarizing, previous research suggests that direct-marketing respondents are more likely than others to hold more extreme political opinions
and support aggressive political behaviors. This occurs despite their higher levels
of education and income. With the exception of the telethon study, however,
these studies did not compare direct-marketing recruits and social network recruits within the same organizations. For that reason, we do not know whether
the observed differences were caused by the nature of the organization or the
method of recruitment. Neither do we know whether direct marketing encourages political extremism and aggressive behaviors or simply appeals to persons who have these characteristics. Comparisons of direct-marketing and social
network recruits to environmental groups answer these questions.

I tested the hypothesis that direct-mail recruits are less knowledgeable about
and less interested in politics by examining the correlation between being recruited through a direct-marketing appeal and through political interest. The
partial correlation coefficient between these two variables is only +.03 and suggests that no relationship exists between them.[44] Given the previous findings,
this is surprising. To assure that the low coefficient was not hiding a more complex relationship, we tested for curvilinear relationships. Table 3.3 shows there
is a relationship between being recruited through direct marketing and political
interest, but the relationship is not linear. Direct-marketing recruits tend to have
either low scores or high scores on political interest, while social network recruits
fall in between.

This pattern repeats itself in comparisons of public environmental activities, political partisanship, and democratic political participation. The partial
coefficients between direct-marketing recruitment and these variables are weak
(.10, −.09, and −.07 respectively), indicating that direct-marketing recruits are
slightly more likely than social network recruits to be activists on environmental issues and slightly less likely to be strongly partisan and to participate in

TABLE 3.3

RELATIONSHIP BETWEEN RECRUITMENT METHOD AND POLITICAL ATTITUDES
(IN PERCENT)

	Kind of Recruit					
	Direct Mail			Social Network		
	Score on Political Variables					
Attitude or Behavior	High	Medium	Low	High	Medium	Low
Political interest	39	20	40	27	46	27
Partisanship	32	24	44	34	29	37
Democratic behaviors	27	31	42	36	35	31
Postmaterial orientation	41	21	38	26	45	29
Opposition to technology	43	14	43	24	42	35
Ideological extremism	42	23	35	25	38	37
Alienation	39	38	23	21	36	43
Support for aggressive actions	36	39	25	24	35	50
Aggressive behavior	46	23	31	21	45	34
Public environmental action	32	28	40	35	38	27
Private environmental action	36	34	30	31	35	34

activities such as voting, campaigning, and contacting public officials. As was true with political interest scores, however, these coefficients mask the true relationship between the variables. In fact, graphing these relationships (see figure 3.1) demonstrates their curvilinear character. Except for individual activities such as recycling and boycotting environmentally damaging products (where there is no relationship), and aggressive political participation and political alienation (which show linear relationships in the hypothesized directions), the curvilinear character of direct marketing to political attitudes and behaviors manifests itself in every comparison.[45]

What do these curvilinear relationships mean? They indicate that marketing attracts two different kinds of people, and social networks reach still another. For one set of recruits, those on the left side of figure 3.1, marketing lowers the costs of joining an organization while alerting them that a threat exists to their values. These new members need not seek out the organization nor worry about going to meetings or becoming active beyond making their contribution. The mail solicitation contains information concerning why the cause and the organization are worthwhile, and it includes the necessary reply card that makes it easy and simple to become a member. Persons responding for these reasons are not as committed to the political cause as other recruits, and they have less political interest, knowledge, and experience. They are generally passive in their political activities, and in the absence of a direct-marketing

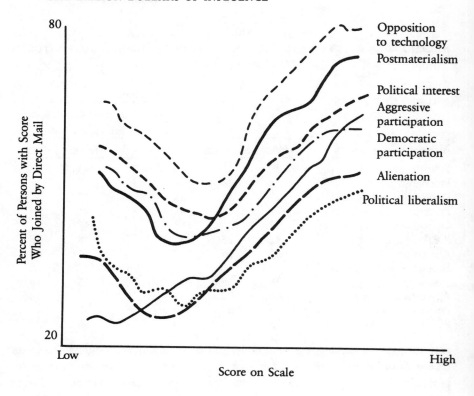

FIGURE 3.1
RELATIONSHIPS BETWEEN KIND OF RECRUITMENT
AND POLITICAL ATTITUDES AND BEHAVIORS

solicitation, they would be unlikely to join a citizen's group or to contribute to a political action committee.

The other kind of direct-marketing recruit, those persons on the right-hand side of figure 3.1, felt strongly about the issue before receiving the direct-marketing appeal. No material or social incentives are required to motivate these individuals. They have a strong commitment to the group's goals and have high scores on measures of political interest, participation, and ideology. Social network joiners fall in between these two kinds of direct-marketing recruits. Social network recruits care more about the political goals and ideals of their group than the passive direct-marketing recruits, but they are less extreme in their attitudes and behaviors than the direct-marketing members who joined solely for political purposes.

The positive linear relationships between direct-mail recruitment and aggressive participation, approval of aggressive participation, and political alienation indicate that persons motivated by direct marketing—regardless of their previous level of political interest or support for environmentalism—are less committed to democratic norms and to the political system itself. Intuitively, this makes sense. Social network recruits are persons whose political interest and commitment are moderately high, but whose opinions are moderated by cross-cutting group memberships and personal friendship ties. This encourages social network recruits to be more tolerant of opposing viewpoints, less supportive of aggressive political behaviors, and less alienated from the political system. In contrast, the attitudes and opinions of direct-mail recruits are not tempered by these influences.

Although these findings support several of the expectations concerning the relationship between direct marketing and increased intolerance and political alienation, they are far from conclusive. We do not know whether direct-marketing appeals cause alienation and aggressive behaviors, or whether direct-marketing recruits persons who already exhibit these attributes; nor do we know whether direct-marketing recruits become more or less aggressive, alienated, and extreme as they receive more and more mailings. To examine these issues we must examine the impact of length of membership on the different kinds of recruits.

Aggressive political behavior (illegal protests, rent strikes, fights with police, and sit-ins) is a product of several factors. Ideological extremism, alienation from the political system, perceived insufficiency of political influence, and youth all encourage aggressive political activity. In contrast, more democratic forms of participation (voting, contacting public officials, taking part in political campaigns, and contributing to political causes and candidates) are encouraged by higher levels of education, political interest, ideological conceptualization, activity in voluntary associations, and perceived political efficacy.[46]

To determine whether recruitment by direct marketing increased or decreased aggressive and democratic participation, these recruits were separated from social network joiners. For each category of recruit, a respondent's level of aggressive and democratic participation was predicted by his scores on the variables previously found to encourage these behaviors plus the length of time he had been a member of his organization. To assure that the impact of membership length was not simply a surrogate measure for age, age was entered into the predictive equation before the introduction of membership tenure.[47]

The results shown in table 3.4 indicate that participation in citizen action groups decreases the level of aggressive participation for both direct-mail and social network recruits. Although the decrease is smaller for persons who joined through direct mail, the longer they remain in their group, the lower their scores on aggressive behavior. Similarly, the democratic participation scores of direct-

TABLE 3.4

DETERMINANTS OF AGGRESSIVE POLITICAL PARTICIPATION
FOR DIRECT MARKETING AND SOCIAL NETWORK RECRUITS

Variable	Beta Elasticities	
	Direct Marketing	Social Network
Ideological extremism	.43	.42
Postmaterial orientation	.12	.09
Age	−.17	−.19
Perceived insufficient influence	.11	.03[a]
Environmental extremism	.08	.02[a]
Number of voluntary associations	−.03[a]	−.12
Democratic participation	−.04[a]	.06[a]
Length of membership	−.07	−.11
R^2 =	.30	.30

a. Beta is not twice the standard error.

TABLE 3.5

DETERMINANTS OF DEMOCRATIC PARTICIPATION FOR
DIRECT MARKETING AND SOCIAL NETWORK RECRUITS

Variable	Beta Elasticities	
	Direct Marketing	Social Network
Political interest	.59	.60
Ideological conceptualization	.12	.15
Number of voluntary associations	.07	−.02[a]
Aggressive participation	.14	.13
Age	.03[a]	.03[a]
Length of membership	.08	.17
R^2 =	.49	.50

a. Beta is not twice the standard error.

marketing recruits increase with membership tenure (table 3.5). The increase is not as great as that enjoyed by social network joiners, but the relationship is statistically significant and it is positive.

As might be expected from looking at tables 3.4 and 3.5, membership tenure is negatively correlated with extreme political ideology, alienation, a perception of insufficient political influence, and opposition to technology. The negative correlations are smaller for direct-marketing recruits than social network joiners, but the coefficients for political interest and ideological extremism are large enough to be substantively significant. Table 3.6 shows these results.

TABLE 3.6

PARTIAL CORRELATIONS BETWEEN LENGTH OF
MEMBERSHIP AND POLITICAL ATTITUDES[a]

Political Variable	Kind of Recruit	
	Direct Marketing	Social Network
Political interest	.23	.19
Ideological extremism	−.19	−.28
Postmaterial orientation	−.09	−.10
Political alienation	−.10	−.23
Perceived insufficiency of influence	−.10	−.14
Opposition to technology	−.08	−.13

a. Effects of group and age have been controlled.

What do these findings tell us about direct marketing and its impact on the political system? Direct-marketing recruits tend to be more alienated than others from the political system, which may make them more susceptible to demagoguery and more willing to circumvent traditional pluralist norms of political behavior. While this supports the view that direct marketing—based as it is on threatened values, fear, and negativism—increases tendencies toward intolerance and political violence, it appears that these tendencies are moderated over time. The longer individuals remain in their organization, the higher they score on measures of political interest, political efficacy, and democratic participation. And as tenure increases, scores on alienation, ideological extremism, and aggressive participation decrease.[48]

MEMBERS' ATTITUDES AND BEHAVIORS TOWARD THEIR GROUP
Although membership in voluntary associations reduces recruits' aggressive and extreme attitudes and behavior, direct marketing may still harm the political system, but in less obvious ways. These negative effects would occur, not because of these recruits' political attitudes and behaviors, but because of the orientations of direct-marketing recruits toward their citizen action groups. If direct-marketing members are only "checkbook members"—persons who think about the association and its goals only long enough to see it as a worthy cause and write a check in the hope that it will do some good, but who neither keep track of the group's political activities nor feel any real loyalty to the organization—then they are supplying extensive resources to national elites without holding them accountable for their actions.

Similarly, if recruits are interested only in the political goals of the association and have no commitment to the group itself, then the national leadership must constantly convince them that the group is actively pursuing the political goals the members value and that it is doing so better than other groups competing for the members' contributions. The leadership must also persuade these members that the threats to their values are sufficiently great to be worth a contribution to the group. To recruit and keep this kind of member, the national leadership may pursue political strategies that are highly emotional and conflict oriented.

To test the hypothesis that direct-marketing recruits are less committed to their political groups, we examined their motivations for joining and remaining in the group. Respondents indicated their motivations for joining their association through completions to the statement "I belong to [name of the group] because . . ." where thirteen completions were provided and respondents ranked each from "very important" to "very unimportant." Analysis of these items showed two distinct kinds of motivations.[49] One was composed of statements that emphasized purposive benefits and personal efficacy responses (e.g., "If the [name of group] achieves its goals, my life and my children's lives will benefit" and "My contribution to [name of group] is helping to influence government action on conservation problems"). The other involved social and material benefits such as the group's publications, wilderness outings, and friendships within the organization.

To measure support for the organization, respondents were asked to indicate whether or not they had made financial contributions during the previous twelve months beyond the required membership dues. To quantify participation in the group's activities, the survey asked members whether or not they had voted in the selection process for local and national officers, taken part in policy discussions within the group, or participated in activist mobilizations and telephone alert systems. To gauge personal attachment to the group, an index was constructed from the respondent's level of agreement with statements such as "I don't think of myself as a member of [name of group], I just send money because I think it's a worthy cause." Respondents' perceptions of the organization's effectiveness were measured by their level of agreement with the statement "[Name of group] is very effective in influencing national conservation-environmental policy." Perceptions that the citizen action group represents their interests and policy preferences were calculated with statements including "I almost always agree with the policy stands taken by [name of group]."

Andrew McFarland, in his study of Common Cause, discovered that members who joined in response to a direct-marketing solicitation did not, in general, want to do any more for Common Cause than contribute their yearly dues.[50] Similarly, John McCarthy found greater group commitment and attachment in citizen action groups recruited through social networks than in organizations that depended primarily on direct mail to solicit new members.[51]

These results are also consistent with the findings of David Knoke and James Wood, who discovered that lower levels of social interaction within a voluntary association lead to lower group activity and lower membership attachment.[52]

Analysis of environmental group members indicates that whether they are checkbook members who are normally apathetic in political matters or members deeply committed to the political goals of their citizen action group, direct-marketing recruits are not committed to their organization. Almost every measure of a member's group attachment and participation found direct-mail recruits to be less positive than social network recruits in their orientations. These variables included length of membership in the group, personal attachment to it, and participation in it. The lower levels of commitment and participation by direct-marketing recruits occur despite the fact that they are more likely to see their groups as politically effective and as representing their political interests. The correlations between having originally joined the organization in response to a direct-marketing solicitation and the above variables are shown in table 3.7.

TABLE 3.7

RELATIONSHIPS BETWEEN KIND OF RECRUITMENT
AND MEASURES OF ORGANIZATIONAL COMMITMENT

Membership	Correlation with Direct Marketing
Length of membership[a]	−.18
Joined for purposive incentives[b]	.15
Joined for social and material incentives	−.22
Participation in group activities	−.34
Participation in selection of issues	−.19
Perception of group effectiveness	.12
Number of friends within the group	−.42
Proximity of group goals to one's own	.16
Attachment to the group	−.33

a. Because most of the direct-mail groups are much younger, the highest value the length of membership was allowed to take was six years.
b. All correlations other than length of membership are partial correlations which have controls for length of membership.

Table 3.7 demonstrates clearly that persons who respond to a direct mailing do so primarily for political reasons, and because they do not participate as much in the social or organizational activities of their association, they have less attachment to it.

These patterns may have serious implications for citizen action groups dependent on direct marketing for members and income. These groups may suffer substantially greater losses than social network associations when an issue loses its position in the political limelight. If this is the case, then voluntary associations dependent on direct mail must pursue policies and strategies that attract media attention to their issue. The results also suggest that organizations built on social networks may not wish to become dependent on mail and other direct-marketing techniques. To do so courts the volatile membership swings and permanent downturns that have created problems for associations such as Common Cause, Zero Population Growth, and more recently, environmental groups after Interior Secretary James Watt and Environmental Protection Agency Director Anne Burford were forced to resign.[53] Social network associations also suffer when their issue is not in the headlines, but their members are not as likely to drop their memberships because they have personal attachments to the organization and friendships within it.

Summary

Our comparisons of direct-marketing and social network recruits indicate that direct marketing increases rather than decreases the political advantages of persons with higher socioeconomic status. Because direct mail requires a list of prospects who are likely to respond to a political appeal and the persons most likely to be on these lists are high-income and professional persons who belong to an existing political or social network, this accentuation of existing patterns is understandable. Somewhat more surprising is the fact that television appeals also increase the advantages of higher-status individuals. Both the Democratic party telethons and the cable television efforts of the Christian Right recruited persons with higher education and income than persons who responded to these same organizations via traditional channels of political enlistment.

Comparison of the political attitudes and behaviors of direct-marketing recruits with those of more traditional social network participants shows that critics of direct mail are correct in their hypothesis that extreme appeals encourage participation by persons who have lower levels of political knowledge and interest or who have more extreme political ideologies. The relationships between direct-marketing recruitment and political attitudes and behaviors are more complex, however, than the simple linear relationship expected. While direct-marketing recruits are more likely to exhibit extreme attitudes and behaviors and are less likely to exhibit high levels of political knowledge than are social network joiners, extremism and lower levels of knowledge apply to different sets of recruits. One set is relatively apathetic and exhibits lower levels of interest and knowledge than traditional activists. These recruits rarely follow the activities of the citizen action group or political action committee to which they contribute, but they provide substantial resources to political elites.

The second set of direct-marketing respondents consists of persons with very high levels of political interest and activity. They hold more extreme political attitudes and are more aggressive and more accepting of aggressive behaviors. Despite these tendencies, these persons probably do not represent a major threat to democratic systems because they become less extreme and less supportive of aggressive political activities the longer they remain in their organizations. It appears, therefore, that at the level of individual activists, direct marketing carries at least a partial antidote for its own political extremism.

Perhaps the greatest danger from direct-marketing respondents is the fact that they respond to negative and extreme messages. It may be that although direct-marketing recruits do not in themselves present a threat to democratic values, the process of recruiting them does. The elites who formulate these appeals may believe that they must use highly emotional, negative, and divisive language to obtain political resources, and they must pursue extreme and uncompromising political tactics to maintain this resource flow. This possibility provides the focus of chapter 4.

Notes

1. Allan Cigler and Burdett Loomis, "Introduction: The Changing Nature of Interest Groups," in *Interest Group Politics,* ed. Allan Cigler and Burdett Loomis (Washington, D.C.: CQ Press, 1983).

2. *Citizen action group* refers to voluntary associations organized for political purposes where membership in the group is not based on occupation. The term refers to groups known in the media as *public-interest groups* and includes organizations such as Common Cause, the National Right to Life, the League of Women Voters, and the Sierra Club. It would not include political interest groups such as the American Medical Association or the Teamsters Union where membership is based on occupation, nor would it include groups such as Boy Scouts of America or church groups where the purposes of the organization normally do not include attempting to influence public policy.

3. Jack Walker, "The Origins and Maintenance of Interest Groups in America," *American Political Science Review* 77 (June 1983): 390-406.

4. Pluralism, competition among groups, is the dominant interpretation of the American political process. It contends that neither majorities nor a single elite controls the government. Instead, political decisions are the result of political competition among organized groups. No single group prevails in all policy areas; different sets of groups become involved in different issues.

5. David Truman, *The Governmental Process* (New York: Knopf, 1958).

6. Antony Oberschall, *Social Conflict and Social Movements* (Englewood Cliffs, N.J.: Prentice-Hall, 1973), 2-28.

7. John McCarthy and Mayer Zald, "Resource Mobilization and Social Movements: A Partial Theory," *American Journal of Sociology* 82 (May 1977): 1212-41.

8. Mancur Olson, Jr., *The Logic of Collective Action,* rev. ed. (New York: Schocken, 1971), 7-16.

9. James Q. Wilson, *Political Organizations* (New York: Basic Books, 1973).

10. Included in these studies are Harriet Tillock and Denton Morrison, "Group Size and Contributions to Collective Action: An Examination of Mancur Olson's Theory Using Data from Zero Population Growth," in *Research in Social Movements, Conflicts and Change,* vol. 2, ed. Louis Kriesberg (Greenwich, Conn.: JAI Press, 1978); Jeffrey Berry, *Lobbying for the People* (Princeton: Princeton University Press, 1977); R. Kenneth Godwin and Robert C. Mitchell, "Rational Models, Collective Goods and Nonelectoral Political Behavior," *Western Political Quarterly* 35 (June 1982): 161-80; Constance Cook, "Membership Involvement in Public Interest Groups," (paper presented at the 1983 meetings of the American Political Science Association); Andrew McFarland, *Common Cause: Lobbying in the Public Interest* (Chatham, N.J.: Chatham House, 1984); and Terry M. Moe, *The Organization of Interests: Incentives and the Internal Dynamics of Interest Groups* (Chicago: University of Chicago Press, 1980).

11. Godwin and Mitchell, "Rational Models"; and Cook, "Membership Involvement."

12. William Riker and Peter Ordeshook, "A Theory of the Calculus of Voting," *American Political Science Review* 62 (March 1968): 25-42.

13. Moe, *Organization of Interests,* 205-18.

14. Robert C. Mitchell, "National Environmental Lobbies and the Apparent Illogic of Collective Action," in *Collective Decision Making,* ed. Clifford Russell (Baltimore: Johns Hopkins University Press, 1979).

15. Olson's analysis does explain the behavior of the 98 percent of persons who receive prospecting letters and do not respond. What Olson does not explain is why the 2 percent who respond are more likely to respond to collective goods and appeals to citizen duty and personal efficacy than to selective incentives. Nor does Olson's analysis indicate why pretests of alternative messages and sets of incentives find that appeals to selective incentives do less well than appeals to purposive goals. An exception to this emphasis on purposive goals is the National Wildlife Federation which stresses material incentives almost entirely.

16. A danger that turned out to be very real when the French government destroyed a Greenpeace ship, killing an activist in the process.

17. Cross-cutting memberships and the tolerance they encourage are two of the most important assumptions of pluralist theory. These assumptions have been empirically tested, and in large part supported, by a number of studies. An excellent book on this subject is John L. Sullivan, James Pierson, and George E. Marcus, *Political Tolerance and American Democracy* (Chicago: University of Chicago Press, 1982).

18. In an interesting experiment to determine who shares mailing lists and how much political direct mail will be sent to a person once he joins a national direct-mail group, Kay Schlozman enrolled her three-year-old son, Daniel, in four citizen action groups using slightly different versions of his name so she could track the trading of the lists. Enrollment in the National Conservative Caucus produced mail from 12 additional conservative groups; enrollment in the Sierra Club yielded mailings from 10 environmental and liberal groups; and enrollment in Common Cause produced prospecting

letters from 10 good government and environmental organizations. In addition, the groups in which young Daniel enrolled sent him a combined total of 103 mailings. Kay Lehman Schlozman and John T. Tierney, *Organized Interests and American Democracy* (New York: Harper & Row, 1986), 94-96.

19. Sylvia Tesh, "In Support of Single-Issue Politics," *Political Science Quarterly* 99 (Spring 1984): 27-44.

20. Center for Political Studies, *American National Election Study, 1976* (Ann Arbor: University of Michigan, 1977).

21. Herbert H. Hyman and C.R. Wright, "Trends in Voluntary Association Memberships of American Adults: Replication Based on Secondary Analysis of National Sample Surveys," *American Sociological Review* 36 (April 1971): 191-206; Sidney Verba and Norman Nie, *Participation in America: Social Equality and Political Democracy* (New York: Harper & Row, 1972); and Sidney Verba, Norman Nie, and Jae-on Kim, *Participation and Political Equality: A Seven Nation Comparison* (Cambridge: Cambridge University Press, 1978).

22. The survey was conducted by Resources for the Future, a Washington-based research organization. The sample was a probability sample drawn from the membership lists of each of the five organizations. Appendix A contains all questions used in the analysis.

23. For detailed reports of these surveys, see James L. Guth and John C. Green, "Political Activists and Civil Liberties: The Case of Party and PAC Contributors" (paper presented at the 1984 meeting of the Midwest Political Science Association), and John Green and James Guth, "Big Bucks and Petty Cash: Party and Interest Group Activists in American Politics" in Allan Cigler and Burdett Loomis, *Interest Group Politics*, 2d ed., (Washington, D.C.: CQ Press, 1987); and Ruth Jones and Warren Miller, "Financing Campaigns: Macro Level Innovation and Micro Level Response," *Western Political Quarterly* 38 (June 1985): 187-210.

24. Correlation analysis was used to test for relationships. Correlation analysis measures the strength of a relationship between two variables. If there were a perfect positive relationship, i.e., a higher score on one variable means a higher score on the other for each individual, then the correlation coefficient would equal 1.0. A perfect negative relationship, i.e., a higher score on one variable would mean a lower score on the other, would show a coefficient of −1.0. If two variables are unrelated in a linear fashion, the coefficient is 0.0. The correlation analysis controls for the group impacts by using dummy variables and then partialing out the group effects before reporting the observed correlations. Although the measures used in this study are ordinal, I feel that correlation procedures are justified because of the large sample size and because the correlation coefficients generally underestimate the strength of relationships. Correlation analysis enables the reader more easily to interpret the relationship between how a person was recruited and the variable of interest.

25. Guth and Green, "Political Activists and Civil Liberties." See also Green and Guth, "Big Bucks and Petty Cash."

26. Berry, *Lobbying;* and Jeffrey Berry, *The Interest Group Society* (Boston: Little, Brown, 1984); McFarland, *Common Cause;* and Cook, "Membership Involvement."

27. John W. Ellwood and Robert J. Spitzer, "The Democratic National Telethons: Their Successes and Failures," *Journal of Politics* 41 (1979): 828-64.

28. For a more complete breakdown of the demographic characteristics of direct-mail joiners see R. Kenneth Godwin and Robert C. Mitchell, "The Impact of Direct Mail on Political Organizations," *Social Science Quarterly* 65 (Fall 1984): 829-39.

29. Larry J. Sabato, *The Rise and Fall of Political Consultants: New Ways of Winning* (New York: Basic Books, 1981).

30. Perhaps the major reason these two voluntary associations have been so successful has been their medical insurance plans, which, for the first time, offered the elderly group rates for medical care and did not require a physical examination. For an in-depth analysis of these groups and their growth see Henry J. Pratt, *The Gray Lobby* (Chicago: University of Chicago Press, 1976).

31. Robert C. Liebman, "Mobilizing the Moral Majority," in *The New Christian Right: Mobilization and Legitimation,* ed. Robert Liebman and Robert Wuthnow (Hawthorne, N.Y.: Aldine, 1983).

32. Verba and Nie, *Participation in America,* 81-90.

33. David Broder, "When Campaigns Get Mean," in *The Fear Brokers,* ed. Thomas J. McIntyre with John C. Obert (Boston: Beacon Press, 1979); Michael Hayes, "Interest Groups: Pluralism or Mass Society," in Cigler and Loomis, eds., *Interest Group Politics;* Peter Fenn, Handout from the Center for Responsive Politics, January 1983; J. Skelly Wright, "Political Big Bucks: Sin Against the Constitution," *Washington Post,* 31 October 1982, C1; Maurice Rosenblatt, "Nov. 7 Vote Was 37.9%, Lowest Since '42," *New York Times,* 19 December 1978, A13, cited in Margaret Latus, "Assessing Ideological PACs: From Outrage to Understanding," in *Money and Politics in the United States,* ed. Michael Malbin (Chatham, N.J.: Chatham House, 1984).

34. This scale was developed by Ronald Inglehart. Inglehart hypothesized that as societies become wealthier, the values that people seek will change from the pursuit of more and more material goods to the pursuit of values such as environmental protection, a more humane society, and greater political equality. For a discussion of the scale and Inglehart's findings, see "Values, Objective Needs, and Subjective Satisfaction among Western Publics," *Comparative Political Studies* 9 (January 1977): 429-58.

35. Stephen Cotgrove and Andrew Duff, "Environmentalism, Middle-Class Radicalism, and Politics," *Sociological Review* 28 (May 1980): 333-51; and Robert A. Stallings, "Patterns of Belief in Social Movements: Clarification from an Analysis of Environmental Groups," *Sociological Quarterly* 14 (Autumn 1973): 465-80.

36. Cook, "Membership Involvement."

37. Jones and Miller, "Financing Campaigns," 202-8.

38. Hayes, "Interest Groups," 116-24; Larry Sabato, *PAC Power: Inside the World of Political Action Committees* (New York: Norton, 1984): 160-81; Frank Sorauf, "Who's in Charge? Accountability in Political Action Committees," *Political Science Quarterly* 99 (Winter 1984-85): 590-93.

39. Green and Guth, "Big Bucks and Petty Cash" and Guth and Green, "Political Activists and Civil Liberties."

40. Green and Guth, "Big Bucks and Petty Cash."

41. Although there is a danger of committing the ecological fallacy in this comparison, the danger is not great. The percentage of party donors in the Green and Guth survey who were originally reached by direct marketing is probably less than half that of ideological and issue PAC contributors, while the percentages of extreme responses on the Likert scale items of ideological and issue PAC donors reported later is almost

twice that of party donors.

42. Green and Guth, "Big Bucks and Petty Cash."

43. Ellwood and Spitzer, "Democratic National Telethons," table 6, p. 854.

44. This is the correlation coefficient after a control for the group effects was introduced. See note 23.

45. The best fitting equation for curvilinear relationships was: $y = b_1 * x + b_2 * x^2$; where y is the predicted percentage of direct-mail members and x is the score on the appropriate scale, and the median score was assigned a value of 0 (zero).

46. Edward N. Muller, "An Explanatory Model for Differing Types of Participation," *European Journal of Political Research* 10 (1982): 1-16; and Edward N. Muller and R. Kenneth Godwin, "Aggressive and Democratic Participation," *Political Behavior,* Fall 1984, 129-46.

47. These predictions were done using two-stage, least-squares regression techniques. Regression is a statistical technique used to determine the extent to which the variation in one set of variables causes variation in another variable. For example, if we wanted to find out how much an individual's educational level and his parents' educational level determined his income, we would regress the income level onto the two education variables. Because parents' education is logically prior to the individual's education, the parents' score would be entered in the equation prior to the individual's own education score. This procedure yields measures of how much of the variation in income parents' education and the individual's education explain. Two-stage least-squares regression was used to analyze democratic and aggressive participation because past research indicates that each of the two kinds of participation is a significant cause of the other.

48. Although the above findings are encouraging in the sense that direct-mail recruits become more tolerant and more democratically oriented the longer they remain in their organization, an important caveat must be made. The survey of environmental group members was conducted during the final year of the Carter administration, an administration with a moderate to strong proenvironmental record. The Reagan administration, including Secretary of Interior James Watt and Environmental Protection Agency Director Anne Burford had not yet arrived on the scene. As we see in later chapters, environmental organizations clearly prospered because of the Reagan Administration, and membership rolls expanded rapidly. At the same time, however, all environmental organizations became more aggressive and radical in their rhetoric and in their tactics. Although current studies indicate that the evaluation of a particular administration's policy does not affect the probability of aggressive political activity or support for such actions, we cannot be sure whether the increased democratic participation and decreased aggressive activities discovered above would have been found if the survey had occurred after President Reagan had taken office. For analyses of the impact of policy evaluation on aggressive behaviors, see Muller and Godwin, "Democratic and Aggressive Political Participation"; Karl Dieter-Opp, "Soft Incentives and Collective Action," *British Journal of Political Science* 15 (1985): 269-94; and Edward N. Muller and Karl Dieter-Opp, "Rational Choice and Rebellious Collective Action," *American Political Science Review* 80 (June 1986): 471-88.

49. The two motivations were discovered through factor analysis, a statistical technique that examines an array of variables for underlying patterns. In the data, responses to the 13 reasons for joining the group were analyzed to determine whether or not a

strongly positive response to one reason for joining was related to strongly positive responses to other reasons for joining the group. In this case, the 13 questions found two underlying factors.

50. Andrew McFarland, *Public Interest Group Lobbies* (Washington, D.C.: American Enterprise Institute, 1976); and McFarland, *Common Cause*.

51. John McCarthy, "Social Infrastructure Deficits and New Technologies: Mobilizing Unstructured Sentiment Pools" (paper presented at the 1982 meetings of the American Sociological Association).

52. David Knoke and James R. Wood, *Organized for Action: Commitment in Voluntary Associations* (New Brunswick: Rutgers University Press, 1981).

53. Tillock and Morrison, "Group Size."

4. Lobbying and Electoral Tactics of Direct-Marketing Groups

All political organizations must make choices concerning which goals to seek and what tactics to use to reach them. This chapter examines whether or not organizations dependent on direct marketing differ in their goals and tactics from organizations based on more traditional sources of funding. Critics of direct marketing suggest that if an organization depends on fear, extremism, and intolerance to generate resources, then these attributes will typify its political tactics as well. This occurs because persons who develop the intemperate and aggressive issue positions for mail appeals will come to believe their own propaganda, and because the persons in charge of the direct-mail programs generate the organization's resources, they will eventually dominate the leadership positions.[1] In addition, to avoid losing the support of persons who originally joined in response to extreme appeals, direct-marketing-based organizations must stress conflict and extremism rather than compromise and moderation. Finally, critics argue that direct-mail-based organizations are neither democratic in their internal structure nor held accountable for their actions. Michael Hayes writes that "these groups offer only the illusion of broad participation, as decisions regarding organizational goals and strategies are made by full-time staff members with little or no input from the membership."[2]

This chapter compares the political goals, tactics, internal organization, and decision-making processes of direct-marketing-based institutions with those of similar institutions funded by alternative means. These comparisons help us answer the questions whether or not organizations based on direct marketing are divisive and destructive forces in American politics, and whether they are less democratic and less accountable than other political institutions.

Citizen Action Groups

Direct mail—in combination with foundation giving, the social protests of the 1960s, a long-term increase in the educational level of the population, and massive governmental assistance—enlarged the number of national citizen action

73

groups from only a handful before the 1960s to well over a hundred in 1980. By 1982, these organizations composed more than one-fifth of the total interest-group population.[3]

Every citizen action group must make four strategic decisions concerning issues and tactics: (1) whether to encourage member input into group decisions concerning issues and tactics; (2) whether to lobby on highly visible issues with extensive media attention and reject compromises, or to work behind the scenes and bargain with opposition groups, as more traditional lobbies have done; (3) whether to use direct lobbying by the organization's staff or rely on grass-roots efforts; and (4) whether to join coalitions with other groups within their social movement or to lobby alone. Although all lobbying organizations must make these choices, they are more critical for citizen groups because these choices have significant consequences for the size of a group's membership and for the amount of political discretion available to its leadership.[4]

If critics are correct, direct-mail-based associations will not encourage member participation in decisions concerning issues and tactics; instead, they will expect contributors to be "checkbook" members who follow the leadership's decisions. In place of rewards for participation in organizational decision making, the groups will offer expressive rewards to members by taking extreme and uncompromising positions on highly visible issues. Such issues are particularly useful to the group's leadership because they require no demonstrable lobbying success to make them credible and they assist the group in its competition with rival organizations for potential members.[5]

Part of the expressive rewards offered by direct-mail based groups may be participation in grass-roots lobbying. The decision concerning whether to involve members in grass-roots lobbying is important because the mobilization of a group's members not only influences governmental decisions but also bonds members to their group and makes them feel a part of the collective effort. As we saw in chapter 3, persons recruited through direct mail are often committed to the cause but not to the organization. Grass-roots efforts tie members to the group by reminding them that *their* group is working for *their* espoused cause and that they can be more effective by working as a part of that effort. If individuals are deeply committed to a cause such as saving the whales, prayer in public schools, or the Equal Rights Amendment, and the group makes it possible for members to see themselves as effectively participating in the achievement of that goal, then they are more likely to become emotionally attached to the group.[6] This attachment may help take the place of the social bonds and material incentives that tie social network recruits to their associations.

The "law of the instrument" provides another reason that citizen action groups may make extensive use of grass-roots lobbying. Having invested heavily in the development of mailing lists and computer capabilities, group leaders may feel that they must justify past expenditures by using these facilities in every possible way. This may be particularly true if a separate unit exists within the organization to write and handle mailings.[7]

The final strategic choice a citizen group must make is whether or not to join coalitions with related groups. These coalitions have become increasingly common among corporate lobbies as more firms establish their own public affairs offices in Washington, and such cooperation makes sense both economically and politically. Coalitions allow the costs of lobbying to be shared by firms with related interests and present at least the appearance of a united front to governmental decision makers. Also, by entering into coalitions, a lobbying organization can work to influence policies that it could never afford to take on by itself.[8]

Citizen action groups within the same social movement are in a different situation from that of corporate lobbies. Where firms within an industry compete in the *economic marketplace* and cooperate in the political arena, citizen groups compete for members and resources within the *political marketplace.* Citizen groups compete for political "customers" in a manner not unlike Ford and General Motors competing for automobile buyers. Each organization must show that it is doing something unique and valuable and therefore has a superior claim to a "customer's" resources and loyalty.[9]

In every coalition, both a group and an individual emerge in leadership roles and use the coalition's resources to stay in the public eye. Given the competition among groups for members and resources, being the leading partner in a coalition constitutes a substantial advantage in gaining media attention. Conversely, contributing resources but not receiving external credit is a significant disadvantage. Because direct-marketing-based groups offer fewer social and material incentives, the importance of staying visible and appearing in the leadership role is particularly important to them. For this reason, we expect that the more dependent a group is on direct marketing for resources, the less likely it will be to join coalitions, unless it occupies the leadership position.

In summary, we hypothesize that direct-mail-based citizen groups will discourage member participation in the decision process, choose highly visible issues, employ extreme political tactics, utilize more grass-roots lobbying, and join fewer coalitions within the same social movement.

To test these expectations, I conducted personal interviews with twenty-four lobbyists and directors from eighteen national citizen action groups. Twelve respondents came from environmental groups and twelve came from organizations within the women's, prochoice, prolife, and consumer movements.[10] I concentrated interviews within the environmental movement because it is among the oldest and largest of the contemporary social movements and it shows the greatest differentiation among its associations with respect to size, age, level of internal specialization, and dependence on direct mail. In addition, our sample of direct-mail and social network members in chapter 3 came from this movement. This allows the examination of possible relationships between membership characteristics and elite strategies.

MEMBER PARTICIPATION AND ISSUE CHOICES

To evaluate the level of member input into decisions concerning which issues a group would lobby and the strategies the group would use, each respondent from the eighteen citizen action groups was asked two questions: "Does your organization have a formal process for obtaining members' input?" and "How important are members' opinions and participation in the choice of issues and tactics?" Each organization then received a score from 1 to 3 based on the answers. If a group had an institutionalized process for encouraging member input, and the respondent indicated that members' opinions were either "very important" or "important" in the choice of issues, then the group received a score of 3. Six groups achieved this score. If an organization had either a formal input process, but indicated that members' opinions were only "moderately important" or "slightly important," or if the group had no formal process but their lobbyist indicated that informal input into issue selection was "very important" or "important," the group received a score of 2. Six organizations fell into this category. The remaining six groups received a score of 1 because they indicated that they had no formal input mechanism and that member input was either "moderately important," "slightly important," or "not important at all" in the choice of issues.

Despite the imprecise nature of this measure, the correlation between member input and the percentage of members originally recruited through direct mail is $-.41$, and the relationship between member input and the percentage of the association's income derived from direct-mail solicitations is $-.30$.[11] These correlations, as well as respondents' elaboration of the way their organizations typically decide issues and tactics, indicate that groups most dependent on direct mail rarely encourage member participation in these activities. Instead, the chief executive officer and a few top staff persons make these choices. The ordinary member in these associations has little or no influence. In sharp contrast, groups that are less dependent on direct marketing for their membership and income encourage members to participate in these choices. Institutionalized input from members occurs either through a mailed ballot listing alternative issues or through the election of an executive board where the candidates indicate their issue preferences as part of the material mailed to members with the election ballot. More informal kinds of input come from special phone lines to the Washington offices, the use of volunteer lobbyists and interns, and communication from local chapter meetings where the local membership meets to discuss priorities and then sends this information to the national office.

Two environmental groups, the Sierra Club and Friends of the Earth, demonstrate the differences between social network and direct-mail groups. A large majority of Sierra Club members joined through social network channels, while almost 80 percent of the contributors to Friends of the Earth joined in response to a direct-mail solicitation. Sierra Club members elect their executive board, and each candidate for the board indicates his or her priority issues on the materials members receive with their ballot. In addition, members have an opportunity each year formally to notify the board concerning which issues they would like to see the club address, and the club has local chapters organized for the express purpose of working on political issues. Members of Friends of the Earth do not elect their executive board, and the leadership does not request members' opinions concerning the choice of issues. David Brower, founder and executive director of Friends of the Earth, and a few staff members make these decisions.

ISSUE VISIBILITY

Citizen advocacy groups depend on the media more than any other form of pressure group. In their survey of 175 interest groups, Kay Schlozman and John Tierney found that 96 percent of all citizens' lobbies spent lobbying efforts meeting with the press and media. More than 26 percent of these groups indicated that these efforts were an especially time- or resource-consuming activity, a figure almost three times greater than any other kind of lobby.[12] The efforts include press conferences, preparing materials for use as news items and giving them to the media, and staging situations that will require press coverage.

Just as there is a strong negative association between dependence on direct marketing and member input into issue choices, there is a strong positive correlation between the degree to which an organization depends on direct mail and the probability that it will choose highly visible and emotional issues. In direct-mail-dependent groups, issues are chosen to maximize media exposure, and the leadership tries to appear radical and innovative in its issue choices by claiming an issue as "theirs" before another association takes it. The chief lobbyist for Friends of the Earth described this strategy:

> We try to stay on the cutting edge of the movement in our selection of issues. That helps us show our members that we are aware of the changes that are occurring in the environment and that we're not standing still. We were the first to go into

international issues, the first to have an anti-nuclear lobby, and the first to have a full-time disarmament lobbyist.

This lobbyist believed that the ability to get to an issue first justified the leadership's decision not to hold elections or request formalized member participation. Without such institutionalized procedures, the group had greater flexibility to move quickly to a new issue whenever circumstances required it. Among the more important "circumstances" was the level of media attention an issue was likely to receive.

Perhaps the most candid statement concerning the significance of media attention to direct-mail-based groups came from a lobbyist who stated, "If the press isn't going to be interested, then neither are we. We have to show our members we're doing something." Another manifestation of the necessity of choosing issues with media exposure was the tendency of direct-mail organizations to call frequent press conferences. The lobbyist quoted immediately above indicated that the reasons for press conferences go beyond influencing policy makers. "Press conferences not only bring us and the issue to the attention of the guys on the Hill and in the agencies, they also look good in the newsletters to the members."

Dependence on direct mail for members and income almost mandates that a group will stress issues that the media find important. With only one exception, if a group obtained at least 60 percent of its members or 40 percent of its income through direct-mail solicitations, the respondent from that organization reported that the group tried to choose emotional issues that were likely to receive substantial attention in the press. For example, a lobbyist from a group with 80 percent direct-mail members commented:

> We have to emphasize emotional issues like toxic chemicals or nuclear waste. Court cases aren't places where the members can get involved and so they have to feel strongly about the issues we choose. Superfund was a great issue for us and EPA helped by keeping the issue hot. DDT and dioxin were good too. James Watt, of course, was the best.

The Sierra Club, the Audubon Society, and the National Wildlife Federation—large groups that rely mainly on either social networks and/or material incentives for recruits and income—contrast sharply with the above pattern.[13] Although issue visibility and press coverage are important, they are not the key considerations. Instead, these groups choose issues that will maximize their expertise and will have substantial environmental impact. These organizations are far more likely to lobby on the implementation aspects of an issue that has been around for some time than to rush to be first with a new issue so they can claim it as their own. For example, a lobbyist from the National Wildlife Federation stated:

> We try to research a piece of legislation and determine exactly which provisions will help to get effective action by the bureaucracy. We've learned that just getting a bill isn't enough. We have to be sure that EPA or Interior will implement it. We hope our members understand this. . . . We don't just pick issues like [another environmental group] because they're good press.

A lobbyist from the Sierra Club indicated that this strategy of choosing issues and lobbying behind the scenes was not always popular with the membership:

> We follow the executive board's direction in our choice of issues and then we try and work behind the scenes because it's easier for us to reach our goals there. Our greatest problem comes in saying no to members who want us to lobby on issues that the board didn't choose. Those are usually backyard issues (i.e., those close to the member's home) or those that the media are concentrating on.

Interviews with citizen action group lobbyists made it clear that the key factor in choosing highly visible issues was the group's dependence on direct marketing for resources. For example, a staff member of the Women's Equity Action League (WEAL) reported that her group does not choose issues on the basis of their emotionalism or their media visibility, except perhaps to stay away from such issues. Despite having a membership of less than 2000, WEAL can do this and concentrate on behind-the-scenes lobbying because it receives more than 90 percent of its resources from foundations and government grants and contracts. The National Organization for Women (NOW), in contrast, is a much larger organization with well over 100,000 members. But NOW, because it depends on direct mail for more than 70 percent of its membership and funding, must choose issues that mobilize its constituency and receive substantial media attention. When the leadership of NOW failed to do this and chose instead to lobby behind the scenes, many local chapters withheld membership dues. Ultimately the national leadership was fired and replaced with more radical persons, who chose more visible and emotional issues.[14]

GRASS-ROOTS OR STAFF LOBBYING

A major change that citizen action groups have brought to the American political system has been the dramatic increase in grass-roots lobbying—the lobbying of public officials by an organization's supporters rather than its staff. Whereas the major resources of corporate and trade association lobbies are their ability to contribute large sums to political campaigns, long-standing relationships with executive agencies and congressional committees, and extensive information-gathering capabilities, the major resources of most citizen action groups are the number and political activism of their members.

Although grass-roots tactics have been utilized throughout America's political history, the computer and direct mail have quantitatively and qualitatively changed the nature of these efforts. A 1981 report investigating the factors that most influence congressional voting found that congressional staff overwhelmingly ranked "spontaneous letters from constituents" as the most effective kind of communication in the lobbying process. Phone calls from constituents ranked second.[15] Because members, rather than money, are the strength of citizen action groups, these organizations have become quite innovative in mobilizing members to "spontaneous" action.

Grass-roots lobbying takes several forms, the most common being letter writing to congresspersons. Other frequent activities include telephone calls and telegrams to members of Congress, the bureaucracy, and the White House, and personal contacts by members who are close friends of congresspersons. Member mobilizations may begin with a special alert where the organization uses a direct mailing or "telephone tree" to contact activists on a particular issue, or the call to action may come in the group's monthly or bimonthly publication.[16] In either situation, the organization provides instructions to its members concerning whom they should write or call and what they should say. In addition to the political effectiveness of grass-roots efforts, this tactic provides a wonderful way for the group to advertise its efforts to its members and tie them more closely to the association.[17]

Given these reasons for choosing grass-roots tactics, why would a citizen lobby not use them? First, they are expensive. Our interviewees indicated that for special alerts, the total cost of each letter or phone call is almost 40 cents. If an association has 10,000 activists, the cost of only five mobilizations would equal the average salary of a full-time lobbyist in many groups. A second reason that citizen action groups eschew grass-roots lobbying is the loss of control that accompanies these efforts. Even when the staff sends careful instructions, members often deviate substantially from the prescribed script. Finally, the career rewards of this activity to the group's paid staff are small, while the time and work involved can be quite large. Grass-roots efforts do not increase a lobbyist's prestige with public officials because the most successful letters are those that appear "spontaneous."[18]

With the exception of representatives from groups that specialize in court action and one organization that specifically disavowed grass-roots activism, respondents from all organizations indicated that about 20 percent of their lobbying budget was devoted to grass-roots tactics.[19] This 20 percent figure is highly misleading, however. If the measure of grass-roots effort is the frequency and size of special mobilizations, then substantial differences emerge. As table 4.1 indicates, groups with separate mailing departments initiate many more special alerts than organizations without such facilities. And the probability that a separate mailing department will exist is directly related to organizational size.

TABLE 4.1

GRASS-ROOTS MOBILIZATIONS AND THE PRESENCE OF AN
INDEPENDENT MAILING DEPARTMENT WITHIN THE ORGANIZATION

Independent Mailing Department	Number of Mobilizations		
	5 or More	2 to 4	0 or 1
Yes	5	2	0
No	1	5	5

Separate mailing departments encourage grass-roots lobbying because they reduce the costs of such efforts to staff lobbyists. If a lobbyist for a group with a separate direct-marketing department wants to mobilize members on an issue, he calls the mailing department and indicates what material the letter should cover and which activists should be contacted. Unless the lobbyist wants to become more intimately involved in the writing of the letter or the contacting effort, the mailing unit takes care of the rest. In smaller groups, the lobbyist must handle most of the tasks involved in the mobilization. He maintains and updates lists of activists on the various issues, writes the mobilization letter, and supervises many of the chores related to its printing and mailing. If a telephone alert is used, the lobbyist handles this activity as well. A lobbyist from a prolife group indicated how taxing these activities could be:

> When I have to organize a letter drive I know that I am going to be working 12 hours a day for more than a week. You have to get the letter cleared upstairs, you have to get the printer moving, you have to update your files, and you have to find the money to do it. The worst part is that we rarely know if we are having an impact. When I go see a congressman at least I have an idea what his reaction is.

Another lobbyist, from one of the women's organizations, voiced similar complaints:

> They're just not worth the effort most of the time. I don't know how many of the people on my list actually do what they're supposed to, but we have to do them [the mobilizations]. The members expect it. Otherwise we wouldn't do it— at least I wouldn't.

Because large organizations are more likely to have a separate mailing department, but at the same time tend to be less dependent on direct mail, those groups most dependent on direct mail engage in the least amount of grass-roots lobbying. This is, of course, the opposite of what was hypothesized.

This tendency for direct-mail-based groups to utilize grass-roots lobbying to mobilize their members less frequently is partially offset by the fact that these groups choose more simple and emotional issues. When the issue is nuclear power, toxic waste, or the "giving away of the Panama Canal"—issues that can be portrayed in black-and-white terms—grass-roots lobbying is easier and more effective. If, however, the issue is one such as what is the best available technology for manufacturing polyvinyl chlorides or how many parts per billion of TCE in drinking water can be considered safe, an issue that is more technical in nature, then lobbying by staff members is the dominant tactic.

Despite the fact that their issues are usually better suited to grass-roots lobbying, the overall relationship between dependence on direct marketing and member mobilizations remains negative. This means that groups that most need to activate their members to keep them committed pursue these activities less frequently. It appears that the maintenance needs of the organization are not sufficient to overcome the short-term expenses of grass-roots efforts and the unwillingness of individual lobbyists to devote their time and effort to these activities.

COALITIONS AND COOPERATIVE LOBBYING

When citizen action groups must compete with one another for members, there are substantial disincentives to cooperative lobbying. In their pioneering work conceptualizing social movements as a competitive industries, John McCarthy and Mayer Zald suggest that competition among groups within the same issue area should be considered normal. Among the best-documented of these struggles are those among groups within the women's and the civil rights movements, but substantial competition occurs within all movements.[20] Anne Costain, describing the difficulties of coalition building within the women's movement, writes, "Unlike other public interest coalitions, the women's lobbies generated no lasting coalition superstructure." She attributes this failure to the mixture of movement groups and traditional voluntary associations such as the League of Women Voters.[21] While Costain is certainly correct that the women's movement has had difficulty in sustaining lasting coalitions and that part of this difficulty reflects the variety among the women's organizations, she is incorrect in seeing such coalitions as standard practice within other social movements.

The civil rights movement—with its often bitter and aggressive rivalry among the NAACP, the Student Non-Violent Coordinating Committee (SNCC), the Southern Christian Leadership Conference (SCLC), the Urban League, and the Black Panthers — indicates that extensive, long-term coalitions are difficult to achieve. The women's movement may, in fact, have a better record than other social movements. In their study of feminist groups, Joyce Gelb and Marian Palley found that if common memberships on directorates indicates cooperation and coalition building, then women's groups engage in substantial cooperative activity.[22]

The Gelb and Palley study showed quite clearly that the factor that most inhibits a group from participating in cooperative lobbying is its dependence on members' dues for income. Just as WEAL could eschew highly visible issues and lobby on implementation aspects of legislation because its funds come largely from foundations and government grants, WEAL can also afford to join coalitions because it does not have the same need to show its members that it is the leading group in any cooperative effort. The National Organization for Women must take a more visible role in any cooperative effort because it depends on member contributions for more than 80 percent of its income.

Interviews with directors and lobbyists from citizen action groups revealed that two additional factors consistently influence the likelihood that a group will lobby cooperatively: the perceived security of the group's income and the perceived prestige of the organization. As table 4.2 shows, with but one exception, the six groups reporting the highest levels of cooperation and coalition formation were the least dependent on direct mail and/or were quite large in comparison to other organizations within the same issue area.[23]

TABLE 4.2

GROUP SIZE, DEPENDENCE ON DIRECT MAIL,
AND COOPERATIVE LOBBYING

	Percentage of Income from	Level of Resources Devoted to Cooperative Lobbying		
Number of Members	Direct Mail	High	Medium	Low
More than 75,000	Less than 40	4	1	0
More than 75,000	More than 40	0	2	2
Less than 75,000	Less than 40	1	3	1
Less than 75,000	More than 40	1	1	2

Comments from interviewees of smaller and less secure groups show why this pattern occurs. These individuals believe that their groups would lose their identity and possibly even disappear if they engaged in extensive cooperative efforts with larger, more established organizations. The associate director of one environmental interest group put this fear most succinctly:

> We can't afford to work with the Sierra Club; they would swallow us up if we did. They have so much more name recognition and they are so much better organized at the local level than we are.

This same person reported that while there was some cooperation with the Sierra Club, it was the latter organization that did the cooperating:

> It's a one-way street. They provide us with information concerning coming issues or candidates . . . but we don't respond with anything for them. We don't have the resources and [the executive director of his organization] doesn't want us to.

When asked why the director did not wish cooperation, the respondent answered that he suspected that the director feared a loss of personal access to the media and to individual congresspersons if the group was seen as having the same goals as the Sierra Club.

A lobbyist from another small environmental group indicated that he personally did not get involved in coalitions because the "larger groups always dominate us. They have a lot more resources and that gives them the advantage when deciding who gets to do what." Similarly, another lobbyist stated that when she did work with larger, more prominent groups, the congressional staff did not give her as much attention as they gave lobbyists from the better-known groups. She felt that this was not as true when her group worked independently.

Lobbyists from the more established groups saw the situation differently. They viewed the groups within their movements as choosing lobbying tactics based on a specialization of labor. For example, a lobbyist from one of the larger and older groups commented that a major task of his organization was to supply research not only to Congress but also to other lobbyists within the movement. It was the job of other groups to handle more of the grass-roots efforts. Similarly, a lobbyist from the Sierra Club saw his group's role as one of supplying "insider knowledge" to congresspersons and their staffs:

> That's what we do. We let other people—congresspersons, other groups, and other people involved with an issue—know what's happening with everybody else. Our influence comes from being the best known group and from keeping a congressman from being embarrassed by an issue. We let them know what's really going on.

A staff member of one of the larger feminist organizations stated that although her group did not engage in as many coalitions as she might like, the various groups did try to emphasize their own special advantages and not get in the way or compete with one another. Each organization was expected to emphasize its own skills and tactics:

We do a lot of grass-roots work and local organizing. That's really our strength. We let other groups handle most of the legal battles. We don't want to compete with them, that would hurt everybody. Anyway, we don't need to compete. Everybody knows who we are and what we stand for.

There was one major exception to the above pattern. Environmental Action (EA), a small and relatively radical citizen action group, ranked second in the number of mentions of cooperative lobbying and first in the percentage of resources it spent on these efforts. When queried about the group's decision to devote so many of its scarce resources to coalitions and cooperative efforts, the director replied:

The natural constituency for us has always been persons who hold strong anti-capitalist, anti-corporation views. But you can't lobby Congress by expressing those views or being known as a representative of them. [Therefore] EA cooperates with other groups and tries to get the whole environmental lobby to take a more radical stance.

At the same time, however, the director reported that she was extremely concerned about losing the distinctive character of Environmental Action as the most radical of the major environmental groups: "All other groups have become increasingly radical because of Reagan and Watt. It's hard for the public to see us as really different." Because of this, the group planned to devote most of its new resources to grass-roots rather than cooperative lobbying.[24]

Although we have emphasized the competitive nature of citizen groups within the same social movement, it would be a mistake to overestimate the level of competition or to underestimate the degree of cooperation that exists. Coalitions among citizen action groups do occur; a few, such as the Clean Air Coalition, have become institutionalized. Most groups within these movements exchange membership lists for prospecting new members because they know that once individuals have shown that they will respond to a mailing in a certain area, they will be more likely to join other groups advocating similar goals. In addition, the staffs of these organizations typically know one another and share similar values and political goals. Hugh Heclo, an authority on interactions among the Washington elites, points out that each issue arena has an "issue network" that encourages cooperation because network members reinforce one another's sense of emotional and intellectual commitment.[25] Jeffrey Berry makes a similar argument when he writes that peer pressure within a social movement often induces participation in coalitions.[26]

To summarize, in all the social movements cooperative lobbying and long-term coalitions follow the same pattern: Larger, well-established groups and groups with resources not based on solicitations of the mass membership are most likely to engage in coalition building. Smaller organizations, particularly those that depend on frequent mail solicitations, are less likely to spend their scarce resources in lobbying coalitions because to do so decreases their visibility to their membership and to decision makers in Washington.

DISCUSSION

What do these patterns tell us about the impact of direct mail on citizen action group elites? Perhaps the most important finding is that the leaders of associations based on direct-mail memberships must choose more extreme positions on highly visible issues. Even elites from the larger direct-mail-based groups such as the National Organization for Women must choose more radical and more visible issues to keep their members attached to the organization. While this finding is not surprising, it is important. Elites from direct-mail-based groups do not have the luxury of working behind the scenes and concentrating on successful implementation. Instead, they must strive for symbolic victories, victories that receive media attention. These organizations must hope that other groups within the movement will stay with the legislation and see to it that the implementing agencies will be faithful to the spirit of the legislation.[27]

The necessity of choosing visible and extreme positions on issues where citizen action groups are organized has led to the politics of confrontation rather than compromise. Abortion, school prayer, civil rights, and the environment—issues that attract citizen group development—are already emotionally charged issues. The constraints that organizational maintenance places on direct-mail-based groups discourages tolerance and makes these issues still more difficult to compromise. One need only look to the 1985 convention of the National Organization for Women to see how difficult it is for moderate tactics to succeed in the competitive atmosphere within which these groups must operate. At that convention, like the 1975 convention, an opposition promising to reject any compromises on women's issues and to "go back to the streets" defeated the incumbent leaders who had pursued moderate, behind-the-scenes tactics. Similarly, the stalemate on environmental issues from 1980 to 1985 is the result of the inability of elites on either side to compromise because their supporters refuse to accept any dealing with the "enemy."[28] In a government accustomed to the bargaining and compromises of pluralism, these issues and tactics have left Congress, the White House, and the bureaucracy in unfamiliar positions where any decision that gains support on one side is balanced by a loss of support on the other. It is not surprising, then, that the most vigorous critics of single-issue politics and direct-marketing-based groups are the politicians, who find themselves caught in the middle of these struggles.

While the greater reliance of direct-mail-based organizations on extreme and visible issues and tactics constitutes the most important of the above findings, the most surprising discovery is the failure of direct-mail-based groups to utilize grass-roots lobbying as often as social network groups. Given the importance of grass-roots activities for keeping members committed to the group, this failure to mobilize members creates long-term losses for direct-mail organizations. Although this absence of grass-roots activity can be explained by the monetary costs of mobilizations and the time and effort costs to individual staff members, this omission is a major opportunity foregone and its importance became abundantly clear to the defeated leaders of the National Organization for Women.

Political Action Committees

Although citizen action groups have a long and distinguished history in American politics, political action committees (PACs) are relatively new arrivals. The Congress of Industrial Organizations (the CIO of the AFL–CIO) formed the CIO–PAC in 1943 to collect and disperse voluntary political contributions from union members. This PAC was followed by another CIO committee in 1944, the National Citizen's Political Action Committee (NC–PAC).[29] The first major business and trade association PACs were created in 1962 and 1963 when the American Medical Association formed AMPAC and the National Association of Manufacturers formed BIPAC (the Business and Industry Political Action Committee).[30]

Not until the 1970s, however, did the real boom in political action committees begin. In 1971 Congress passed the Federal Election Campaign Act for the purpose of tightening the required disclosures of campaign contributions and expenditures. This act specifically legitimized PACs by allowing corporations and labor unions to create, administer, and raise funds for their PACs and to cover organizational expenses from corporate and union treasuries.[31] In 1974 Congress, incensed by the revelations of Watergate and the role played by both legal and illegal corporate giving, amended the 1971 legislation to limit individual contributions to political candidates to $1000 per election and placed a cumulative limit of $25,000 on the amount that an individual could give to all federal candidates.[32] This legislation also limited PAC contributions to $5000 per candidate per election, but it did not limit the total amount a PAC could give to all candidates. The impact of these "reforms" was to increase the number of registered PACs from 608 in 1974 to over 4200 in 1987. PAC campaign contributions rose from $8.5 million in the 1971-72 electoral cycle to over $139 million in the 1985-86 cycle. And PAC giving in 1987 was up 44 percent over 1985.[33]

Direct mail has made much of this increase possible. In his survey of political action committees, Larry Sabato found that 82 percent of all corporate and 73 percent of all trade association PACs utilize direct mail to raise funds. Even labor, where only 36 percent of the PACs employ direct mail as a fund-raising technique, has increased the number and sophistication of its mailings. The AFL-CIO's political arm, COPE, has personalized and refined its mailing lists by categorizing union members by occupational specialty as well as by congressional district. This allows COPE-supported candidates to make personalized appeals indicating that they are aware of the special problems particular trades face.[34]

Although corporate, trade association, and labor PACs utilize direct mail extensively in their fund-raising efforts, the political action committees most dependent on direct mail are the nonconnected PACs. These include purely ideological PACs, such as the National Conservative Political Action Committee (NCPAC), PACs associated with citizen action groups (e.g., Sierra-PAC), and PACs affiliated with particular politicians, including Ronald Reagan's Citizens for the Republic and Senator Helms's Congressional Club. These organizations, which numbered over 1000 in 1987, are forced by Federal Election Commission (FEC) regulations to utilize direct mail to survive. While corporate, trade association, and union PACs can rely on their parent organizations to pay their overhead and fund-raising expenses, ideological PACs must pay these costs themselves. Because the FEC limits individual contributions to PACs to $1000, ideological PACs must attract large numbers of small donations. Direct mail is the most effective way of doing this.

Ideological PACs have been quite successful in meeting the challenge of reaching thousands of small donors. Margaret Latus, in her study of ten large ideological PACs, found that they raised an average of $1.9 million during the 1981-82 electoral cycle; almost all of this was generated through mail solicitations.[35] During the 1983-84 cycle, NCPAC raised more than $19 million, the National Congressional Club and the Fund for a Conservative Majority each raised over $5 million, and a total of twenty different ideological PACs raised more than $1 million each.[36]

These vast amounts of funds have not gone unnoticed by critics of direct mail. Ideological PACs have received extensive media coverage and have been accused of numerous sins against the political system. Influential writers for major newspapers and magazines, such as David Broder of the *Washington Post,* Robert Timberg of the *Baltimore Sun,* and Elizabeth Drew of *The New Yorker,* have suggested that directors of ideological PACs use the contributions of their members for personal gain rather than political influence, intentionally lie and mislead the public, and create a mean and negative milieu around political campaigns.[37] In fact, almost every charge directed against single-issue groups, the direct marketing of politics, and political junk mail has been made specifically against ideological PACs.

For the most part, charges that directors of ideological PACs use contributions for personal gain are unfounded. For example, Robert Timberg, in a series of articles for the *Baltimore Sun,* called attention to the fact that NCPAC contributes less than 5 percent of the funds it raises to candidates and calculated that of the funds raised by NCPAC between 1975 and 1982, over one-third was channeled to individuals and firms closely linked to NCPAC's then national chairman, Terry Dolan. Most of these funds paid for printing and mailing costs.[38] What Timberg did not make clear was that these expenses were not significantly higher than those of other PACs or of direct-mailing costs in general. In addition, because corporate, labor, and trade association PACs have their overhead expenses and mailing costs paid for them by the parent organizations, it is not really fair to compare the percentage of donations that these PACs spend on elections with the percentage that ideological PACs disperse for the same purposes.[39] If corporate and trade PACs had to pay these costs, the differences between them and ideological PACs in the percentage of total receipts spent on political campaigns would not be significant.

ACCOUNTABILITY

While the leadership of ideological PACs spend funds in ways that their contributors would approve and rarely use contributors' funds for personal financial gain, it is certainly true that there are few controls on what leaders of these PACs can do with the contributions they receive. The reality of the situation is that directors of ideological PACs are responsible to no one. Frank Sorauf, a leading expert on PACs, believes that the most critical issue that PACs raise is that of accountability:

> . . . PACs have become major organizers of political power in American politics. And therein lies another major policy issue: their accountability. . . . As an emerging form of political organization, PACs raise many of the same questions of accountability that parties and lobbyists raised decades ago: who controls their political decisions, and to whom do they answer for the political choices they make?[40]

Ann Lewis of the Democratic National Committee finds the absence of PAC responsibility particularly objectionable. She argues that "unlike the parties, many of the independent PACs are essentially computer-driven mail-order operations that have no membership and are accountable to nobody."[41] Larry Sabato writes that there are "shockingly few controls on groups like NCPAC and PRO-PAC [the Progressive Political Action Committee]."[42] He found that nonconnected PACs are responsible only to themselves and that, at most, a few persons decide which candidates will receive money and how independent expenditures will be spent. Vic Kamber, director of PROPAC, acknowledged this absence of external controls when he stated: "I guess in the simplest sense . . . they've [the contributors] got to trust, yeah, I guess they do, Vic Kamber."[43] This absence of accountability presents a problem for democratic theory because while no one holds directors of ideological PACs and citizen action groups responsible for their actions, these same leaders have exercised significant political influence. Vic Kamber may be deserving of his contributors' trust, and Terry Dolan might have been doing exactly what NCPAC's contributors wanted but they (and we) have no effective means of holding these leaders responsible for what they say and do.

It might be argued that if the leadership of these organizations does not pursue the policies their contributors desire, then these persons will stop contributing and the PAC leaders will lose their resources. This argument misses the critical point: Contributors know little about their organization's policies and goals beyond what the leadership tells them in its mailings, newsletters, and media appeals. It is quite possible for a political action committee to obtain resources by promising one set of actions and then turn around and do the opposite. The probability that the contributors will know of this deception is small. There are no opposition candidates to point out to contributors that they are being misled. Only those persons creating the deception know whom they are deceiving.

STRATEGIES AND TACTICS OF PACs

As with citizen action groups, substantial differences can be seen in the strategies and tactics of PACs dependent on direct marketing for the majority of their income and PACs that have other sources of income and support. For all PACs, contributors provide legitimacy and grass-roots support, but these resources are particularly important to ideological PACs. In 1976, for example, PACs from the New Right generated over 700,000 letters to President Ford urging him to veto a common-site picketing bill. Three years later, the same organizations mailed more than 7.5 million letters to supporters urging them to demand that their senators vote against President Carter's Panama Canal Treaty. Like citizen action groups, PACs sell their mailing lists at low rates to favored candidates at election time. If a senator wants to alert only conservatives, he can buy NCPAC's house list for his state. If he wishes to alert only liberals, he can purchase PROPAC's list.

Although ideological PACs have many critics, the directors and supporters of these direct-mail-based organizations see them as having a beneficial impact on the political system. Richard Viguerie, the best-known and most notorious of all direct-mail fund raisers, is not afraid to speak out on the value of direct mail to the New Right and its PACs. In his book *The New Right: We're Ready to Lead,* Viguerie writes:

> Without direct mail, there would be no effective counterforce to liberalism, and certainly there would be no be no New Right. . . . We sell our magazines, our books and our candidates through the mail. We alert our supporters to upcoming battles through the mail. We find new recruits for the conservative movement through the mail.
>
> Without the mail, most conservative activities would wither and die. . . . You can think of direct mail as OUR TV, radio, daily newspaper and weekly magazine. . . . It is the advertising medium of the underdog. It allows organizations or causes not part of the mainstream to get funding. It is the advertising medium of the nonestablishment candidate.[44]

Certainly Viguerie is correct in pointing to direct mail's effectiveness in challenging the establishment and forcing issues onto the political agenda that are unpopular with elected officials. In her analysis of ideological PACs and direct mail, Margaret Latus suggests that an important contribution of these institutions is their capacity to make elected officials deal with divisive issues. But, she argues, *divisive* issues are not necessarily *destructive* issues.

In fact, considering the paucity of information that voters have about candidates, ideological PACs may be enhancing democratic representation by holding elected officials responsible for their actions.[45] Certainly ideological PACs have increased participation in politics through monetary contributions to candidates and causes. In the first two elections of the 1980s, the percentage of persons who contributed to a political candidate or cause climbed to an all-time high.[46]

A comparison of ideological PACs with corporate, labor, and trade association PACs — PACs that need not depend as heavily on direct mail — finds three factors distinguish the strategies and tactics of ideological PACs: (1) their willingness to fight and lose a political struggle in order to fight the pure fight; (2) their readiness to spend money in behalf of challengers rather than incumbents in congressional elections; and (3) their widespread use of independent spending in electoral contests, instead of giving contributions directly to candidates.

The New Right was willing to spend millions to mobilize persons against the Panama Canal Treaty, despite knowing that the chance of defeating the treaty was small. Although they lost the fight, the leadership of the New Right felt that this effort set the stage for future victories, especially the election of Ronald Reagan and a Republican majority in the Senate in 1980.

Richard Viguerie stresses the importance to the New Right of being will-ing to lose, and he believes that this attribute is one of the major differences between the New Right and the Republican party:

> We're so irresponsible we don't even mind losing a fight. We fight anyway. Where the "responsible" Republican tries to appease and compromise, we try to win. Or if we lose, we want to come out of the fight with an issue to use against the liberals in the next election. . . .
> When you battle for a principle, you may lose the battle—but not the principle. The principle lives on, to shame and embarrass the winners.[47]

Just as the leadership of the New Right PACs spent money on the Canal treaty knowing that the battle probably could not be won, ideological PACs on both the right and the left typically have spent a larger proportion of their campaign expenditures on challengers than incumbents, even though they know that incumbents win almost 90 percent of their races. In 1986, while corporate and trade association PACs spent 76 and 75 percent respectively for incumbents, and gave only 8 and 9 percent each to assist challengers, ideological PACs spent only 51 percent on incumbents and 25 percent on challengers.[48]

Ideological PACs are willing to spend on losing causes and on challengers because of the advertising value of these expenditures and their strategic uses in future political confrontations. Money spent on losing efforts today are an investment in tomorrow's fund raising. By campaigning against the Panama Canal Treaty, the New Right added thousands of names to its house list, names that responded well to future mailings. It also forced politicians to take a clear and well-publicized position that could be used against them in the next elec-tion. Similarly, left-wing PACs lost in their attempt to unseat Jesse Helms in 1984; but Roger Craver, the direct-mail expert for Helms's Democratic oppo-nent, added thousands of liberal donors to his house list and gained visibility and legitimacy among them.

The extensive use of independent spending[49] constitutes the third factor that sets ideological PACs apart from other political action committees. Al-though ideological PACs accounted for only 15 percent of all PAC expenditures in 1986, they accounted for 53 percent of all independent expenditures.[50] This emphasis on independent spending occurs for four reasons: (1) the limit on campaign contributions to $10,000 per election cycle; (2) the desire to start early campaigning against an incumbent; (3) the need to disassociate their mes-sages from their candidates; and (4) the advertising value of independent ex-penditures to the PACs.

The $10,000 contribution limit necessitates independent expenditures be-cause ideological PACs typically focus their attention on only a few races. Part of their strategy for these races is to show that an incumbent is vulnerable and thereby encourage strong challengers to enter the contest. For this reason, ideological PACs often begin spending heavily against incumbents as much as a year before the general election.

One of the often heard criticisms of ideological PACs is their emphasis on the negative rather than positive aspects of candidates. This criticism is certainly justified. Negative messages against candidates, rather than positive advertisements for them, accounted for 78 percent of all independent expenditures on the 1982 congressional elections, and over 80 percent of these expenditures were directed against incumbents.[51] To do the most damage to their opponent without harming the reputation of their preferred candidate, ideological PACs often disassociate their message from their candidate. The late Terry Dolan summarized this with his often cited quote about NCPAC: "A group like ours can lie through its teeth, and the candidate it helps stays clean."[52] Similarly, Vic Kamber, director of PROPAC, stated, "If you plant the seeds of doubt about a senator, and back it up with facts and figures, then someone else can capitalize on it. I don't like it, but it's effective."[53]

Leaders of ideological PACs expect that their independent expenditures will not only help their chosen candidate but also the PAC. One reason for this is the extensive media attention that negative expenditures attract. Although negatively oriented independent expenditures account for only a small portion of all PAC campaign spending, they probably receive the majority of media attention. This coverage constitutes free political advertisement for organizations that need to stay in the public's eye in order to survive.

Just as the political strategies of ideological PACs set them apart from other political institutions, the character of their mailings also differs from that of the political parties and economically oriented PACs. While party mailings stress broad, long-term partisan issues, and corporate, labor, and trade association PACs emphasize economic and regulatory issues important to them, two-thirds of ideological PACs use as their major appeal social issues such as abortion, the ERA, school prayer, and homosexual rights. Perhaps the best (or worst!) example of this stress on social issues coupled with the use of extremism and fear was a NCPAC letter signed by Senator Jesse Helms that read, "Your tax dollars are being used to pay for grade school classes that teach our children that CANNIBALISM, WIFE-SWAPPING and the MURDER of infants and the elderly are acceptable behavior."[54]

Mailings from ideological PACs are also more likely to personify the chosen peril in a familiar name. For example, a mailing from a conservative PAC put on the outside of its envelope the message, "Teddy Kennedy doesn't want you to open this letter." It would certainly be fair to say that Teddy Kennedy has raised millions for NCPAC and the New Right, while Jerry Falwell and Jesse

Helms have given comparable assistance to PROPAC and other liberal causes. Similarly, the environmental citizen action groups and PACs grew at an unprecedented rate during the period when James Watt was the secretary of the Department of the Interior and Anne Burford headed the Environmental Protection Agency. Sabato, in his book *Pac Power,* summarized the mailings of ideological PACs as "pure emotion, lightening-rod issues, and 'hot' names."[55] One of the more interesting developments in the mailing strategies of ideological PACs is their use of one another as threats and enemies. For example, PROPAC asks for money to "expose groups like NCPAC," and Independent Action requests money to help end PAC influence.[56]

Although independent expenditures, negativism, and emotionalism characterize the vast majority of messages sent by ideological PACs, not all such organizations use these tactics, and there is considerable disagreement among their leaders concerning the merit of this approach. Some ideological PACs refuse to spend money on negative, independent campaign efforts. The League of Conservation Voters refuses to spend money on any form of independent campaign expenditures, and only $477 of the $237,797 spent independently by the National Rifle Association Victory Fund in 1982 was used for negative messages. Leaders of PACs also disagree over the extensive use of emotionalism and fear in direct-mail appeals. One reason that the League of Conservation Voters discontinued its direct-mail program was the belief of its leaders that direct-mail "success" requires "guilt, fear, and distortion."[57]

The absence of moderation among most ideological PACs is not limited to direct mail. Extreme appeals also work well on television. Norman Lear's People for the American Way, a PAC formed to oppose the Moral Majority, produced "Life and Liberty . . . For All Who Believe," a half-hour documentary against the "radical right." This program attacked the Christian Right as a threat to liberty, freedom, and democracy; it generated almost $250,000 in pledges and added nearly 10,000 names to its membership rolls and house mailing list. In sharp contrast, the more moderate appeals found in the 1983 Democratic party national telethon lost $2.8 million and placed the party still further in debt.[58]

DISCUSSION

Ideological political action committees, when taken as a group, exhibit the characteristics that have caused so much criticism of the direct marketing of politics. As we saw in our content analysis of direct mailings in chapter 1, ideological mailings are more likely than those of political parties to stress negativism, fear, and guilt, and to use propaganda techniques such as ad hominem arguments rather than more factual communication. It is impossible to defend letters such as the one cited above from Senator Helms stating that tax dollars are being used to teach cannibalism, wife-swapping, and murder. In addition, the campaign messages funded by ideological PACs are more likely to employ extremism, intolerance, and vitriolic personal attacks.

An equally disturbing attribute of nonconnected political action committees is the absence of financial and political responsibility. Each year, millions of dollars flow into the treasuries of these institutions, and except for the financial statements that they must file with the Federal Election Commission, there are no institutionalized checks on what they communicate or on how they spend their funds. As long as PAC mailings and independent political advertisements have to be neither reasonable nor accurate, the temptation to use misleading statements is exceptionally strong. The critical issues, however, are not whether ideological PACs are encouraging intolerance and extremism, or even whether they are politically accountable. The more important questions concern what the overall impact of these tactics on public policy and the American political system may be.

Despite the problems that ideological PACs create, they also produce several positive effects. Among them are an introduction of social or moral questions onto the political agenda, an increase in public awareness of issues, and greater citizen participation. While elected officials, particularly those who have been the target of negative independent expenditures, may argue that issues such as abortion and prayer in public schools have no place in politics and should not become politicized, democratic theory argues that the political system must decide such issues. Certainly it is more appropriate for the electorate and their representatives to determine these issues than for the economic system to determine moral choices or for the public to ignore such issues entirely. To argue that all ethical or moral questions should be individual rather than social choices evades the issue. In a democracy it is up to the citizenry to determine which issues should be left to the individual and which should fall under the purview of the state. The criminal code in every nation, state, and city embodies these decisions, and for liberals to argue that abortion or school prayer is beyond the bounds of public discussion is no different from southerners arguing in the 1960s that segregation was beyond the bounds of political decision, or from conservatives in the 1930s maintaining that child labor conditions must be left to the private sector.

Ideological PACs also help to educate the public concerning how their elected officials have voted on issues. Less than 15 percent of the voting public knew how their congressperson voted on any issue during the most recent session of Congress and how his opponent would have voted on that same issue. Only 36 percent of adult citizens could identify their two home-state U.S. senators.[59]

Political action committees such as the Life Amendment PAC, NCPAC, the League of Conservation Voters, and PROPAC spend millions of dollars to change this situation, and to the extent that an effective democracy depends on the public's being aware of the issues and candidates, ideological PACs are helping to increase citizen control over government.

Finally, as I discuss more fully in chapter 6, the traditional economic lobbies and their associated political action committees may be doing far more harm to the democratic process than ideological PACs. Those PACs that further the interests of doctors, realtors, bankers, farmers, retired persons, schoolteachers, and union members provide huge contributions to political campaigns. These contributions are often more important than ideology, party, or constituency preferences in determining congressional voting patterns.[60] And, whereas ideological PACs do their best to keep their issues and the congresspersons' voting record in the public's eye, economic PACs often try equally hard to keep their issues and votes out of the public's view. Such a strategy reduces citizen knowledge and involvement.

Summary

In both citizen action groups and political action committees elites who depend on direct mail are more extreme and less tolerant in their strategies and tactics. They try to keep high profiles and to utilize the media to keep their issues and their organizations before the public. Our comparison of elites who are more dependent on direct marketing with their counterparts whose resources come largely from other sources shows clearly that the former are much more vulnerable to changes in public opinion. Because of this, it is no accident that the largest ideological PACs are the most extreme in their strategies and statements. Moderation reduces resources. This pursuit of uncompromising tactics is changing the nature of American politics at the elite level. In the following chapters I will examine how these changes are affecting political parties, elected officials, and ultimately, public policy.

Notes

1. Xandra Kayden, "The Nationalizing of the Party System," in *Parties, Interest Groups and the Campaign Finance Laws*, ed. Michael Malbin (Washington, D.C.: American Enterprise Institute, 1980), 279.

2. Michael Hayes, "Interest Groups: Pluralism or Mass Society," in *Interest Group Politics*, ed. by Allan Cigler and Burdett Loomis (Washington, D.C.: CQ Press, 1983), 111.

3. Jack Walker, "The Origins and Maintenance of Interest Groups in America," *American Political Science Review* 77 (June 1983): 390-406.

4. For studies of groups making these choices see Jeffrey Berry, *Lobbying for the People* (Princeton: Princeton University Press, 1977); Allan Cigler and J.M. Hansen, "Group Formation through Protest: The American Agricultural Movement," in *Interest Group Politics,* ed. Cigler and Loomis (Washington, D.C.: CQ Press, 1983); Anne Costain, "The Struggle for a National Women's Lobby: Organizing a Diffuse Interest," *Western Political Quarterly* 33 (December 1980): 476-91; and Anne Costain, "Representing Women: The Transition from Social Movement to Interest Group," *Western Political Quarterly* 34 (March 1981): 100-113; Joyce Gelb and Marian Palley, *Women and Public Policies* (Princeton: Princeton University Press, 1982); M.R. Hershey and D.M. West, "Single-Issue Politics: Prolife Groups and the 1980 Senate Campaign," in Cigler and Loomis, eds. *Interest Group Politics;* R.C. Liebman, "Mobilizing the Moral Majority," in *The New Christian Right,* ed. Robert Liebman and Robert Wuthnow (Hawthorne, N.Y.: Aldine, 1983); Andrew McFarland, *Common Cause* (Chatham, N.J.: Chatham House, 1984); R.C. Mitchell, "National Environmental Lobbies and the Apparent Illogic of Collective Action," in *Collective Decision Making,* ed. C. Russell (Baltimore: Johns Hopkins University Press, 1978); and Walker, "The Origins and Maintenance"; Hayes, "Interest Groups"; Robert Salisbury, "Interest Representation: The Dominance of Institutions," *American Political Science Review* 78 (March 1984): 64-76; Kerry Smith, "A Theoretical Analysis of the Green Lobby," *American Political Science Review* 79 (1985): 132-37; and John M. Hansen, "The Political Economy of Group Membership," *American Political Science Review* 79 (1985): 79-96.

5. Hayes, "Interest Groups," 113-19.

6. R. Kenneth Godwin and Robert C. Mitchell, "The Impact of Direct Mail on Political Organizations," *Social Science Quarterly* 65 (1984): 829-39.

7. As Anthony Downs points out in *Inside Bureaucracy* (New York: Harper & Row, 1967), separate units within organizations lobby internally to increase their own budget, staff, and duties.

8. Berry, *Lobbying;* Donald Hall, *Cooperative Lobbying* (Tucson: University of Arizona Press, 1968); and Kay Schlozman and John Tierney, *Organized Interests and American Democracy* (New York: Harper & Row, 1986), 278-88.

9. John McCarthy and Mayer Zald, "Resource Mobilization and Social Movements: A Partial Theory," *American Journal of Sociology* 82 (1977): 1212-41.

10. The 12 environmental respondents came from 9 interest groups: the League of Conservation Voters, Defenders of Wildlife, Environmental Action, the Environmental Defense Fund, Friends of the Earth, the National Audubon Society, the National Wildlife Federation, the Sierra Club, and the Wilderness Society. We have not listed the other 9 organizations because some respondents requested anonymity. Because no more than 3 associations were chosen from each of the other issue arenas, it is not possible to protect this pledge and identify the issue area at the same time.

11. In this case the measure of association is Kendall's tau_c, a measure of association appropriate to ordinal level data. Just as with Pearson's correlation coefficient, a tau of 1.0 would indicate a perfect positive relationship, and a tau of -1.0 would indicate a perfect negative relationship.

12. Schlozman and Tierney, *Organized Interests,* 173.

13. The National Wildlife Federation (NWF), the Sierra Club, and the Audubon Society all rely heavily on direct mailings for membership renewals and to encourage new members, but the pattern of how members originally joined is quite different. For

example, one-third of NWF members originally received their memberships as a gift.

14. See Costain, "Representing Women," 104-5. A number of excellent accounts of the development and diversification within the women's movement have been written: the Costain articles and the Gelb and Palley book cited in note 4; Barbara Deckard, *The Women's Movement* (Harper & Row, 1979); Maren Lockwood Carden, *Feminism in the Mid-1970's* (New York: Ford Foundation, 1977); and Jo Freeman, *The Politics of Women's Liberation* (New York: David McKay, 1975). The Gelb and Palley volume is particularly useful in that it gives the membership size, sources of support, and issue-selection processes of the more influential women's groups.

15. Burdett Loomis, "A New Era: Groups and the Grass Roots," in Cigler and Loomis, eds. *Interest Group Politics*.

16. A telephone tree mobilization is similar to a chain letter. The staff member initiating the mobilization calls several persons and indicates what he wants the activists to do (e.g. write a letter or phone their congressperson); each of these individuals then calls several other persons and gives them the message; then these individuals call others, who continue until the entire list of activists has been contacted.

17. For discussions of how grass-roots lobbying helps tie members to associations, see Richard Viguerie, *The New Right: We're Ready to Lead* (Falls Church, Va.: The Viguerie Company, 1981); Godwin and Mitchell, "The Impact," 836-37; and Sheldon Eckland-Olson, "Social Networks and Social Movements: A Microstructural Approach to Differential Recruitment," *American Sociological Review* 45 (1980): 787-801.

18. R. Kenneth Godwin, "Lobbying Choices of Citizen Action Groups" (paper presented at the annual meeting of the Midwest Political Science Association, Chicago, 1984).

19. The only exceptions to this were representatives of groups such as the Environmental Defense Fund, which spends a substantial portion of its budget (about 20 percent) in litigation, Environmental Action, which reported spending almost half of its lobbying budget in grass-roots efforts, and the Sierra Club, whose lobbyist indicated that only 10 percent of its budget was devoted to grass-roots efforts. This latter figure is misleading, however, in that the Sierra Club charges most of these expenses to its direct-mail department rather than its lobbying budget.

20. McCarthy and Zald, "Resource Mobilization." For discussions of the women's and civil rights movements see Jo Freeman, "A Model for Analyzing the Strategic Options of Social Movement Organizations," in *Social Movements of the Sixties and Seventies,* ed. Jo Freeman (New York: Longman, 1983); Anne Costain, "The Struggle for a National Women's Lobby"; Costain, "Representing Women"; and Joyce Gelb and Marian Palley, *Women and Public Policies* (Princeton: Princeton University Press, 1982). For discussions of the New Christian Right, see James L. Guth, "The New Christian Right," in *The New Christian Right*, ed. Robert Liebman and Robert Wuthnow (Hawthorne, N.Y.: Aldine, 1983).

21. Costain, "The Struggle," 478-79.

22. Gelb and Palley, *Women and Public Policies*.

23. To measure an organization's level of cooperation, we asked each respondent to estimate the percentage of the group's lobbying effort that went into cooperative lobbying with other groups within the movement. We also asked each respondent to rank all other groups within the movement on their level of cooperative lobbying. Group size was determined by membership rolls; dependence on direct mail was determined

by a combination of the percentage of members originally recruited by direct mail and the percentage of the group's total budget supplied by these memberships plus additional funds that came to the organization in response to mail solicitations of members.

24. Approximately nine months after this interview, the director's fears were partially realized. When James Watt resigned as the secretary of the interior and Anne Burford was replaced at EPA, all the environmental interest groups suffered substantial declines in membership renewals and new recruits. The most severely hit groups were those that were dependent on direct marketing for their resources. In response to this drop in resources, Environmental Action initiated a plan to merge with another relatively radical environmental group, Friends of the Earth. The staff of Friends of the Earth accepted the merger plan, but David Brower, its founder, went to court to stop the merger.

25. Hugh Heclo, "Issue Networks and the Executive Establishment," in *The New American Political System,* ed. Anthony King (Washington, D.C.: American Enterprise Institute, 1978).

26. Berry, *Lobbying,* 260.

27. As Murray Edelman and others have shown, symbolic victories often fail at the implementation stage as other organized interests, which do not have to concentrate on visible politics, work behind the scenes to negate or change the legislation. See, Murray Edelman, *The Symbolic Uses of Politics* (Urbana: University of Illinois Press, 1964); and Roger W. Cobb and Charles D. Elder, *The Political Uses of Symbols* (New York: Longman, 1983).

28. For a discussion of such a stalemate during the 1980s on environmental issues, see Mary Etta Cook and Roger H. Davidson, "Deferral Politics: Congressional Decision Making on Environmental Issues"; in *Public Policy and the Natural Environment,* ed. R. Kenneth Godwin and Helen M. Ingram (Greenwich, Conn.: JAI Press, 1985); and Henry C. Kenski, "The President, Congress and Interest Groups," in the same volume.

29. No relationship, except an ironical one, exists between the CIO's NC–PAC and today's NCPAC (the National Conservative Political Action Committee).

30. Larry J. Sabato, *PAC Power: Inside the World of Political Action Committees* (New York: Norton, 1984), 6.

31. Ibid., 8.

32. Ibid.

33. *Common Cause News,* 23 February 1988; Frank Sorauf, *Money in American Elections* (Glenview, Ill.: Scott Foresman, 1988), 79.

34. Sabato, *PAC Power,* 61-69.

35. Margaret Ann Latus, "Assessing Ideological PACs: From Outrage to Understanding," in *Money and Politics in the United States,* ed. Michael Malbin (Chatham, N.J.: Chatham House, 1984).

36. Federal Election Commission press release, 1 December 1985, Washington, D.C.

37. David Broder, "When Washington Gets Mean," *Washington Post,* 31 October 1982, C7; Robert Timberg, "The PAC Business," *Baltimore Sun,* 11-19 July 1982; and Elizabeth Drew, *Politics and Money: The New Road to Corruption* (New York: Macmillan, 1983).

38. Timberg, "The PAC Business."

39. *National Journal,* 15 December 1983, 2628.

40. Frank Sorauf, "Who's in Charge? Accountability in Political Action Committees,"

Political Science Quarterly 99 (Winter 1984-85): 591-92.

41. Quoted in Sabato, *PAC Power,* 151.

42. Ibid., 52.

43. Ibid.

44. Viguerie, *The New Right,* 90-93.

45. Latus, "Assessing Ideological PACs," 166-67. Although some critics of ideological PACs argue that the forcing of issues and positions leads to a lower quality of political debate and possibly to public disillusionment, the persons who direct these PACs believe that their efforts help to educate the public by bringing important issues to their attention. Directors of PACs are not the only ones who see their efforts as improving the levels of political participation and knowledge in the United States. Latus reaches the same conclusion, as does Sylvia Tesh, "In Support of Single Issue Politics," *Political Science Quarterly* 99 (Spring 1984): 27-44.

46. Herbert Alexander, *Financing Politics: Money, Elections, and Electoral Reform,* 3d ed. (Washington, D.C.: CQ Press, 1984), 422.

47. Viguerie, *The New Right,* 90-93.

48. FEC Reports, 1987.

49. Independent spending is campaign spending by a PAC for or against a candidate. The PAC does not contact the candidate it is trying to help concerning the expenditures and is not supposed to coordinate its efforts with those of the candidate.

50. FEC Reports, 1987.

51. Gary Jacobson, "Parties and PACs in Congressional Elections," in *Congress Reconsidered,* 3d ed., ed. Larry Dodd and Bruce Oppenheimer (Washington, D.C.: CQ Press, 1985). This emphasis on negative expenditures decreased in the 1984 elections because conservative PACs were more interested in protecting past Republican gains and the negative expenditure strategy did not work well in 1982.

52. Myra MacPherson, "The New Right Brigade," *Washington Post,* 10 August 1980, F1.

53. Quoted in Sabato, *PAC Power,* 101.

54. Ibid.; emphasis in the original mailing.

55. Ibid., 57.

56. Ibid.

57. Personal interview with a league official in Washington, D.C.

58. Sabato, *PAC Power,* 158.

59. Poll taken by the Roper Organization, 6-13 December 1975.

60. Among the studies that indicate a strong relationship between economic PAC contributions and congressional voting behavior are those of John Frendreis and Richard Waterman, "PAC Contributions and Legislative Behavior: Senate Voting on Trucking Deregulation" (paper presented at the 1983 meetings of the Midwest Political Science Association); and Kirk Brown, "Campaign Contributions and Congressional Voting" (paper presented at the 1983 meetings of the American Political Science Association).

5. The Impact of Direct Marketing on Political Parties

Between 1964 and 1984, direct mail emerged from a little-used method for special situations to the dominant means of political fund raising. The most successful of all political direct mailers, the national committees of the Republican party, raised over $200 million for the 1984 electoral campaign, almost six times the amount collected by their Democratic counterparts.[1] Senator Helms's direct-response programs generated over $12 million for his 1984 campaign, while his opponent, James Hunt, raised almost $8 million;[2] and most presidential candidates utilize personal direct-mail-based political action committees to finance not only their campaigns but those of other candidates whose assistance will be important at the national conventions. The huge sums of money, tremendous Republican advantage, and generous contributions of PACs have changed dramatically the role of the national parties, the personnel who work for them, and campaign funding for candidates. This chapter examines these changes and their effects on politics in the United States.

The Republican Advantage

Although Dwight Eisenhower was the first Republican presidential candidate to use direct mail effectively to raise funds and determine which issues he should stress in the 1952 presidential election, the Republican party's current direct-mail program began with Barry Goldwater in 1964. The Goldwater campaign mailed over 12 million letters, raised $4.7 million, and created a list of over 221,000 contributors.[3] The Republican National Committee (RNC) used this list to begin a direct-response program that continues intact today.

Senator Goldwater's direct mailings appealed to persons who felt disenfranchised by both the national political system and their own party. His letters combined an emotional appeal and a threatened good—"Extremism in the defense of liberty"—and gave his supporters an opportunity to feel politically efficacious. These mailings argued that if the conservatives did not win in 1964, they might never have another chance; liberals would dominate both parties.

But if conservatives supported Goldwater's candidacy, they could achieve an important victory. This blend of emotion, threat, and appeal to political efficacy reflected Goldwater's own beliefs; it was also the perfect recipe for successful direct mailing.[4] This fortuitous correspondence accounts for much of the Republican party's current direct-mail success.

Between 1976 and 1984, the RNC increased its contributions from direct mail by more than 1000 percent and tripled its house list of contributors. By 1980, the combined direct-marketing receipts of the three national committees — the RNC, the Republican National Senatorial Committee (NRSC), and the National Republican Congressional Committee (NRCC) — exceeded $100 million; in the 1981-82 electoral cycle, this total reached over $130 million and represented 77 percent of the party's receipts.[5] By 1984, the RNC had built a house list that peaked at over 1.1 million contributors and in the 1985-86 electoral cycle raised $201 million.[6] The three committees currently send over 30 million pieces of mail annually and work continuously to broaden the party's basis of support.[7]

Democratic national committees have not been nearly as successful as their Republican counterparts. Their three national committees raised only $31.4 million for the 1982 elections, or about 16 cents for each Republican dollar.[8] Herbert Alexander, a leading expert on money and politics in the United States, found that from 1976 to 1980, the Democratic National Committee (DNC) raised only $8.3 million through direct mail, less than one-third the amount the RNC received in response to its direct-marketing solicitations in 1980 alone![9] Only in George McGovern's campaign in 1972 — a campaign that reflected a similar situation and appeal to the 1964 Goldwater campaign — and in the 1984 Senate race in North Carolina — where Governor Hunt was able to capitalize on liberals' intense dislike of Jesse Helms — have the Democrats come close to matching the Republicans in direct-mail receipts.

How Party Elites View Direct Marketing

The directors of the Republican and Democratic direct-marketing programs suggest that a major cause of the imbalance between the two parties is the failure of the Democrats to identify a cohesive set of ideas or ideology to which recipients of direct mailings can respond.[10] While the GOP can appeal to fight the "Teddy Kennedy liberals," inflation, and the growth of big government, the Democrats do not have an easily identifiable enemy. Ronald Reagan is not the bogeyman to Democrats that Senator Kennedy is to Republicans, and the "fairness" issue does not threaten and mobilize upper-middle-class Democrats the way "big government" and "high taxes" activate Republicans. The success of

Democratic mailings against Jesse Helms indicates, however, that Democrats can raise money through direct-response programs, if they find the right enemy and threat.

A second reason given by both Democrats and Republicans for the failure of the DNC to copy the success of the RNC is that, with the exception of McGovern, all Democratic presidential candidates are too moderate. Morris Dees, one of the leaders of McGovern's 1972 direct-mail drive, believes that direct marketing will not work for the current Democratic leaders because they lack the extreme appeal necessary for effective direct marketing.[11]

Although Teddy Kennedy is the ultimate liberal enemy to conservatives, he does not appeal to the more radical liberals McGovern reached. Democratic party leaders feel that part of this problem stems from the heterogeneity of their party.[12] If a candidate makes a radical appeal to one sector, he alienates another. This sentiment was echoed by David Adamany, who wrote that "mass-mail appeals appear to be most successful when pitched to ideological groups, the Democrats may find responses to their mass-mail fund raising limited to the party's liberal activists, but the party is so diverse that it includes important groups of moderates and conservatives as well. It would therefore risk alienating important constituencies if it pitched its financial appeals to one ideological group within the party coalition."[13]

The unenthusiastic attitude of liberal elites toward direct marketing also reduces the Democrats' success. A direct mailer for several liberal citizen action groups stated: "Most liberals fail to understand the advertising benefits of direct mail and only see it as a way of raising money." A direct-marketing specialist within the DNC argued that the Democratic party leadership neither understood the advertising benefits of mailings nor did it find the work that must go into effectively mining the membership as exciting as other aspects of politics. This opinion was repeated by Roger Craver, the leading direct-mail expert for liberal causes and the head of Governor Hunt's very successful direct-response program.[14]

A common explanation of Democratic and liberal respondents for the greater success of Republicans and conservatives was their more extensive use of extremism and emotionalism. Comparisons of the actual mailings of Republicans, Democrats, conservatives, and liberals do not support this explanation; instead, the reverse is true. As we saw in table 1.1, Democrats are slightly, but not significantly, more likely to use extremism and emotionalism than Republicans; and liberals are more likely to utilize these techniques than are conservatives. Part of the reason that extremism by conservatives is a popular and plausible explanation is the visibility of the National Conservative Political Action Committee (NCPAC). This PAC's mailings score extremely high in fear and emotionalism, and between 1980 and 1984 NCPAC sent more mail than any political organization other than the Republican National Committee.

The earlier start of the Republicans and the budgetary constraints that have plagued the Democratic party in recent years provide final explanations of the differences in their direct-marketing success. The Republican direct-mail program began in 1964; the Democrats began almost a decade later, and their efforts were temporarily halted a number of times because of the party's massive debt problems. Because direct marketing requires a substantial initial investment and prospect mailings often lose money, an organization needs investment capital to mail effectively. The Republicans had the necessary capital, made the investment, and received substantial dividends. Even if the Democrats liked direct marketing, were more homogeneous, and had a readily identifiable national target, their late start and huge party debt would have placed them far behind the Republicans in direct-mail fund raising.

Although the political resources that direct marketing generates for the Republican party are much greater than those generated by the Democrats' direct-response program, the real question, as Elizabeth Drew points out, is not how well one group or another does with it, but how does this imbalance affect the political system? Does the inequality produce different kinds of candidates? Does it make effective government more difficult? Does it change public policy?[15]

Not surprisingly, the directors of the parties' direct-marketing fund raising efforts see the impact of *their* programs as a positive influence. They believe that the direct mail sent by the political parties educates the public, increases political interest and party loyalty, encourages more ideological parties, and makes politicians more responsive to the electorate. Not all direct-marketing and direct-mail experts within the two major parties see all of these positive things happening, but most believe that direct mail increases participation and democracy in America.

When asked whether direct mail generates more extremism in the political system, the directors of both parties' direct-marketing programs responded affirmatively. Each believed that because threat and a sense of urgency had to be created in every mailing, the number of extreme groups and individuals had increased. At the same time, however, the Republican leaders did not feel that direct marketing had polarized either the electorate or national politics. Instead, they saw direct mail from the parties as leading to a more responsible party system. They expected these beneficial consequences because party mailings impart information that helps the citizenry integrate issues into a coherent political ideology and alerts them to the party's positions on major issues.

For example, the letter from the Republican Task Force quoted in chapter 1 used the typical direct-mail tactics of threat and appeal to personal efficacy. In this instance, the threat was the potential loss of the Republican majority in the Senate and the return of high levels of government spending. Although the appeal began with a threat, the letter also informed the recipient of the importance of having the Republican party control the Senate and showed the pattern of Senate control for the previous twenty-five years. In addition, the letter alerted the prospective contributor to three basic Republican stands: low inflation, lower taxes, and higher defense spending.

One significant characteristic of both Republican and Democratic party mailings is an absence of single issues. In our sample of party mailings the closest a Republican letter came to stressing a single issue was an appeal based on balancing the budget—an issue central to the Republican party platform under Ronald Reagan. Democratic mailings accentuated the traditional party issues of fairness in taxation and the failure of the Republicans to concern themselves with the poor.

All the party elites we interviewed reported that they intentionally stayed away from single issues and stressed instead loyalty, belonging, and traditional partisan issues. This decision not to use single issues was a pragmatic one, according to Phil Smith of the RNC. He stated that if there were single issues that the RNC could use, it would, but that contributors to the Republican party had not responded well to single issues in the past. Rod Smith of the National Republican Senatorial Committee pointed out that even if a single-issue prospect mailing had a good response, these persons did not make good house-list members because they had no loyalty to the ideals of the Republican party. They gave as a "knee jerk" response to a particular threat, but rarely gave again.

Partially because of their lack of success in direct marketing, Democratic party respondents were far more likely than their Republican counterparts to see direct mail as detrimental to the political system. The Democratic leadership believed that this political tool not only led to political extremism but also reduced opportunities for compromise among competing interests. As was true with Republican respondents, however, the Democrats we interviewed distinguished between direct marketing by the parties and that by single-issue citizen action groups and ideological PACs. In fact, a majority of the respondents from both political parties felt that some nonparty groups abused direct mail by emphasizing only negativism, extremism, and fear; and both Republicans and Democrats were likely to suggest that the mailings of Richard Viguerie and NCPAC were the worst offenders.[16] This perception by party elites that their mailings differ substantially from ideological PACs is correct. As was seen in table 1.2, when we combine the mailings of the parties into one category and those of both liberal and conservative ideological PACs into another, substantial differences emerge. Ideological PACs are more likely to stress fear and guilt, threatened values, and to use the propaganda techniques of card stacking and glittering generalities. Party mailings place much greater emphasis on citizen duty, political efficacy, and future values that a contributor can gain by donating to the party.

To summarize the perceptions of the party fund raisers, there was universal agreement that direct mail has helped the Republicans and conservatives much more than the Democrats and liberals, and a major reason for this was the absence of emotional issues that directly threaten potential Democratic and liberal contributors. There was close to complete agreement among interviewees from both parties that Democrats do not like direct marketing and that it will always be a better tool for the Republicans. And there was consensus among these party officials that the direct-marketing efforts of the political parties have had a positive impact on the political process. Although a consensus concerning the impact of other political direct mailers did not emerge, a majority of Democrats and Republicans felt that ideological PACs, particularly NCPAC, had hurt the political system through the use of extremism and negative independent expenditures.

The Changing Party Roles

Perhaps no set of events surprised political observers in the late 1970s as much as the emergence of the Republican party as a dynamic and effective institution. In 1975, for example, Joyce Gelb and Marian Palley wrote of American national parties:

> . . . the national parties have little power vested in them and possess no real authority over state and local party organizations or elected officials. . . . [They are] little more than paper organizations during the years between presidential campaigns.[17]

Frank Feigert and Margaret Conway wrote in 1976:

> The national party organization can best be described as a loose coalition of local and state parties which agree to work together when it is in the interests of state and local parties to do so.[18]

Despite the fact that the RNC entered the 1980 campaign with over 350 full-time employees and the NRCC and the NRSC employed 100 more, Charles Longley wrote in 1980 that "the national party organization is at best regarded as an ephemeral and episodic adjunct."[19] And as recently as 1986, Martin Wattenberg echoed this perception that the national parties are becoming increasingly weaker while candidate organizations become more independent and less oriented toward national issues.[20] By the early 1980s, however, many political scientists had caught up with the reality of the Republican success and were writing of the rise of national parties and greater party ideology and power.[21]

Direct marketing was not the only factor in the emergence of the Republican national organizations; campaign finance laws also encouraged this process. The 1971 and 1974 campaign finance laws forced the centralization of presidential campaigns because of the many requirements related to the size and disclosure of contributions. Direct mail made the generation of large numbers of small contributions possible, and computer-readable numbers on return envelopes made the recording of contributions much simpler. The 1979 amendments to the campaign finance legislation accelerated the centralization process by allowing the national party organizations to fund the state and local party contributions to candidates and by permitting unlimited transfers of funds from the national parties to state and local organizations for use in voter registration, voter mobilization, and other grass-roots activities.[22] These changes in election finance legislation, coupled with the development of the modern technologies of direct marketing and the importance of campaign polling, made the emergence of stronger national parties and the fund-raising domination by direct mail inevitable.

As might be expected, direct marketing has had different effects on the two parties. The Republican party has become more centralized, ideologically cohesive, and staffed by technical specialists in marketing, polling, and media presentations; the Democratic party has become more fragmented, state and local oriented, and centered on individual candidates. Local GOP parties and candidates have become increasingly dependent on national party assistance while local Democratic organizations and candidates have become increasingly independent of national party organizations and more dependent on nonparty organizations such as labor and citizen action groups.[23]

Bill Brock, chairman of the RNC, saw the opportunities that direct mail presented for the Republican party. He developed a strong national organization funded by direct mail and controlled by a centralized party that could assist state and local parties and individual political campaigns.[24] Brock's direct-mail program was a stunning success. In the 1977-78 electoral cycle, an expenditure of $7,973,000 brought a return of $25,128,000. In the 1979-80 cycle, an investment of $12.1 million returned $54.1 million.[25] The Republican party was so productive in its mailings that, contrary to other direct mailers, the overhead costs of direct mail were cheaper than all other kinds of party fund raising.[26]

Two factors stand out when comparing the national party organizations before 1970 and the national parties today. First, the characteristics of party professionals has changed dramatically. In the past, party officials were persons whose expertise was in generating money from large donors and in developing coalitions; today's professionals are skilled in computers, direct marketing, and public opinion polling. Second, the central bureaucracy of the Republican party has greater independence from contributors than any party in American history. The small donors who provide more than 70 percent of the national GOP's budget have little or no say in party decisions. Their contributions, however, sharply curtail the influence of large donors. David Adamany writes of this independence:

> Those who contribute the money to support the Republican party apparatus, largely in response to ideological appeals, have no direct voice in selecting party leaders or making decisions about party organization or activities. At most, they can withdraw their financial support if they become discontented. . . . As a consequence, the Republican party is able to maintain a professional bureaucracy that directs vast resources and activities that are largely insulated from state and local party organizations.[27]

Despite its ability to ignore state and local parties, the RNC has chosen not to do so. Instead, the RNC hired full-time regional coordinators to coordinate and encourage state and local inputs and established extensive training programs for state and local party elites. The national party organizations, however, did begin to exert substantial control over state and local party organizations through contributions to their treasuries and candidates at all levels and by directly hiring campaign consultants for candidates. In the 1984 elections, for example, the GOP national committees gave an average of almost $27,000 in either direct or coordinated expenditures to candidates for the House of Representatives, a figure that represented 10.5 percent of the candidates' total expenditures. In sharp contrast, Democratic candidates received less than 3 percent of their campaign funds from their party.[28]

Contributions and coordinated expenditures represent only a portion of what the Republican national party has been able to do for its candidates. The party committees employ a permanent staff of pollsters, media specialists, direct-mail advisers, and advertising specialists who train party workers and prepare sophisticated campaign packages. In addition, the party finances national advertising campaigns with common themes, provides press releases, and polls local districts to determine issues on which Democratic incumbents might be vulnerable.[29] During the 1980 elections the RNC staff wrote more than 700 computer programs for candidates and state party organizations, surveyed data from 175,000 precincts, and handled more than 20 million names for get-out-the-vote drives.[30]

The national Republican political action committee that assists local and state GOP candidates, GOPAC, raised $2.64 million for state races in 1984 and almost doubled that amount in the 1986 elections. In 1985, the RNC made cash grants totaling $400,000 to 214 key counties to assist county organizations in changing voters' registrations from Democratic to Republican, mailed 1.2 million pieces of mail to registered Democrats, and spent $350,000 on a media campaign as part of this same project.[31] In October 1985, the RNC chairman, Frank Fahrenkopf, announced his 1991 plan, which included funneling $1.4 million to state parties to assist their fund-raising efforts. Obviously none of these activities would be possible in the absence of the tremendous influx of funds that the GOP derives from its direct-response campaigns.

As the above paragraphs suggest, the thrust of the Republican national committees is unmistakable: They are encouraging more modern technology in all sectors of party activities and a more ideological approach to politics. The national organizations are dominated by technicians who have taken over almost all the functions traditionally filled by volunteers and local party regulars. Even in the area of voter mobilization, direct mail has taken charge. Xandra Kayden writes of this transformation:

> changes in communication technology . . . have eliminated the need for door-to-door activities: direct mail and paid media enable the party . . . to communicate directly and fully with voters in a far more sophisticated and complete manner than volunteer message carriers, however well-trained and articulate.[32]

The Republican national organizations have far outdistanced their Democratic counterparts. While the Republican organizations were becoming stronger, more centralized, and increasingly dominated by direct-marketing professionals and other technicians, the national Democratic organizations were actually becoming weaker.[33] Plagued by debt, the Democrats were unable to invest heavily in direct marketing. Even the Democratic national telethons, the party's major direct-marketing fund raiser in the 1970s, lost money in its most recent effort and deprived the Democratic National Committee of the major source of revenue that it previously used to assist state and local party organizations.

For the Democrats, this absence of national party strength has meant the rise of candidate organizations and increasing reliance on nonparty groups. Although the national organizations cannot afford to hire the necessary media, direct-marketing, and polling specialists, strong candidates can; but they must raise the necessary funds from sources not traditionally associated with Democratic party support and ideology. The most significant of these new sources are corporate and trade association PACs. These PACs increased their contributions to Democratic incumbent candidates for the House from an average of $33,800 in 1980 to $72,500 in 1984, more than ten times the amount the average candidate received from his or her party.[34]

At local and state levels, Democratic party organizations have fared better. Although the GOP strategy to capture state offices is heavily influenced by the national party and its resources, the local Democratic parties utilize not only the small contributions from the national committees but from many nonparty organizations such as the National Committee for an Effective Congress, the American Federation of State, County, and Municipal Workers, and labor unions. As John Bibby points out, the Republican and Democratic strategies at state and local levels clearly reflect the differences in the parties' strengths and orientation. The GOP effort is a party effort directed from the national level; the Democratic endeavors are joint operations with nonparty groups, with the latter in control of many major responsibilities.[35]

In the long run, the reliance of state and local Democratic organizations on nonparty institutions may strengthen the party. The Republicans' dependence on paid professionals and the national committees reduces opportunities for providing solidary benefits to local workers. Although the number of volunteers is declining in both parties, and this decrease has occurred not only because of increasing professionalism within the parties but also because of major social changes,[36] many nonparty organizations continue to offer the solidary and purposive incentives that can tie individuals to the parties if they see their organization's goals as partisan issues.

The Recent Decline in Party Contributions

Both Democrats and Republicans enjoyed increasing direct-mail success from 1974 to 1984, but in the 1985-86 election cycle both parties received substantially fewer contributions than in past years. In the 1985-86 cycle the net receipts of the national party committees fell dramatically. The Republicans fell from over $289 million in 1984 to less than $210 million in 1986. The Democrats dropped from over $90 million to just over $50 million. What accounts for this decline?

Several reasons have been put forth. First, it is possible that people on the house lists simply became tired of giving. The Republican party had been working the same list for more than a decade. Contributors may have become tired of hearing the same old threats. An alternative explanation is that the scandals within the administration and the Iran-*Contra* affair disenchanted many GOP donors. While these explanations no doubt have some validity, the fact of the matter is that the drop in Democratic giving was more precipitous than that of the Republicans.

An alternative possibility is that PACs have won the competition for contributors' dollars. PACs continued their growth during the 1985-86 cycle, and it may be that this increase was at the expense of the parties. This explanation also falls short in that although PAC receipts continued to rise, their growth was much less dramatic than during the period prior to 1984.

I believe that the campaign finance figures can best be explained by a general complacency of the American electorate. Democrats and Republicans were, by and large, better off financially in 1986 than they were in 1980 (if we exclude the amount owed to the national debt). There were no major domestic crises to provide the necessary enemies and threats for successful direct mail. The numerous scandals and the Iran-*Contra* affair were probably sufficient to disenchant many Republican donors but were not enough to make Democrats open their pocketbooks. These factors, combined with the general burnout of the house lists, probably account for the majority of the dropoff in party contributions.

If the above explanation is correct, we should see a substantial increase in party giving in the second six months of 1988. Although George Bush appears too moderate to inspire the contributions that Ronald Reagan did, Michael Dukakis should inspire both Democrats and Republicans to give. Republicans will contribute because the threat of the loss of the Presidency is a real one. Democrats will donate because, for the first time in eight years, they have a shot at winning the White House. If this expected increase does not occur, we can probably conclude that the parties have lost the competition with PACs in the race for donor dollars and that the rise in party strength during the last half of the 1970s and the first half of the 1980s was a short-term aberration in the long-term decline of national parties.

Direct Mail and Nonparty Organizations

Despite the fact that the national party mailings typically do not utilize single issues, parties and individual candidates use the house lists of single-issue and other citizen action groups and political action committees to obtain volunteer workers and to mobilize voters at election time. Party elites actively seek the endorsements of citizen groups and PACs, and ask these organizations to send mailings to their members and contributors that encourage them to vote, to contribute, and to campaign for the party's candidates. In the 1984 elections, Ed Blakely, director of the NRCC, indicated that it designed PAC solicitation strategies for about a hundred GOP candidates. This included arranging meetings between candidates and leading PACs and designing "PAC-Kits" to solicit PAC contributions and PAC mailings to their members.[37]

The Democratic Congressional Campaign Committee (DCCC) also attempted to assist its candidates in obtaining PAC contributions, but because of limited funds, it could not provide the same levels of assistance as the NRCC. Rather than develop individualized strategies and meetings for congressional candidates, the DCCC held luncheons and dinners where many candidates were introduced to many PACs. From the candidates' perspective, this strategy was not effective. In his survey of candidates for the House, Paul Herrnson found that Republican candidates rated the assistance of the NRCC much more highly than Democratic candidates rated the DCCC.[38]

The parties also request citizen action groups to utilize their mailing lists to assist candidates. The director of the National Abortion Rights Action League estimated that more than 10,000 of its members worked for prochoice candidates in the 1982 elections,[39] and an official of the League of Conservation Voters stated that environmental citizen action groups put more campaign volunteers into the 1982 and 1984 elections than any other group except organized labor.[40] One of the more sophisticated efforts to assist parties and candidates is the Prolife Voter Identification Project in the Midwest. Prolife volunteers use voter registration lists and survey by phone a voting member of each family concerning his or her opinions on when abortion should be permitted. When respondents give strong antiabortion responses, their names are placed on computer lists by precinct and party identification. Because candidates who take public stands on the abortion issue are likely to lose a vote for each vote they gain, the Voter Identification Project allows parties and candidates to send direct-mail messages only to families that support the prolife position and only to voters in their precincts.

Direct Marketing and Individual Candidates

Just as political parties have placed increasing reliance on direct marketing, individual candidates have learned to use it effectively. Perhaps more than any other politician, President Reagan has been direct mail's most innovative user. In January 1977 Reagan formed a personal direct-mail-based political action committee, Citizens for the Republic. The purpose of this PAC was to help Reagan gain influence with Republicans nationwide by providing candidates with financial assistance and electoral expertise. During the 1977-78 election cycle, Citizens for the Republic raised and spent $4.5 million and contributed almost $600,000 to Republican candidates.[41] Other presidential aspirants quickly followed Reagan's lead. In the 1980 presidential race Ted Kennedy, George

Bush, and Robert Dole all established personal PACs that used direct mail as the basic fund-raising technique. Howard Baker began his 1988 presidential campaign by establishing a personal PAC in 1982. This move allowed him to contribute over half a million dollars to Republican candidates during the 1984 elections. Senator Kennedy also started early for the 1988 race. His PAC raised $2.5 million and contributed almost $200,000 to Democratic candidates during the 1984 elections. By January 1985, Baker's house list contained the names of over 200,000 contributors; Kennedy's list had reached almost 100,000.[42]

Presidential hopefuls are not the only persons who use direct-mail-based PACs to assist their political operations. In 1978 Jesse Helms raised over $5 million through direct mail for his Senate race. The Congressional Club, Helms's personal PAC, raised $5.3 million during 1981, more than two years before Helms had to face reelection. In addition, the senator has used direct mail to establish and fund a number of auxiliary organizations — the Institute of American Relations, the Center for a Free Society, the Institute on Money and Inflation, and the American Family Institute — organizations that assist him in getting his political message across to both Congress and the general public.[43]

Although most candidates for public office do not form personal PACs they do utilize direct mail heavily during their campaigns.[44] The obvious advantages of mailings to individual candidates are that direct mail is one of the few campaign advertisements that has a possibility of paying for itself. It can be directed to specific audiences, such as prolife activists, without alerting activists on the other side of the issue; and it can be directed to geographic areas as small as a voting precinct or to a narrow, but nationwide, audience relatively inexpensively.

The recent Senate candidacies of Governor James Hunt, Tom Harkin, and Robert Packwood supply useful examples of how candidates utilize these advantages. Hunt had the advantage of running against an incumbent who was well known and strongly disliked at the national level. Because of the national reputation of Jesse Helms, Hunt was able effectively to solicit contributions from several house lists of nationally organized liberal citizen groups and political action committees. Harkin, who ran successfully against Senator Jepsen in Iowa, mailed to the house lists of prochoice groups and described how prolife groups were disrupting his political campaign by dressing someone in a Teddy Bear suit and having him appear at all of Harkin's campaign appearances to remind voters that Harkin supported abortion. Harkin wrote to members of prochoice organizations:

> There's a Teddy Bear following me all around the state of Iowa.
> Most people think Teddy Bears are sweet and cuddly.

This one isn't! He's mean and vicious.

His name is Teddy Tomorrow.

Let me tell you *what Teddy Tomorrow is doing to me, and how it affects you as well as me.*

In January, in my hometown of Cumming, Iowa, I announced that I was running for the Senate. When I announced, Teddy Tomorrow was there, carrying a sign that said:

I'M TEDDY TOMMOROW. BECAUSE OF TOM HARKIN'S VOTES ON ABORTION, 15 MILLION BABIES WILL NEVER HUG A TEDDY BEAR LIKE ME.

"So what," you say, "how can one human being dressed up like a Teddy Bear play a major role in a political campaign?"

I'll tell you.

Teddy Tomorrow has friends.

Like the National Conservative Political Action Committee (NCPAC) which has targeted my campaign as one of three races on which they will spend $2 million for negative advertising this year.

Like the gun nuts . . . and the radicals who want to ban *all* abortions . . . and the defense contractors . . . and the millionaires who have benefitted from Ronald Reagan's tax cuts. . . .

Harkin went on to call prolife and NCPAC supporters cowards who hide behind a mask and distort his record. By aggressively attacking prolife tactics, Harkin turned Teddy Tomorrow into a fund-raising advantage for his own direct mailings.

Packwood also used opposition groups to raise money for his campaign. In a letter to house lists of Jewish organizations, Packwood wrote the following:

Like most Senators, I like to see my name in the newspapers.

But I didn't like seeing this headline: *"Death Threat Aimed at Senator Packwood."*

And I didn't like the story behind the headline—that the FBI had been told that the Aryan Nations—a virulent, anti-Semitic group—wanted to kill me and my family.

The FBI took that threat seriously.

As a result, my wife, my children and I spent the week after Christmas last year under armed guard.

It was one of the longest weeks of my life.

And it didn't make it any easier that this wasn't the first time.

In 1977, radical Arabs threatened to kidnap and kill my children.

Their reason?

My support in the United States Senate for Israel.

But I am not writing to tell you sad stories about my life. I know that I'm not alone in being the subject of threats by extremist groups.

At some point in your life, you've probably been touched by a part of this river of hate. You've seen the cheap mimeograph sheets which warn of "the international Jewish conspiracy" and "the blood sucking Jewish bankers" and "the threat the Jews pose to the white race.". . .

And somewhere, some kid who has never known a Jew and doesn't understand the Holocaust, sits in the dark of the night and listens to this filth. And to that kid, their message may make sense.

Senator Packwood transforms a threat against himself into a threat against the Jewish community. He employs the powerful symbols of the Holocaust, the family, and children who can be easily misled and converts them into a strong appeal for political support and campaign contributions:

> *My re-election campaign will be tough—very tough.* As the target of the hate groups and the right wing and the anti-Israel lobby, I'm going to have to work a lot harder than I ever thought I would.
>
> And I'm going to have to spend a lot more money than I hoped I would need to. So I'm asking, now, for your help.
>
> If you could send me a check—for $100, $50 or even $30—I'll be thankful. Your contribution will do more than help me—it will also help beat all the hate mongers who want to get to me as a way of getting at you.
>
> I hope to hear from you today.

As the above letters indicate, when direct mail moves from the party to the candidate level, the levels of extremism, fear, and "enemy orientation" increase. This tendency for candidates to be more aggressive and negative reflects political learning from past races. In 1976, 1978, and 1980, NCPAC and prolife independent negative campaigning were given credit for defeating a number of liberal candidates.[45] Beginning in 1980, however, targets who fought back aggressively seemed to do substantially better than candidates who attempted to ignore the negative campaigns against them. The above letters of Senators Harkin and Packwood indicate that, at least at the candidate level, extremism and the labeling of opponents will continue to escalate. As one Democratic campaign consultant stated, "People say they hate negative campaigning. But it works. They hate it and remember it at the same time. The problem with positive is that you have to run it again and again to make it stick. With the negative, the poll numbers will move in three or four days."[46]

The Harkin and Packwood letters are indicative of another trend in candidate mailing: the expectation that for people on house lists of citizen action groups and political action committees issues will be tied together ideologically. If a person is liberal on one issue, he or she will be liberal on others. Harkin strikes out at gun control, military spending, and tax breaks for the wealthy in a letter to prochoice groups. Packwood's letter includes not only an attack against the Ku Klux Klan and the American Nazi party but also lashes out at the prolife groups that labeled him "Senator Death." This combining of single-issue opponents into negative coalitions is new in direct mailings. Studies of the relative success rates of multiple-issue versus single-issue letters should provide political scientists with important information concerning the ideological structure of political activists.

Summary

This chapter examined how the increased use of direct marketing has affected political parties. Four important trends emerged. First, the Republican party has a distinct advantage over Democrats. Republicans raise more than four times as much money through direct mail as Democrats do, and these funds — and the independence from large contributors that direct mail makes possible — have led to an increasingly powerful national Republican party. Second, party mailings are seen by party elites as different from nonparty appeals. The parties stress traditional party issues, party loyalty, and citizen duty. They leave the more emotional, single-issue appeals to political action committees, citizen action groups, and individual candidates. Third, individual candidates are making increasingly effective use of direct mail to support their political ambitions. This use of direct mail is not limited to single races but includes the development of personal PACs to gain their party's presidential nomination. Finally, mailings for individual candidates tend to be more extreme and negative than party mailings. Part of this reflects the success that targets of negative campaigns have had in turning these attacks into support for themselves.

In the next chapter we examine how these changes, particularly the Republican party's financial advantage, have changed public policy in the United States.

Notes

1. Interviews with direct response program personnel of the three Republican national committees. For data on previous years see Herbert Alexander, *Financing the 1980 Election* (Lexington, Mass.: Lexington Books, 1983); Larry Sabato, *PAC Power: Inside the World of Political Action Committees* (New York: Norton, 1984); and Gary C. Jacobson, "The Republican Advantage in Campaign Finance," in *The New Direction in American Politics,* ed. John Chubb and Paul Peterson (Washington, D.C.: Brookings Institution, 1985).

2. Personal communications with members of the Helms and Hunt campaign committees. The total amounts spent by the two candidates were $16.5 million by Senator Helms and $9.5 million by Governor Hunt. Gary Jacobson, *The Politics of Congressional Elections,* 2d ed. (Boston: Little Brown, 1987), 79.

3. Herbert Alexander, *Financing the 1964 Election* (Princeton, N.J.: Citizens' Research Foundation, 1966), 71.

4. Constance Cook, in her article "Participation in Public Interest Groups: Membership Motivations," *American Politics Quarterly* 12 (1984): 409-30, found that the single most important reason persons joined these groups was to increase their personal political efficacy.

5. Xandra Kayden and Eddie Mahe, Jr., *The Party Goes On* (New York: Basic Books, 1985), 81.

6. The GOP committees' house lists have fallen substantially since 1984. Leah Geraghty, finance chairman of the RNC, reports that its house list has fallen from 900,000 in 1984 to 700,000 in 1986. This drop appears to be the result of a saturated market. It currently costs the RNC 35 cents for every dollar it receives compared with 22 cents in 1980. Cited in Janet Novack, "The Gold Mine Is Playing Out," *Forbes Magazine,* 6 April 1987, 146-47.

7. Interviews with direct-response program personnel of the three national committees.

8. David Adamany, "Political Parties in the 1980s," and Gary Jacobson, "Money in the 1980 and 1982 Congressional Elections," in *Money and Politics in the United States: Financing Elections in the 1980s,* ed. Michael Malbin (Chatham, N.J.: Chatham House, 1984). Marjorie Hershey, *Running for Office: The Political Education of Campaigners* (Chatham, N.J.: Chatham House, 1984), 122.

9. Herbert Alexander, *Financing Politics: Money, Elections, and Political Reform,* 3d ed. (Washington, D.C.: CQ Press, 1985), 70-74.

10. Unless otherwise noted, comments from Republican and Democratic party leaders come from interviews with the direct-response program staffs of the two national parties. The first set of interviews were carried out by Margaret Latus and a followup set of interviews were conducted by the author in 1986.

11. Cited in *Newsweek,* 6 November 1978.

12. While 56 percent of Republican party identifiers classify themselves as conservative, Democrats are much less cohesive. Twenty-seven percent describe themselves as liberal, 38 percent as moderate, and 29 percent as conservative. Harris survey, *Boston Globe,* 11 November 1984. Cited in Kayden and Mahe, *The Party Goes On,* 177.

13. Adamany, "Political Parties in the 1980 Election."

14. Quoted in the *National Journal,* 10 October 1984, 1983.

15. Elizabeth Drew, *Politics and Money: The New Road to Corruption* (New York: Macmillan, 1983).

16. The perception among party elites that ideological PACs are detrimental to the political system has been prominent since Richard Richards was director of the RNC. Richards believed that the elimination of extremist groups, especially NCPAC, would be in the best interest of the political system. *White House Weekly,* 20 July 1981, 3.

17. Joyce Gelb and Marian Lief Palley, *Tradition and Change in American Party Politics* (New York: Crowell, 1975), 211.

18. Frank B. Feigert and M. Margaret Conway, *Parties and Politics in America* (Boston: Allyn and Bacon, 1976), 141.

19. Charles Longley, "Party Nationalization in America," in *Paths to Political Reform,* ed. William Crotty (Lexington, Mass.: Lexington Books, 1980), 167. For other data on Republican national organizations, see Adamany, "Political Parties in the 1980s."

20. Martin Wattenberg, *The Decline of American Political Parties: 1952-1984* (Cambridge, Mass.: Harvard University Press, 1986).

21. See A. James Reichley, "The Rise of National Parties," in *The New Direction in American Politics,* ed. John Chubb and Paul Peterson (Washington, D.C.: Brookings Institution, 1985); Kayden and Mahe, *The Party Goes On;* Christopher Arterton, "Political Money and Party Strength," in *The Future of American Political Parties,* ed. Joel Fleishman (Englewood Cliffs, N.J.: Prentice Hall, 1982); John Bibby, "Party Renewal in the National Republican Party," in *Party Renewal in America: Theory and Practice,* ed. Gerald Pomper (New York: Praeger, 1980); and Gary Orren, "The Changing Styles of American Party Politics," in Fleishman, *The Future of American Political Parties.*

22. Reichley, "The Rise of National Parties," 73; and Jacobson, *Politics of Congressional Elections,* 68-73.

23. John F. Bibby, "Political Party Trends in 1985: The Continuing but Constrained Advance of the National Party," *Publius* 16 (Summer 1986): 79-91.

24. James Reichley argues that the most important decision Brock made as chairman of the Republican National Committee was to emphasize direct-mail fund raising. In an interview with Reichley, Brock indicated that the decision was an easy one: "There was really no other way to build an effective national party." Quoted in Reichley, "The Rise of National Parties," 187.

25. Ibid.

26. Xandra Kayden, "Parties and the 1980 Election," in Campaign Finance Study Group, *Financing Presidential Campaigns* (Cambridge, Mass., John F. Kennedy School of Government, Institute of Politics, Harvard University, 1982), 11. Even with the increase in overhead costs of the GOP's direct mailings, direct mail is still much cheaper per dollar generated than other fund-raising efforts.

27. Adamany, "Political Parties in the 1980s," 108.

28. The national and state party organizations are limited by the FECA as to how much they can contribute directly and spend in behalf of candidates. State organizations, however, rarely have sufficient funds to make significant expenditures. The GOP has taken advantage of a loophole in the FECA that allows the national party to give funds to the state party which in turn can contribute these funds to candidates or use them in coordinated expenditures. By 1986, the total limits on party contributions to House candidates had risen to $73,620. Jacobson, *Politics of Congressional Elections,* 69.

29. Ibid., 71-72.

30. "Chairman's Reports," Republican National Committee, Washington, D.C., 1981 and 1985.

31. Bibby, "Political Party Trends," 90.

32. Kayden, "Parties and the 1980 Presidential Election," 613.

33. James Gibson, Cornelius Cotter, John Bibby, and Robert Huckshorn, "Whither the Local Parties? A Cross-Sectional Analysis of the Strength of Party Organizations," *American Journal of Political Science* 29 (February 1985): 139-60.

34. Federal Election Commission press release, December, 1985.

35. Bibby, "Political Party Trends," 88.

36. These changes would include the increasing participation of females in the workforce, the more isolated living patterns within neighborhoods, and alternative organizations (e.g., health clubs) for meeting people.

37. Paul Herrnson, "Do Parties Make a Difference? The Role of Party Organiza-

tions in Congressional Elections," *Journal of Politics* 48, no. 3 (1986): 589-615.

38. Ibid., 595.

39. Frank Sorauf, *Money in American Elections* (Glenview, Ill.: Scott, Foresman, 1988), 145-47.

40. Margaret Ann Latus, "Assessing Ideological PACs: From Outrage to Understanding," in *Money and Politics in the United States,* ed. Michael Malbin (Chatham, N.J.: Chatham House, 1984), 163.

41. Personal interview with the league's associate director.

42. Sabato, *PAC Power,* 115.

43. Maxwell Glen, "Starting a PAC May Be Candidates' First Step Down Long Road to 1988," *National Journal,* 16 February 1985, 374-77. It is interesting to note that neither Baker nor Kennedy actually campaigned for President in 1988.

44. *Congressional Quarterly Weekly Reports,* 6 March 1982, 499-503. The Congressional Club became almost an alternative Republican party in North Carolina during the 1970s. It went out and recruited candidates for political offices and, at times, worked in opposition to the state party when Senator Helms believed the party's candidates were too moderate.

45. Larry J. Sabato, *The Rise of Political Consultants* (New York: Basic Books, 1981), 220-63; and Marjorie R. Hershey, *Running for Office.*

46. Marjorie Randon Hershey and Darrell M. West, "Single-Issue Politics: Prolife Groups and the 1980 Senate Campaign," in *Interest Group Politics,* ed. Allan Cigler and Burdett Loomis (Washington, D.C.: CQ Press, 1983).

47. Quoted in Alan Ehrenhalt, "Technology, Strategy Bring New Campaign Era," *Congressional Quarterly Weekly Report* 43, 7 December 1985, 2561.

6. Direct Marketing, the Electoral Connection, and Public Policy

To understand how direct mail is changing American public policy, we must first comprehend some of the basic facts concerning how Congress is structured, which candidates for Congress are elected, and the manner by which public policies are determined. This chapter briefly examines these questions and then discusses how the rise of political direct marketing alters which candidates are likely to win electoral contests and which interests have higher probabilities of reaching their political goals.

Congressional Structure and Elections

The structure of Congress assures, not that the national interest will be served, but that the vast majority of incumbents will win in the next election by serving the important interests in their districts. Members of Congress know that voters will judge them, not so much on the basis of how well things are going for the country, but on how well things are going in the home district and what special projects the district has received.

Each year Congress passes numerous projects that benefit specialized interests: auto makers, dairy farmers, tobacco growers, defense contractors and so on. Farmers obtain subsidies and price supports, auto makers and auto workers receive quotas on foreign imports, cities secure federal grants for urban projects, and western states gain large water projects for their arid lands. These subsidies provide particularized benefits to almost every congressional district, and incumbent congresspersons work hard to guarantee that voters credit them with obtaining those benefits.

The structure of Congress encourages this emphasis on district rather than national interest. Members of Congress serve on committees important to their district and utilize their committee positions to benefit their constituents. Jesse Helms, the senior senator from North Carolina, is the chairman of the Senate Agriculture Committee — the legislative unit that determines tobacco subsidies. Similarly, Morris Udall, the representative from Tucson, Arizona, heads the

House Interior Committee—the committee that decides whether federal funding will be provided for the huge federal water projects so important to the state. The overall results of such subsidies and projects are a huge budget deficit, a large number of policies that cost the country more than they benefit it, and an increased probability that the incumbent will win reelection.

As a rule, voters in each congressional district give credit for "their" benefits to "their" congressperson; they do not blame him, however, for the long-term costs that the nation bears.[1] Tobacco farmers in North Carolina do not censure Senator Helms for voting for the Central Arizona Project, nor do water users in Tucson vote against Morris Udall for supporting tobacco subsidies; voters in both states would, however, hold their representative responsible for not obtaining the highest possible benefits for their district or state. Thus the electoral incentives to serve constituency interests and the committee system that places members of Congress in positions where they protect their districts rather than their nation produce the logrolling and pork-barrel policies for which Congress is famous.[2] Gary Jacobson summarized this problem of constituency interest taking precedence over national interest when he wrote, "The structure of Congress and its recent committee reforms reinforce the fundamental flaw in electoral politics: great individual *responsiveness* and equally great collective *irresponsibility.*"[3]

To ensure that they will win again, congresspersons provide numerous constituency services and make frequent trips back home to their districts. These activities help the representative maintain the image of a member of the community who shares its attitudes and values. In his perceptive analysis of congressional behavior, *Home Style: House Members in their Districts,* Richard Fenno describes how congresspersons encourage constituents to trust and identify with their representative.[4] "Home style" refers to the image a member of Congress creates to show the folks back home that he knows their needs and wants, and that he is in Washington to serve them.[5]

Members of Congress also work on home style through extensive service work for constituents, such as helping someone in the district apply for a special loan for a minority business, assisting a trucking firm in obtaining approval from the Interstate Commerce Commission, alerting a company in the district of potential tax changes that might help it, providing a constituent's child with an appointment to West Point or Annapolis, and helping citizens obtain entry visas for relatives.

The local press and broadcast media assist incumbents in developing their image by covering their visits home and assisting representatives in demonstrating how much they are doing for their districts. Edie Goldenberg and Michael Traugott have documented the extent of this cooperation between the local press and incumbents, particularly incumbents who are vulnerable to defeat. Goldenberg and Traugott's analysis found that a vulnerable incumbent will receive three times the press coverage of the challenger.[6]

Direct mail, particularly the franking privilege, plays a critical role in developing the incumbent's advantages. Between 1954 and 1970, the flow of mail from Congress to constituents increased by 600 percent and then more than doubled again between 1970 and 1973. Congressional mail cost the taxpayer over $62 million for 12 months during 1976 and 1977—excluding staff salaries, the cost of paper for printing Senate newsletters, and the office overhead expenses! In 1980 that figure was at least $100 million, and in 1984 the average congressperson sent over 1 million pieces of mail to his constituents. The General Accounting Office estimates that the cost of franking in 1986 exceeded $144 million![7]

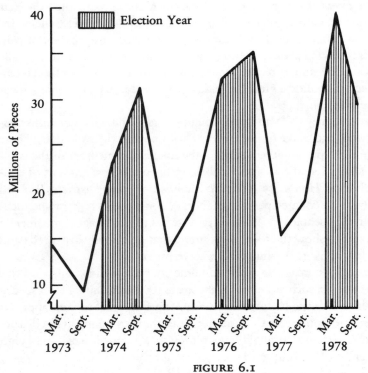

FIGURE 6.1

TIMING OF FRANKED MAIL BY CONGRESSPERSONS

SOURCE: *Congressional Quarterly Weekly Report* 38 (16 August 1980), 2387. Copyright © 1980. Congressional Quarterly, Inc. Reprinted by permission.

Three separate studies of contacts between members of Congress and their constituents found that mail contacts have a greater impact on the election than any other communication.[8] Through the use of the frank, the congressperson can tell constituents of the work he is doing for them, his desire to hear their opinions, and his willingness to provide them with individualized benefits. The example given in chapter 1 of the representative who sent all new parents in his district a congratulatory message and then followed this in a second mailing with the baby book from the National Institutes of Health is but one of many kinds of mailings that incumbents use to encourage trust, identification, and an image of caring. And, as figure 6.1 on page 122 indicates, as election time nears, the level of franked mail increases dramatically.

Figure 6.2 shows the first page of the first piece of franked mail sent by first-term congressman Jim Kolbe of Arizona. By having his photograph taken with President Reagan, Representative Kolbe tries to ally himself with a popular President and to give the impression that he has access to the most important politician in Washington. In the text of the letter Kolbe indicates that he cares about his constituents, wants to look out for their interests, and tells them how to get in touch with him should they need help with a special problem.

In addition to developing an effective home style, incumbents follow two other strategies to improve their probability of re-election: They move to an ideological position closer to their expected opponent, and they amass a large campaign fund early in the electoral cycle. By changing their ideological position toward that of their opponent, incumbents hope to prevent the opposition from taking advantage of any dissatisfaction in the district. This typically means that as the election draws near, members of Congress move to a less ideological and less partisan position on roll-call votes.[9] In 1978, for example, one Republican and five Democratic senators found that they were on the "hit list" of the Life Amendment Political Action Committee for the 1980 election. The response of the Democrats was to take a *less* liberal position in the next congressional session, while the Republican took a *more* liberal position.[10] Members of Congress hope that changes in their voting behavior will mollify any groups alienated by previous votes and will increase the relative importance of incumbency by decreasing the importance of issue positions.

The second strategy incumbents use to discourage potential challengers is to amass a large campaign fund long before the general election. As discussed in chapter 4, with the exception of ideological political action committees, PACs give the majority of their money to incumbents. Goldenberg and Traugott, in *Campaigning for Congress,* and Jacobson, in *The Politics of Congressional Elections,* found that incumbents use surpluses from their previous campaign and actively solicit PAC contributions early in the electoral cycle to discourage

Congressman Jim Kolbe Reports

5TH DISTRICT, ARIZONA | **February, 1985** | **99TH CONGRESS**

PRESIDENT'S BUDGET REACHES CONGRESS

During the next 9 months, the House and Senate will be deciding budget priorities for the 1986 fiscal year. The President has said that adoption of the new budget would "change the course of history".

The President has called for over $973 billion in federal spending, the largest budget to date. While attempting to cut some $50 billion from the previously projected '86 budget deficit, the package sent to Congress would still be $180 billion in the red. The Pentagon budget of $277.5 billion represents a 12.7% increase in outlays for defense.

The President has made a convincing case for continuing the buildup of our nation's defenses. But I believe that an immediate, across-the-board spending freeze can be implemented without harming America's national security interests. By holding next year's spending to 1985 levels — in every area of the budget — we can reduce the deficit by approximately $30 billion. A spending freeze would require everyone to share equal responsibility for reducing the deficit.

At the same time, it would be wrong to view either a spending freeze or reductions in the defense budget as a panacea for our deficit woes. In the course of the last generation, too many people have come to rely on the government to fulfill the basic responsibilities of the family. The federal government cannot and should not be expected to fill roles better left to individuals, families and volunteer organizations, or to other levels of government closer to home. It is a

mistake to reduce control over our economic destinies by insisting on a government that consumes a third of all the goods and services consumed in this country. To the extent that our income is reduced by taxation, our ability to make individual economic choices is reduced. Finally, running up an enormous deficit, leaving the bills for our children to pay, would indeed be a cruel legacy.

With these thoughts in mind, I ask for your guidance in the task of lessening the deficit. I will be conducting frequent town hall meetings, and encourage you to attend, or contact one of the Congressional offices in your area to express your views on the various elements of the budget.

WASHINGTON:
1222 Longworth HOB
Washington, D.C. 20515
202/225-2542

TUCSON:
4444 E. Grant Rd., Suite 125
Tucson, AZ 85712
602/323-1467
Toll Free 1-800-824-7844

SIERRA VISTA:
Billie Fabijan
District Representative
77 Calle Portal, Suite B160
Sierra Vista, AZ 85635
602/459-3155

CASA GRANDE:
Susan Marler
District Representative
222 Cottonwood Lane, Suite 113
Casa Grande, AZ 85222
602/836-6364

FIGURE 6.2

CONGRESSMAN KOLBE'S FIRST FRANKED MAILING TO CONSTITUENTS

strong challengers.[11] Many congresspersons amass more than $200,000 as much as a year before the primary elections in the hope that this large war chest will convey the message that the incumbent has too many resources to be defeated and that potential challengers should choose an easier target to advance their political ambitions. Goldenberg and Traugott write, "Incumbents have the ability to spend 'preemptively' to structure the nature of the contests they will face. . . . They have the potential to use early money to affect decisions about who their challengers might be."[12]

THE UNKNOWN CHALLENGER

The advantages of incumbency combined with the low levels of political information among voters normally prove too difficult for challengers to overcome. For example, while 97 percent of persons who vote in congressional elections can recognize the name of their congressperson on election day, only 63 percent can recognize the name of the person who is challenging him.[13] Only 37 percent of the general public can place their congressperson on a liberal-conservative scale.[14] Only 5 percent of the voters who belong to the same party as the incumbent vote for the candidate of the other party, while over 50 percent of the voters from the challenger's party vote for the incumbent.[15] The thermometer ratings of incumbents in the House of Representatives average 68.9; the ratings for their challengers average 51.3, or only 1.3 points above neutral.[16] These ratings signify that incumbents are not only well known, they are also well liked. Challengers are neither known nor liked. All these factors create an electoral situation where more than 90 percent of all incumbents in the House of Representatives who run, win. Even in years that are extremely unfavorable to their party, incumbents still win four out of five races. In 1974, the first election after Watergate, 78 percent of all Republican incumbents won. Similarly, in 1980 and 1984, despite the large electoral majorities for Ronald Reagan, over 85 percent of Democratic incumbents were reelected.

Direct Marketing and Running for Office

Although direct marketing obviously has not reduced the chances that incumbents in the House of Representatives will win again, it has affected which challengers are likely to win. Jacobson has shown that the most important variable in House and Senate elections has been the amount of money the challenger has been able to raise and spend on his campaign.[17] A major reason for this is that there is a strong relationship between the availability of money and the likelihood that a challenger will be found who has the attractive personal qualities necessary to run an effective race. Although a challenger would have to spend more than $350,000 to become as familiar to the voters as the typical incumbent, the money that direct mail and political action committees generate makes it far more likely that challengers will find the money to run an effective race.[18]

Republican challengers have benefited most from direct marketing. The Republican National Committee (RNC), the National Republican Senatorial Committee (NRSC), and the National Republican Congressional Committee (NRCC) give substantial assistance to GOP candidates. In 1982, while the Republican national committees contributed directly and through coordinated expenditures an average of $283,000 to each Senate race and almost $24,000 in House races, the Democratic national committees averaged only $74,000 and $2000. In addition, the RNC set up GOPAC, a political action committee for state elections that raised over $1.5 million. Its Democratic counterpart, DEMPAC, could raise only $40,000.[19]

The Republican party's fund-raising advantage goes far beyond candidate contributions. During the 1980 elections, the RNC helped candidates conduct surveys, produce radio and television advertisements, and schedule events, and it provided research on public policies. Bill Brock, the RNC Chairman, made the Republican party's computer facility available to state parties to analyze polls, design surveys, and pinpoint where state candidates should concentrate their campaign resources. In fact, through the use of existing computer routines and volunteer services, the RNC was able to conduct polls for state congressional candidates for a charge of only $250. The NRCC could put together a complete broadcast advertising package for a House candidate for under $5000.[20] These costs are less than 20 percent of what a Democratic candidate had to pay private firms for similar services. The RNC spent over $15 million for nationwide Republican television advertising, and because of its relative wealth, was able to make productive use of campaign schools where candidates, campaign directors, and local and state party officials were taught to utilize direct marketing and other campaign techniques effectively.[21]

Although party contributions to House and Senate candidates represent, on the average, less than 25 percent of total campaign expenditures, they are clearly important to Republican candidates, particularly to those who are not incumbents. Goldenberg and Traugott found that party contributions to Republican challengers allowed them to spend money much earlier than Democratic challengers could; and this early spending encouraged still other contributions from individuals and PACs. Their study showed that if sure winners and sure losers were omitted from the analysis, Republican challengers spent more than Democratic incumbents![22] The party's assistance assured that by 1982, "no Republican candidate with any reasonable chance of winning was inadequately funded."[23]

This influx of money, campaign assistance, and party advertising has substantially helped the Republican party at election time. In 1982, because of the severe recession and high rates of unemployment, the Republican party would normally have lost twenty-five more seats in the House of Representatives than it ultimately did.[24] The tremendous financial assistance that the three national committees were able to provide, combined with the shrewd and well-financed national advertising campaign urging voters to "stay the course," helped the Republican party prevent most of the expected losses.[25]

Close races, those in which the challenger has a legitimate chance of defeating the incumbent, provide the best example of the Republican advantages. In 1980—a year of high inflation and in which an unpopular President was the Democratic nominee and the Republicans had a strong, popular challenger in Ronald Reagan—twenty-five Democratic incumbents in the House of Representatives were defeated. In nineteen of those races, despite all the advantages that incumbents have in raising money, the Republican challenger spent more than the Democratic incumbent. In two other races, where the Democratic incumbents were chairmen of powerful House committees, the level of spending was approximately equal. In 1982, a good year for the Democrats because of high rates of unemployment, twenty-one Republican incumbents were defeated. In those races, only four Democratic challengers raised more money than the Republican incumbent. The financial contrast between the parties is even more evident when we examine the close races the GOP incumbent won. There were twenty-nine of these, and in them the Republicans outspent their Democratic opponents by almost two to one.[26]

While direct marketing enabled the Republican national party leadership to raise millions of dollars, to gain dominance over the state and local parties, and to play an active role in recruiting and financing attractive candidates for the Republican ticket, the organizational strength of the Democratic party was actually declining.[27] In contrast to the Republican party's extensive assistance, candidates on the Democratic ticket had to find their own funds and campaign consultants. Corporate and trade association PACs were the logical place to turn. During the 1970s, labor PACs were the chief source of institutional funding for Democrats, while corporate and trade association PACs played this role for Republicans.[28] By 1982, the direct-marketing success of the Republican party and the increased contributions by trade and corporate PACs had changed this situation substantially. Republican candidates could count on receiving as much money from their party as they received from PACs, while Democratic incumbents received only 1.8 percent of their campaign contributions from their party and 21 percent from corporate and trade association PACs—a sum significantly higher than the funds provided by labor and equal to the amount received by Republican incumbents.[29] *This increasing dependence of Democratic candidates on corporate and trade association PACs is the most important political consequence of the Republican party's direct-marketing success.*

Part of the business and trade contributions to Democrats can be accounted for by the fact that PACs, especially corporate and trade PACs, prefer to give money to incumbents, and there are more Democratic than Republican incumbents.[30] In the 1984 election, Senate incumbents received 78 percent of all PAC contributions to Senate races where incumbents were standing for election; in the House, 89 percent of all PAC contributions to races involving incumbents went to them. In the Senate, PAC contributions through 31 December 1987 represented 30 percent of incumbents' total receipts (compared with 18 percent in 1982); in the House, 44 percent of incumbents' campaign contributions were from PACs (compared with 31 percent in 1982).[31] Even though there were more Democratic than Republican incumbents, the Democrats still received far more than one might expect given the conservative orientation of most business-related PACs.

Policy Consequences of Partisan Imbalance

If we can assume that business-oriented PACs expect some return for their contributions, the critical question becomes, How has the increasing Democratic reliance on corporate and trade association contributions affected public policy? Although corporate and trade association contributors anticipate a return for a political contribution, it would be naive to think that just because a candidate receives money from a group that he will always vote for that interest. Nevertheless, as Jacobson wrote in 1984:

> One need not assume that campaign contributions buy the souls of congressmen to find these figures (the increase in business contributions to Democrats) significant. . . . The shift to the right in national politics after the 1980 election was not simply a consequence of more Republicans in Congress (or a Republican in the White House). It depended as well on a large number of Democratic votes, particularly in the House. . . .
> *A broader implication of this argument is that it is possible to have policy realignments without having partisan realignments.* Republicans did not have to become the majority party for traditional Republican concerns . . . to dominate the political agenda.[32]

Direct marketing has helped to bring about this policy realignment. Democratic congresspersons, because they must rely more and more on business-related contributions to combat well-financed Republican challengers, have become increasingly supportive of the organized business and trade association interests that can provide them with the campaign funding to win again.

CONSERVATIVE OR SPECIAL-INTEREST POLICIES?

Jacobson's conclusion that public policy is moving to the right may be too optimistic. If the consequence of greater Democratic dependence on business-related PACs were simply and only a move toward a more conservative government, then it is possible that the Republican solutions to the problems of special-interest politics could be attempted and possibly achieved. The federal government might be able to reduce its budget deficit, eliminate unnecessary regulations, and lower taxes. But these are not the outcomes that the Democrats' reliance on corporate and trade association PACs encourage. The increasing reliance on contributions from corporate and trade association PACs will lead to an even more unbalanced budget and even less attention to conservative ideologies!

Critics of pluralism such as Theodore Lowi, Grant McConnell, Sheldon Wolin, E.E. Schattschneider, and Mancur Olson, Jr., have argued that the domination of politics by organized business and trade association interests leads not to conservative policies but to interest-group liberalism where government policies exploit the unorganized interests in society to benefit the organized.[33] This exploitation occurs through the logrolling and pork-barrel policies discussed above and for which the congressional committee system is so well suited.

It makes a major difference in America's political and economic well-being whether a PAC gives to obtain access and special consideration for economic interest or gives to encourage a particular ideology. If PACs give, *and congresspersons respond,* for narrow economic interest, then the political system will exhibit the negative attributes that the critics of pluralism attribute to it. The most important are these: (1) Members of Congress will evaluate legislation on the basis of what their vote will do to benefit their campaign fund rather than what it will do to benefit the nation; (2) there will be a reduced level of democracy and equality in society; and (3) there will be a reduction in economic efficiency. In contrast, if PACs give, *and congresspersons respond,* on the basis of party platforms and political ideology, then public policy will reflect at least some conception of the national interest.

VOTING FOR DOLLARS

Congressional support of the organized interests in society at the expense of the unorganized typified Congress long before the rise of direct marketing. Nevertheless, if Democrats are voting for narrow special interests to obtain the necessary campaign funds to combat well-financed Republican challengers, then this tendency to support organized interests will have intensified, for the funding edge of the Republican party has increased as the treasuries of business and trade association PACs have grown.

Evidence from a number of sources indicates that this tendency is increasing. Maxwell Glen, a writer for the *National Journal,* interviewed directors of corporate and business-related PACs such as Macon Freeman of the Tenneco PAC and Bernadette Budde of the Business and Industry Political Action Committee (BIPAC). Glen's interviews revealed that these leaders perceived Democratic members of Congress as increasingly probusiness, and for that reason, corporate PACs were more likely to support Democratic incumbents than Republican challengers.[34] Corporate PAC directors reported a dearth of vulnerable Democratic incumbents with voting records that their corporate community opposed, and during the 1984 elections, the total contributions to incumbents by corporate and trade PACs was over $40 million for Republicans and over $30 million for Democrats.[35]

It is important to note, however, that the beneficiaries of a corporate PAC's largess are incumbent Democrats, especially those who sit on committees important to the particular business interest or those who are from its home district. Corporate and trade PACs rarely support the Democratic challengers or candidates for open seats. Business and trade association PACs typically give to gain access to members of Congress and to reward previous votes. If an electoral contest does not include an incumbent, then business-oriented PACs support the more conservative candidate, and this will be the Republican.[36] Although most business and trade association giving to Democratic incumbents may be to gain access, the standards set for Democratic incumbents to receive money are distinctly different from those set for Republicans. In 1982, for example, the Republican party could advocate antibusiness taxes to reduce the deficit without fear that corporate PACs would withdraw their support. On 7 July of that year, the Senate Finance Committee approved legislation restricting tax breaks in multiyear construction contracts by a vote of 13 to 7. All seven members of the minority that voted to retain the tax breaks, and thereby supported the position of the major PAC involved, the Associated General Contractors (AGC), were Democrats. Eleven of the thirteen persons voting to restrict the tax loophole were Republicans. Despite this impressive support of Democrats for the AGC position and the fact that the Democrats who supported them were rewarded, the AGC did not punish the Republicans. In the AGC's next newsletter to members, listing the candidates to whom it was giving money, 94 percent of the recipients were Republicans.[37]

The tremendous rise in campaign funds available to corporate and trade association PACs has made it possible for them to bid against organized labor for Democrats' votes. The most important piece of labor legislation during the 1970s was the common-site picketing bill. In 1975 a Congress controlled by Democrats passed this legislation only to have President Ford veto it. In 1977 labor was assured by President Carter that he would sign the legislation if Congress passed it. The legislation failed in the House by ten votes; there were eleven Democrats who voted for the legislation in 1975 and then defected in 1977. Labor punished these eleven Democrats by reducing contributions to them by almost $70,000, but this decrease was more than made up for by a corporate and trade PAC increase of almost $170,000.[38]

THE EXPLOITATION OF UNORGANIZED INTERESTS

Although the common-site picketing bill indicates that some Democrats will defect to business even when the opposition is organized, most of the pro-business votes come when the opposition is not organized. This is particularly true with respect to tax legislation. From 1978 to 1984, the Democratic-controlled House of Representatives voted to support business-oriented policies at the expense of unorganized sectors of society. During this period there was a dramatic decline in the percentage of the U.S. Treasury receipts supplied by corporate taxes. In 1968, at the beginning of the direct-mail era and before the 1971 and 1974 campaign finance reforms, corporate taxes supplied over 18 percent of total tax receipts. By 1984, because of major changes in the tax laws in 1978 and 1981, corporate taxes provided only 6.2 percent of the total.[39] In 1981 the House passed one of the largest business tax breaks in history when it allowed corporations to sell their tax losses to other corporations. This single tax break cost the federal treasury almost $750 billion before it was repealed in 1984. At the same time that the Democratic-controlled House of Representatives was supporting tax reductions for business, it was increasing the tax burden of the less advantaged sectors of society through increases in social security taxes on wages and salaries, which supplied 23 percent of the total receipts in 1970 and 37 percent in 1984.[40]

Of course, neither the impressions of business and trade PAC leaders nor the precipitous decline in the percentage of Treasury receipts from corporate taxes proves that either Republican or Democratic congresspersons are "selling out" to special interests. The more probusiness votes of Democrats could reflect their response to a sagging economy; they may have perceived the mood of the country as being probusiness and responded to this change in public opinion; or the Democrats might have accepted the arguments of the business community that they were overregulated and overtaxed and that these problems were creating economic difficulties. Similarly, the reduced revenues from corporate taxes could reflect lower profits by business rather than the response of congresspersons to increasing campaign contributions.

Although the question whether the increasing Democratic dependence on corporate and trade association PACs is leading us to a more conservative political system or to one built on subsidies for organized interests is difficult to answer definitively, it is the critical question concerning the impact of direct marketing on the American political system.

Members of Congress can vote in favor of particular interests for several reasons; because of this, we must look for ways to differentiate a vote for electoral advantage from one that reflects a probusiness ideology. If Democrats are increasingly supporting business not because of ideology but to obtain electoral contributions, then they will be more likely to vote for organized business and trade interests only when these interests are confronted by an unorganized opposition. Democrats will not support business interests when they are pitted against an organized group that can provide an alternative source of electoral support more in line with traditional Democratic ideology. In contrast, if congresspersons are supporting business and trade positions for ideological reasons, then the member of Congress will vote with business's position even when there is an organized opponent.

For example, if a bill sets trade association interests against consumers, then Democrats voting to obtain campaign contributions will vote for the trade association rather than with the unorganized consumers. If, however, a piece of legislation directly pits business against labor, these same representatives are far less likely to defect. Similarly, when organized industrial and environmental interests conflict, a Democrat who is seeking electoral advantage will continue to support environmental interests because their support has been critical in recent elections. If, however, business interests are opposed by unorganized interests such as the poor—people traditionally supported by the Democratic ideology and platform but whose political knowledge and participation are such that a representative need not worry about voting against them— then the Democratic representative will support business interests despite his party's platform and liberal ideology.

Perhaps the clearest examples of Democratic incumbents responding to well-funded PACs were two resolutions passed by the House of Representatives during 1982. The resolutions vetoed the Federal Trade Commission's (FTC) regulation of used cars and exempted professionals (doctors, lawyers, and dentists) from FTC regulation.[41] The National Automobile Dealers Association (NADA) and the American Medical Association (AMA), the two major PACs requesting the resolutions, are also two of the most aggressive and wealthy PACs in American politics.[42] In 1982, NADA contributed $917,295 to congressional candidates while the AMA contributed $2,132,888.[43]

When the votes were counted and the resolutions passed, Common Cause accused legislators of being "the best Congress money can buy," and of being "a Government of, by and for the PACs."[44] A number of major newspapers, including the *Wall Street Journal* and the *Washington Post,* ran stories showing the strong relationship between campaign contributions from NADA and the AMA and voting on the two issues.[45] The two political action committees, as well as the accused congresspersons, were quick to respond that the relationship between the votes and the contributions was spurious. The AMA and NADA claimed they contributed to these individuals, not to buy their votes on the FTC regulations, but simply because they opposed unnecessary government interventions.

Kirk Brown carefully studied these claims and statistically analyzed the voting patterns. He found that although the two PACs contributed in part because of the political ideologies of the congresspersons, they also rewarded substantially those congresspersons who voted for them and against the FTC *regardless of political ideology!*[46] From the point of view of this author, an even more important finding of Brown's study was that *Democrats were more likely than Republicans to respond to political action committee contributions* after the impact of ideology had been accounted for statistically. If two congresspersons, one a Democrat and the other a Republican, each had a liberalism rating of 50 by the Americans for Democratic Action[47] and received a $1000 contribution from NADA, the probability that the Republican would vote for the car dealers was .63, and the probability for the Democrat was .80! Even more dramatic was the fact that a Democrat with a liberalism rating of 50 and a contribution of $2500 from the AMA had a .61 probability of voting to exempt doctors from FTC regulations; his Republican counterpart's probability was only .23. If the two congresspersons received $10,000, the Democrat had a .79 probability of voting to exempt the doctors, while the Republican's probability was only .43.[48] In short, despite their party's pledge to support consumer protection, Democrats rather than Republicans were more likely to respond to PAC money.

Car dealers and doctors are not the only economic PACs to benefit from the imbalance between the treasuries of Republicans and Democrats. Two recent studies of the trucking industry and dairy producers show similar findings. John Frendreis and Richard Waterman studied Senate responses to PAC contributions and found that, just as in the House, Democrats were more likely than Republicans to support positions favored by PACs that make large campaign contributions. The issue that Frendreis and Waterman examined was the 1980 Motor Carrier Act, an act favored by President Carter and opposed by the trucking industry.[49] The industry opposed deregulation and supported their position with substantial campaign contributions. Once again, the political ideology of senators did not affect the probability that they would support the trucking industry nearly as much as being a Democrat did. And this pattern occurred even after the effects of ideology were controlled and despite the fact that the party's leader, President Carter, lobbied strongly against industry's position.

The Public Voice for Food and Health Policy, a Washington-based policy research firm, examined votes on the 1983 Dairy and Tobacco Adjustment Act and PAC contributions by the dairy industry. The study categorized congressional districts by their level of dairy production and attempted to determine how much money a prodairy vote would bring for the next electoral campaign. Public Voice found that representatives who voted in favor of the dairy industry could expect a contribution at least fifteen times larger than that received by similarly placed representatives who voted against the industry. For our analysis, the interesting question concerns whether there were partisan differences in the probability that a congressperson would support the industry rather than the consumer. Table 6.1 shows clearly that at every level of dairy production in a district, the Democrat is significantly more likely to support the position of the dairy PACs than the Republican.

The findings in table 6.1 are particularly useful in that the issue of dairy price supports is a continuing one and therefore allows the study of congresspersons' voting over time. Welch studied the 1975 vote on dairy price supports to discover which variables most influenced a congressperson's vote.[50] Welch included five variables in his analysis: the contributions of dairy PACs, the level of milk production in the district, ideology, the vulnerability of the incumbent in the next election, and political party. In the 1975 vote, the major determinants of a congresspersons' votes were the level of dairy production and ideology. Although political party and campaign contributions were statistically significant predictors of a favorable vote for the dairy industry, and Democrats and congresspersons who received higher contributions were more likely to favor higher price supports than were Republicans or persons who received lower contributions, neither party nor contributions was a substantively significant factor.

Using the same statistical procedures and variables as Welch's study of the 1975 vote, an analysis of the 1983 dairy vote found that the factors influencing it were quite different from those affecting the earlier vote. Political party replaced milk production in the district as the most important determinant of a favorable vote, and Democrats were far more likely to side with the dairy industry than were similarly placed Republicans. In 1983 ideology was no longer a statistically significant factor, while the size of the dairy PACs' contribution was second only to political party in significance.[51]

To determine if the above issues were unique or were in fact representative of a growing trend by Democratic incumbents to obtain additional contributions from political action committees, I analyzed key Congressional votes in

TABLE 6.1

LEVEL OF DAIRY PRODUCTION IN THE DISTRICT, POLITICAL PARTY,
AND VOTING FOR THE DAIRY INDUSTRY
(IN PERCENT)

Level of Milk Production

Supported the Dairy Industry	None		Low		Medium		High	
	Democratic	Republican	Democratic	Republican	Democratic	Republican	Democratic	Republican
Yes	57	9	66	41	75	38	88	52
No	43	91	34	59	25	62	12	48
TOTAL	100	100	100	100	100	100	100	100

1975, 1980, and 1983. Votes were included in the analysis if they affected an interest represented by a corporate or trade association PAC that was among the top ten contributors in their category and the majority position received less than two-thirds of the votes cast.[52] If the Republican fund-raising advantage in direct marketing is making Democratic incumbents increasingly dependent on corporate and trade association money, then Democratic support of corporate and trade positions should increase over time.

Issues were divided into two categories, those on which there were significant organized interests on both sides of the issue and those where only one side had organized support. For example, the auto dealer, medical regulations, dairy subsidy, and trucking deregulation issues discussed above fall into the category of "no organized opposition." The 1975 common-site picketing bill, where labor and business interests were organized, and all major environmental issues provide examples of "organized opposition" issues.[53]

The results of the analysis show a clear and increasingly significant trend for Democrats to support political action committees and oppose their party's ideology when there is no organized opposition to a bill. In 1975 ideology was the most significant factor in predicting how a member of Congress would vote on seven of the ten issues studied. There were no significant differences between Republican and Democratic members of the House once ideology was controlled. The impact of campaign contributions in either the previous election or the following election usually was statistically significant, but small.[54] In 1980 ideology remained the major predictor of votes for Republicans. Among Democrats, however, the size of the campaign contribution had replaced ideology as the most important predictor on four of five issues without organized opposition. On issues with organized opposition, ideology remained the most important predictor. Three years later, the importance of campaign contributions had increased for Democrats, but had remained unchanged for Republicans.

The above results show clearly that Democratic members of the House of Representatives are increasingly supportive of business and trade association interests and that this support occurs because the representatives are seeking campaign contributions. The findings also indicate that the unorganized interests in America have a much lower chance of being represented in Congress than was the case before the development of direct marketing and the campaign reforms of 1971 and 1974.

Economic Inefficiency

The negative consequences of the growing dependence of Democrats on corporate and trade association PACs are not limited to the political sphere. This dependence creates negative economic impacts as well. Economist Mancur Olson, Jr., has shown that when the political system responds to special interests through the creation of subsidies, tax breaks, tariffs, and other incentives that increase the economic returns in one industry rather than another, investment capital flows to economic activities favored by the government rather than those that the marketplace would find most efficient in the absence of governmental intervention. In addition, entrepreneurs find that a dollar invested in political activity provides a higher rate of return than a dollar invested to increase economic productivity. These forces create a situation where profit-seeking individuals invest in lobbying and in economic activities that are politically advantaged rather than in activities that are efficient in an economic sense. The result, then, of politically created economic advantages is economic inefficiency for the entire country and policies that have negative benefit-cost ratios for the entire society.

Briefly, Olson's argument has two parts and works as follows. First, if in the absence of governmental intervention Industry A has an expected rate of return on investment of 10 percent and Industry B has an expected rate of 8 percent, then investment capital will flow into Industry A until the marginal rate of return drops below or equal to that of Industry B. If, however, Industry B receives a governmental subsidy or special tax incentive that increases its expected return to 11 percent, then capital will flow into Industry B despite the fact that economic efficiency would favor Industry A. The second part of Olson's argument is that when government responds to narrow economic interests, not only will economic investment flow into less efficient enterprises, but also entrepreneurs will spend increasing amounts of funds on political action rather than investing in producing economic goods and services. This movement of resources from economic to political investment occurs because the rate of return is higher in the political sphere. And, Olson argues, the more narrow the interest that is favored, the greater the probability that the policy will lead to economic inefficiency for the entire society.

For example, if a particular policy will benefit 100 percent of the population and the costs of the policy are shared equally by the entire population, then only if the expected benefits of the policy exceed its costs will anyone support it. The situation is entirely different, however, if a policy benefits only 2 percent of the population and its costs are shared by 100 percent. In this situation, even if the costs of the policy to society are much greater than the benefits, the 2 percent who benefit from the policy will want the government to implement it because they will be better off. An example of such a situation might be an irrigation project that costs the nation $100 million to build but creates only $10 million in benefits. If, however, only 2 percent of the population receive these benefits, while its costs are shared by everyone, then even though the total benefits of the project are only $10 million, the 2 percent who directly benefit could spend millions lobbying the government to have the project built and still gain economically.

The tremendous increase in campaign contributions and lobbying by corporations and trade associations indicates that these institutions and the people they represent are increasingly finding the return on a dollar invested in politics to be greater than a dollar invested in economic productivity. Just how much better this return can be is demonstrated by the political efforts of milk producers. In 1971 the dairy industry pledged $2 million to President Nixon's election campaign and almost immediately realized a $500 million increase in dairy subsidies for its efforts.[55]

The numerous subsidies, special tariffs, tax loopholes, construction projects, and guaranteed loans that government provides are part of the reason that the United States has a negative balance of trade, huge budget deficits, and relatively slow increases in economic productivity. The political sphere has become the most profitable place to invest resources and protect oneself from setbacks in the marketplace. And to the extent that the direct-marketing success of the Republicans and conservative PACs force Democrats to increase their support for narrow economic interests, the nation as a whole suffers.

The 1986 Tax Reform

In many respects, the 1986 tax legislation exhibits characteristics that are contrary to the preceding analysis. Numerous narrow economic interests lost their tax breaks, and the tax burden of many corporations was increased. Because of this, the 1986 tax legislation provides an illustration of how Congress can overcome what Jacobson calls its "great collective irresponsibility."[56]

Lobbyists and PACs of interests affected by the proposed tax reforms worked hard and contributed huge amounts of money to defeat the legislation. The PACs had given Senator Packwood, chairman of the Senate Finance Committee, more than $900,000 during the 1985-86 electoral cycle and had contributed more than $3.7 million to members of the House Ways and Means Committee, more than triple the amount the members of this committee received two years earlier.[57] Despite these large contributions, both the House and the Senate passed substantial tax reform measures. How did this happen?

First, the President, the congressional leadership of both parties, and a number of peak associations such as the National Chamber of Commerce had to support the bill and give it the highest priority. Even with such support, the bill went nowhere until Senator Packwood dropped his opposition and became a major supporter of the legislation. In addition, Congress had to adopt a very special decision rule to ensure that the tax bill did not fall prey to the individual responsiveness of congresspersons to the special interests in their districts. In the Senate Finance Committee, on the floor of the Senate, and in the conference committee, any legislator who wanted to amend the bill and give a tax break to some particular interest had to identify where taxes would be increased to meet the revenue lost by the proposed tax break. This decision rule meant that congresspersons could no longer give a benefit to one set of interests and pass the costs on to an unknowing general public through greater deficit spending. Instead, a specific set of losers had to be identified. By requiring that the losers be clearly marked, the political costs of any tax break increased dramatically, and logrolling became much more difficult.[58]

Summary

The Republican party's direct-mail efforts, particularly when combined with the assistance that Republican challengers and candidates for open seats have received from political action committees, have helped that party increase their number of congresspersons. Despite these Republican gains, the impact of direct mail has not led to the programs and policies for which economic conservatives had hoped. The budget is further out of balance and the government is more deeply involved in the economy.

The great irony of the successes that the New Right and the Republican party have achieved in direct marketing may be that these accomplishments have brought more, rather than less, government spending; more, rather than less, government intervention in the economy; and less, rather than more, political responsibility of Congress to any political platform or ideology.

Notes

1. For studies illustrating this point, see Gary Jacobson, *The Politics of Congressional Elections* (Boston: Little, Brown, 1983); and Louis Maisel and Joseph Cooper, eds., *Congressional Elections* (Beverly Hills, Calif.: Sage, 1981).

2. *Logrolling* and *pork barrel* refer to the exchanging of votes among congresspersons so that each representative achieves subsidies or special projects for his or her district. For example, Morris Udall may vote for tobacco subsidies in return for the votes of North Carolina congresspersons for the Central Arizona Project. For an excellent analysis of how logrolling and pork barrel work with federal grants to state and local governments, see John E. Chubb, "Federalism and the Bias for Centralization," in *The New Direction in American Politics,* ed. John E. Chubb and Paul E. Peterson (Washington, D.C.: Brookings Institution, 1985).

3. Jacobson, *Politics of Congressional Elections,* 189.

4. Richard Fenno, *Home Style: House Members in Their Districts* (Boston: Little, Brown, 1978).

5. While most members of Congress encourage their constituents to see them as being similar to the folks back home, they also strive to appear sufficiently different to gain the respect of the voters. Perhaps the congressperson who went to the greatest lengths to appear different from his constituents was the late Adam Clayton Powell, who represented Harlem.

6. Edie Goldenberg and Michael Traugott, *Campaigning for Congress* (Washington, D.C.: CQ Press, 1984), 127.

7. "Frankly Outrageous," *Tucson Citizen,* 5 November 1985, A14.

8. Alan Abramowitz, "Party and Individual Accountability in the 1978 Congressional Election," in *Congressional Elections,* ed. Maisel and Cooper, 187; Gary Jacobson, *Money in Congressional Elections* (New Haven: Yale University Press, 1980), 229; and Thomas Mann and Raymond Wolfinger, "Candidates and Parties," in *Congressional Elections,* ed. Maisel and Cooper, 225.

9. Martin Thomas documented this ideological shift in the Senate for the years 1959-76. See Martin Thomas, "Election Proximity and Senatorial Roll Call Voting," *American Journal of Political Science* 29 (February 1985): 96-111.

10. David Tarrant, "Liberal Senators Facing Tough Re-Election Fights Moderated Their 1979 Votes," *Congressional Quarterly Weekly Report,* 26 April 1980, 1111-15; and Marjorie Randon Hershey, *Running for Office: The Political Education of Campaigners* (Chatham, N.J.: Chatham House, 1984), 178.

11. Goldenberg and Traugott, *Campaigning,* 90-94; and, Jacobson, *Politics of Congressional Elections,* 37-44; and Elizabeth Drew, *Politics and Money: The New Road to Corruption* (New York: Macmillan, 1983), 20.

12. Goldenberg and Traugott, *Campaigning,* 94.

13. Abramowitz, "Party and Individual Accountability," 187.

14. Ibid., 138-39.

15. Mann and Wolfinger, "Candidates and Parties," 142.

16. Barbara Hinckley, "House Reelections and Senate Defeats: The Role of the Challenger," in Maisel and Cooper, eds., *Congressional Elections,* 205. Thermometer ratings theoretically can vary between 0 and 100. A rating of 0 would mean that the respondent recognized the candidate and viewed him in a completely negative manner. A rating of 100 would mean recognition and a completely positive evaluation. A rating of 50 could mean either that the respondent did not know anything about the candidate or that he rated the candidate in a completely neutral way.

17. Gary Jacobson, "Money in the 1980 and 1982 Congressional Elections," in *Money and Politics in the United States,* ed. Michael Malbin (Chatham, N.J.: Chatham House, 1984).

18. The $350,000 is adjusted for inflation since 1980. The original figure was $300,000 in 1980 and is from Gary Jacobson, "Congressional Elections, 1978: The Case of the Vanishing Challengers," in Maisel and Cooper, eds., *Congressional Elections,* 230.

19. Christopher Buchanan, "National GOP Pushing Hard to Capture State Legislatures," *Congressional Quarterly Weekly Report,* 25 October 1980, 3188.

20. Larry Light, "Republican Groups Dominate in Campaign Spending," *Congressional Quarterly Weekly Report* 38 (1 November 1980): 3234-39; and Goldenberg and Traugott, *Campaigning,* 72-74.

21. Hershey, *Running for Office,* 132-36.

22. Goldenberg and Traugott, *Campaigning,* 84.

23. Gary Jacobson, "Parties and PACs in Congressional Elections," in *Congress Reconsidered,* 3d ed., ed. Lawrence Dodd and Bruce Oppenheimer (Washington, D.C.: CQ Press, 1985), 141.

24. For estimates on the number of seats that the President's party loses in the midterm congressional elections, see Edward R. Tufte, "Determinants of the Outcome of Midterm Congressional Elections," *American Political Science Review* 68 (1975): 812-26. For expectations concerning the 1982 election, see Alan Abramowitz, "National Issues, Strategic Politicians, and Voting Behavior in the 1980 and 1982 Congressional Elections," *American Journal of Political Science* 28 (1984): 710-21.

25. Ibid.; Jacobson, "Money in the 1980 and 1982 Congressional Elections," 50, 59; and Gary Jacobson, "The Republican Advantage in Campaign Finance," in Chubb and Peterson, eds., *New Direction in American Politics.*

26. Thomas Edsall, *The New Politics of Inequality* (New York: Norton, 1984), 80-82.

27. James Gibson, Cornelius Cotter, John Bibby, and Robert Huckshorn, "Whither the Local Parties? A Cross-Sectional Analysis of the Strength of Party Organizations," *American Journal of Political Science* 29 (February 1985): 139-60.

28. Jacobson, "Money in the 1980 and 1982 Congressional Elections," 40-49.

29. Jacobson, "Parties and PACs," 137-47; and Maxwell Glen, "Democratic Candidates Got a Larger Share of the Corporate PAC Pie in 1984," *National Journal,* 19 January 1985, 156-59. In 1984, labor caught up with corporate PACs in contributions to Democratic incumbents, but it was still far behind the contributions of corporate and trade association PACs combined. Federal Election Commission press release, May, 1985.

30. Numerous books, articles, and papers document this tendency. For perhaps the best summary tables of PAC giving from 1974 to 1982, see the tables in the appendix of Malbin, ed., *Money and Politics in the United States.* For an excellent disaggregation of which business and corporate PACs follow an incumbency strategy, see David Gopoian, "What Makes PACs Tick? An Analysis of Allocation Patterns of Economic Interest Groups," *American Journal of Political Science* 28 (May 1984): 259-81.

31. *Common Cause News,* 7 and 23 February 1987.

32. Jacobson, "Money in the 1980 and 1982 Congressional Elections," 44-45. Italics added.

33. E.E. Schattschneider, *The Semisovereign People* (New York: Holt, Rinehart, and Winston, 1960); Theodore Lowi, *The End of Liberalism,* 2d ed. (New York: Norton, 1979); Sheldon Wolin, *Politics and Vision* (Boston: Little, Brown, 1965); Grant McConnell, *Private Power and American Democracy* (New York: Knopf, 1966); and Mancur Olson, Jr., *The Logic of Collective Action* (Cambridge, Mass.: Harvard University Press, 1965); and Mancur Olson, Jr., *The Rise and Decline of Nations* (New Haven: Yale University Press, 1980).

34. Glen, "Democratic Candidates," 156-59.

35. Federal Election Commission Reports, 1987.

36. Glen, "Democratic Candidates," 158-59; Gopoian, "What Makes PACs Tick"; and W.P. Welch, "Campaign Contributions and Legislative Voting: Milk Money and Dairy Price Supports," *Western Political Quarterly* 35 (1982): 478-95. FEC figures show that in 1986 corporate and trade PACs gave over $12 million to Republican challengers

and candidates for open seats and only $7.2 million to Democratic challengers and candidates for open seats.

37. Edsall, *New Politics*, 90-91.

38. Ibid., 135.

39. *Statistical Abstracts of the United States, 1968-1983; National Journal,* 29 December 1984, 2466. Slightly different figures are given in *Time,* 10 June 1985, 17; and in Edsall, *New Politics,* 212. It should be noted that the observed decline cannot be totally attributed to direct marketing, as the decrease began earlier than 1972. The decline rapidly accelerated, however, in the mid-1970s.

40. Ibid., 213.

41. The FTC ruling required automobile dealers to inform the buyer of a used car if he, the dealer, knew that the car had any of 52 major defects and to sign a statement indicating the presence and extent of the warranty, if any, that accompanied the car. The regulation did not require a warranty or an inspection. It was designed to provide potential buyers with the information that the dealers had obtained through normal business practices.

42. This discussion of the FTC legislation is taken from Kirk F. Brown, "Campaign Contributions and Congressional Voting" (paper presented at the 1983 meetings of the American Political Science Association).

43. Ibid., 3.

44. Common Cause, *People Against PACs: A Common Cause Guide to Winning the War Against Political Action Committees* (Washington, D.C.: Common Cause, 1983).

45. Patricia Theiler, "Can the Used Car Lobby Sell Congress?" *Washington Post,* 22 November 1982, C2; and Albert Hunt, "Special-Interest Money Increasingly Influences What Congress Enacts," *Wall Street Journal,* 26 July 1982, 1.

46. Brown, "Campaign Contributions," tables 4-10.

47. A rating of 50 by the Americans for Democratic Action would mean that the congressperson ranked exactly in the middle of the liberal-conservative continuum; that is, he was a complete moderate.

48. These figures are derived from the probit equation coefficients in tables 9 and 10 of Brown, "Campaign Contributions," 47-48.

49. John P. Frendreis and Richard W. Waterman, "PAC Contributions and Legislative Behavior: Senate Voting on Trucking Deregulation," *Social Science Quarterly* 66 (June 1985): 410-12.

50. Welch, "Campaign Contributions and Legislative Voting," 478-95.

51. To make a more direct comparison with Welch's findings I used probit regression to predict a congressperson's vote and the same variables as Welch except that instead of using the actual contributions of the dairy industry I used the contribution a congressperson would expect for his support. Expected contribution was the average level of contribution to a similarly-placed congressperson who supported the dairy industry in the previous session of congress. For example, the dairy industry rewards persons who are on the Agriculture and Rules committees more than representatives who are not on these committees. Therefore, the average contribution to a member of the Agriculture Committee who supported the dairy industry in the previous session was my measure of the expected contribution for a supportive member of the Agriculture Committee during the current session. Using dairy production in the district, ideology, political party, and expected contribution, I could correctly predict 90.3 percent of con-

gresspersons' votes. Ideology was not statistically significant and political party and expected contribution had standardized betas more than four times as large as dairy production.

52. Issues were chosen from the list of important votes for each year as designated by the *Congressional Quarterly Weekly Report*. Data on PAC giving were compiled from figures supplied by the Federal Election Commission, and all PAC donations from an industry were aggregated to choose the top ten PACs.

53. The analysis was conducted as follows: Issues were included if they had been identified by the *Congressional Quarterly* as key votes, at least one-third of the members of the House of Representatives voted for the minority position, and PACs from the interests affected were among the top ten contributors in their category. These issues were then classified as having either no organized opposition or as having organized opposition based on records of the congressional hearings and reports by the *Congressional Quarterly*. Using probit regression, each issue was analyzed separately for Democrats and Republicans.

54. The reader may question using contributions made after the vote as a cause of the congressperson's vote. If, however, the member of Congress and the PAC both know that the general tendency is to reward past votes, then the anticipated contribution becomes a causal variable despite the fact that the actual contribution occurred after the event being explained.

55. The dairy lobby never had to deliver the full $2 million to Nixon's campaign, but several officers of the dairy cooperatives were sentenced to jail for illegal campaign contributions. See Graham Wootton, *Interest Groups: Policy and Politics in America* (Englewood Cliffs, N.J.: Prentice-Hall, 1985); and William Manchester, *The Glory and the Dream* (Boston: Little, Brown, 1974), 1233.

56. Jacobson, *Politics of Congressional Elections*, 189.

57. FEC Reports, 1987.

58. The tax reform legislation of 1986 provides an interesting illustration of congressional attempts to reduce subsidies, budget deficits, and economic inefficiencies. While it is no accident that the members of the House Ways and Means Committee and the Senate Finance Committee averaged higher PAC contributions than members of any other committees, these committees worked hard to overcome many of the pressures of these interests. Both the House and the Senate passed substantial tax reform measures. The Senate bill, where the Republican party with its greater party assistance and ideological consistency was the majority party, was both simpler and less favorable to particular special interests. Even though big gas and oil interests and specialized interests in Senator Packwood's home state received favorable treatment—Packwood was the chairman of the Senate Finance Committee in 1986—the Senate bill represented major simplification at both the individual and corporate levels. The tax bill shows that Congress can, under special circumstances, overcome interest-group liberalism. For an excellent history of the fight for tax reform, see J.H. Birnbaum and A.S. Murray, *Showdown at Gucci Gulch: Lawyers, Lobbyists, and the Unlikely Triumph of Tax Reform* (New York: Vintage, 1987).

7. Future Prospects for Direct Marketing

Direct marketing has become a major participant in the political process and substantially influences who wins and who loses in politics. Citizen action groups, political action committees, interest groups, and political parties utilize direct marketing to recruit members, to communicate with supporters, to mobilize grass-roots lobbying, and to generate funds for political campaigns. Direct mail has become the dominant fund-raising technique of the above institutions as well as presidential hopefuls and it is a vital part of almost every congressional candidate's quest for office. Finally, direct marketing has allowed the Republican party to become a truly national party during the past decade with greater ideological consistency than political commentators ever thought would be possible.

We began this book by examining the fears of direct marketing's critics and the hopes of direct marketing's supporters concerning whether this new technology might decrease or increase democracy in America. We also asked several "how" questions: How does the direct marketing of politics work? How have the users of these new technologies attempted to change political participation and the way political decisions are made? And how has direct marketing altered public policy?

Our investigation of these issues indicated that, for the most part, the fears of direct marketing's critics have not been realized. Direct marketing does not fragment the political parties; it does not replace democratic participation with ersatz participation where the public is manipulated by national elites; it does not increase significantly political extremism among the public (although it does increase participation among persons who hold extreme opinions). Just as the worst fears of direct marketing's critics have not been realized, neither have the hopes of its supporters. Direct mail, closed-circuit television, and teledemocracy have not led to greater participation by minorities, the poor, and other previously disadvantaged sectors of our society. In fact, the new technologies appear to have increased rather than decreased the disparities between the "haves" and "have nots" of politics.

144

How Does Direct Marketing Work?

Direct marketing, particularly direct mail, became the principal political fund raiser and recruiter because of its technical advantages. Its use of key numbers on return envelopes allowed the sender to compare the effectiveness of alternative messages and greatly facilitated recordkeeping. By addressing the salutation to a particular person or persons and by citing specific characteristics of the addressee in the letter, direct mail personalized political appeals. Direct mail could also send its appeals to persons who had the attitudes or characteristics that made them susceptible to the message sent. Concentration allowed the sending of the message only to those persons who could make a difference in a political outcome. Finally, direct-marketing techniques encouraged an immediate response by providing the necessary response materials with the appeal.

In addition to these technical advantages, every successful direct mailing begins and ends with a threat to recipients' values and provides them with a means to do something to alleviate this menace. Fundamentalist Christians receive appeals that alert them to threats to the family and traditional values; civil libertarians find in their mailboxes messages that warn them of perils to free speech; and environmentalists get letters telling them of impending doom from chemical disasters. After alerting recipients to the intolerable threat to their values, the mailings then reveal to the recipients how they can become efficacious political actors by performing in ways outlined in the direct mailing. The most important way is to give money to the organization that sent the mailing.

How Has Direct Marketing Affected Mass Political Behavior?

Critics object to the use of threats and extreme language in direct mail and fear that the increased use of direct mail may lead to intolerance and a mass society. Our examination of persons who joined citizen action groups and contributed to political action committees in response to direct-mail appeals found two basic kinds of respondents: (1) persons who knew little about the issue or issues addressed in the mailing but responded because it was simple to do and because the issues were portrayed in terms that were easy to understand; and (2) persons who already felt strongly about the issue and saw it in the black-and-white terms portrayed in the mailing. Neither kind of respondent, however, felt committed to the political organization that sent the message. In this respect, direct-marketing respondents differ substantially from persons who join an organization through friendship networks. Whereas the individual who participates in an organization because of occupational or friendship ties may remain in the organization even when its issues do not have high visibility, persons who participate in response to a direct-mail appeal are not likely to continue contributing when the issue fades from the public eye. This lack of commitment to the organization presents a real problem for the elites whose resources depend on direct-marketing appeals.

Our comparisons of people who joined political organizations in response to direct-mail appeals with persons who joined through social network ties discovered that direct-mail recruits are less knowledgeable about politics, less tolerant of opposing ideas, more alienated from American political institutions, and more supportive of aggressive political behaviors. The differences between direct-marketing and social network joiners are not, however, particularly large.[1] In addition, direct-mail joiners become increasingly tolerant and more likely to participate in traditional democratic behaviors the longer they remain in their organization. These more democratic orientations occur despite the fact that the literature they receive from their organizations continues to emphasize extreme threats and characterizes the opposition in ways that often appear unreasonable and even fanatical.

How Has Direct Marketing Affected Elite Behavior?

While the impact of direct marketing on mass behavior does not seriously threaten democracy, its impact on elite behavior may present serious problems. Comparisons of direct-mail-based elites with similarly placed elites who were not as dependent on direct-marketing resources found substantial differences in the political tactics of the two groups. Demagogic appeals, innuendo, and half-truths typically characterized the tactics of direct-mail elites. Rather than portraying their political adversaries as persons who hold opposing views, direct-marketing elites characterized their opponents as "enemies" who have little or no regard for their country or common decency. Instead of attempting to deal with the complexity of issues by balancing competing claims, direct-mail-based elites simplified the issues into black and white alternatives where each side depends more on warlike rhetoric than reason.

The extremism that characterizes direct-marketing elites occurs in large part because these elites fear the loss of public support. Because persons who respond to direct-marketing appeals are not committed to the organization that made the appeal, elites who are dependent on these resources choose tactics that make for good media coverage and easily understood issues. Direct-marketing elites do not have the luxury of compromise or of working behind the scenes. Their issues must remain "hot" so that contributions continue.

Direct marketing has changed not only elite tactics but also the composition of the elites. The introduction of low-cost computers and high-speed printers has encouraged the emergence of marketing entrepreneurs: persons who initiate national political organizations that do not depend on preexisting social networks. If astute political entrepreneurs such as Richard Viguerie, Betty Friedan, or John Gardner can obtain quality prospecting lists, they can create a national base of support. This support need not rely on local institutions or leaders; instead, it may rely on the effectiveness of the marketing messages sent to the prospects by the national leadership. Persons who have never seen one another and who have little in common except for their support for a particular issue or cause can join together to provide resources to a person or persons whom they do not know. This has created a new category of political elites—those whose power stems not from their knowledge of issues or their connections with other political leaders but from their ability to market a political cause successfully.

How Has Direct Marketing Changed Political Decision Making?

The essence of representative democracy is political accountability. If democracy is to work, the elites who make the political choices for the society must be responsible to the citizenry for those choices. As we learn more about direct marketing, we realize that an essential difficulty with it is the lack of accountability. Many elites funded by direct mail are accountable neither to their contributors nor to any set of public institutions. The data presented in chapter 3 and the findings of previous studies of citizen action group members and political action committee contributors indicate that persons who respond to direct-marketing appeals rarely have any real knowledge of the politics and policies made possible by their donations. Contributors' information is limited largely to that contained in the mailings and newsletters sent by the elites they fund. There are no institutions forcing elites to be accurate in the portrayal of their activities; because of this, it is quite possible for leaders of citizen action groups and political action committees to obtain resources by promising one set of actions and then acting in ways quite different from those promised. The probability is small that contributors will discover the deception because there are no opposition candidates to tell of the duplicity. Only the persons creating the deception know whom they are deceiving.

The accountability issue is most severe in political action committees. In most of these institutions, the director and a few staff members decide the issues they will address, the tactics they will use, and the ways they will spend contributors' funds. Given the current ineffective penalties for inaccurate information in political campaigns, it is not surprising that organizations such as the National Conservative Political Action Committee have repeatedly used their funds to perpetrate lies and half-truths during political campaigns. Citizen action groups also have misled their supporters. One environmental group sent its members letters discussing how successful its lobbyists had been during the previous year, despite the fact that it had not employed a single lobbyist during most of the period.

The issue of accountability of elites to donors is not as great within the major political parties because opposition candidates and existing governmental regulations increase the probability that misinformation and wrongdoing will be discovered.

Although direct marketing does not create as great an accountability problem for political parties, it has changed dramatically the relative strength of the two parties, their fund-raising techniques, and the kinds of persons who control the parties. As we saw in chapter 5, the national Republican organizations have made much better use of direct mail than their Democratic counterparts have. The GOP raises five times as much money as the Democrats through direct marketing, and in terms of political activities these funds make possible, the difference is even greater. In 1981, for example, less than 5 percent of the $6.4 million raised by the Democratic National Committee was spent on actual political activities; 95 percent went to fund raising and administrative costs. In contrast, the Republican National Committee, while raising five times as much money as the Democrats, spent more than twenty times as much on political activities.[2]

Because direct marketing plays such an important role in Republican fund raising, the GOP has become increasingly dominated by marketing, polling, and fund-raising professionals—technicians who have taken over almost all functions traditionally filled by volunteers and local party regulars. The tremendous success of these professionals made possible the development of a truly national party with more than 350 full-time employees in the Republican National Committee alone, permitted generous support for Republican candidates, allowed the development of national party advertisements such as the "Stay the Course" campaign in 1982, and encouraged a national orientation and greater ideological coherence among the party's elites.

While direct mail was creating an avenue for growth in the GOP and increasing the relative power of the national party organizations, it was fragmenting the Democratic party and encouraging candidate-centered campaign organizations where candidates were forced to fend for themselves. Whereas Republican candidates in close elections could count on the maximum possible support from their party, Democratic candidates had to obtain their funding from nonparty sources. In the 1982 Senate races, Republican candidates received four times as much party funding as their Democratic counterparts. In the House, the Republicans received almost twelve times as much.[3] As we discussed in chapter 6, this funding inequality often forced Democratic candidates to turn for support to corporate and trade association PACs and to disregard the interests of the disadvantaged sectors of society.

The causes of the Republican advantage in direct marketing are complex. The widely believed claim of Democrats and liberals that the success of Republicans and conservatives stems from their greater extremism is not supported by the data. Part of the GOP's advantage stems from its earlier start and better initial financial situation, but these advantages cannot in and of themselves account for the tremendous disparities that exist. The Republicans have a more coherent ideology, their appeals better fit the social class of political contributors, and their leadership is more positive toward the idea of direct marketing.

Although the past records of the two parties in direct marketing indicate that the GOP will continue to hold a substantial edge in this form of fund raising, Democrats and liberals can prosper using direct mail. The senatorial campaign of Governor James Hunt of North Carolina and the presidential bid of Senator George McGovern of South Dakota demonstrate that, if the right threats or enemies can be identified, Democratic fund-raising efforts can be successful.

One important change that is occurring in direct mailings, by both the national parties and by many candidates, is the greater ideological consistency among issues within the same mailings. The national parties have eschewed single issues and emphasized their traditional positions with respect to taxation, the correct role of government in the economy, and the appropriate distribution of wealth in society. In addition, candidates, particularly those who are the target of negative campaign spending by ideological PACs have counterattacked with mailings of their own that emphasize broad ideological issues. A liberal Democrat such as Tom Harkin in Iowa may fight Right to Life, pollution, high defense spending, and may appeal to support for the disadvantaged sectors of society all in the same letter. Similarly, conservative Republican candidates will include not only antiabortion statements in their mailings but also raise the issues of deficit spending and stronger defense. This increased attention to multiple issues within the same mailings, coupled with the ideological character of the national party mailings, may lead to the greater issue consistency among voters that makes broad coalitions possible and increases political accountability.

How Has Direct Marketing Altered Public Policy?

While the absence of political accountability is direct marketing's major challenge to democracy, the differential success that the various interests have had with the new technology presents its major challenge to equity in public policy. The inequality in party funding has forced Democratic candidates to seek campaign contributions from business and trade association PACs. To obtain these funds, Democrats have increasingly supported public policies that favor those interests. These policies have redistributed the benefits of government increasingly toward the wealthy and redistributed the costs of government toward the lower and lower-middle classes. For example, the changes in social security and income taxes in 1981 and 1982, changes approved by a House controlled by the Democratic party, led to an average net tax increase of $95 for persons earning less than $10,000 per year and a net tax decrease of more than $400 for persons earning between $75,000 and $100,000. Similarly, the percentage of governmental revenues from corporate taxes fell from 18 percent in 1968 to 6.2 percent in 1984.[4]

As we saw in chapter 6, the impact of PAC contributions is particularly significant when a political issue pits a well-financed organized interest against a disorganized set of individuals such as consumers or the poor. In these situations Democratic congresspersons often neglect their party's platform and ideology and support the corporate or trade association positions.

The consequences of direct marketing on public policy not only encouraged the redistribution of income from the poor to the rich and from the disorganized to the organized, they also fostered a number of economic inefficiencies. Organized special interests obtain higher profits not through greater economic productivity and technological advances, but through favorable governmental policies. Increasingly these policies are supported by Democratic congresspersons who have turned to PACs for funds to combat the better-financed Republican candidates.

Advantages of Direct Marketing

The answers to questions about how direct marketing works and how it has changed political participation, political decision making, and public policy indicate that direct marketing creates a number of deleterious consequences for the American political system. But not all of its effects are negative. While direct mail and other new marketing technologies may have led to participation by persons who hold extreme and divisive opinions, "divisive" need not mean "destructive." Moral and ethical issues have an important role in democratic theory and practice. In a democratic society, the political system must decide which behaviors are morally and legally correct. Issues such as abortion, the death penalty, prayer in public schools, the availability of basic levels of medical and nutritional care, and the necessity of sending young persons to war in Vietnam or Nicaragua should be decided, not by elites who are not answerable to the public or by the economic marketplace, but by citizens and their elected officials. The absence of morality and ideology in political discussion can be far more dangerous than their presence, and direct-mail-based ideological political action committees have encouraged greater attention to social, ethical, and moral issues.

Not only has direct marketing led to increased attention to important moral issues, it has also increased the overall levels of knowledge about and participation in political affairs. The direct mailings of the two national parties have helped citizens understand the importance of factors such as which party has majority control of the House or Senate and have increased citizens' knowledge of the ideological differences between the parties.

The fund-raising strength of the Republican party has helped its elected officials resist the temptation to vote for organized special interests, even business interests, when to do so would harm the country as a whole. In addition, the fact that the GOP relies mainly on small contributions from thousands of donors, rather than large contributions from a few, has increased the independence of Republican officials from the influence of the very wealthy in society— a feat that the campaign finance reforms of the early 1970s could not accomplish.

Possible Institutional Changes

Given that direct marketing has both negative and positive effects on the American political system, what changes would help diminish the harms while maintaining the benefits? I believe that two institutional changes would increase the accountability of direct-marketing elites, discourage them from utilizing simplistic and demagogic appeals, and at the same time not infringe on civil liberties.

First, the penalties for inaccurate statements by political action committees and citizen action groups should be augmented substantially. Currently, if a PAC sends out materials that are incorrect and damage a candidate's electoral chances, the likelihood that the PAC will be punished is small, and the penalties are not severe. The reason for this is that by the time the Federal Election Commission can evaluate any complaints, the election is over and the damage is done. If, however, the penalties for knowingly disseminating inaccurate information were increased, then PACs would have much stronger incentives to be accurate in their messages. Penalties might include a substantial fine; the suspension of reduced postal rates; and the requirement that, for a specified period, all communication by the offending organization would include a statement indicating that its previous political communications had been found to include information that was not true and violated election laws.[5]

To encourage accountability by direct-mail-based elites, all political action committees and citizen action groups should provide financial statements to their contributors. These statements would indicate how the organization spent its funds during the previous year, would be checked by the Federal Election Commission for accuracy and completeness, and would provide contributors with information concerning what percentage of their contributions actually reached political candidates and which candidates received donations. Given the direct-mail capabilities of these organizations, and the fact that they currently must file these materials with the federal government, this requirement would not be particularly onerous.

The advantages of the above proposals are that they require no advance screening by governmental agencies and do not limit the rights of freedom of speech and press through prior censorship. They do, however, provide substantially greater information to contributors concerning how their funds are being spent and they provide very strong incentives to political organizations to be accurate in the information that they send to potential voters and contributors. The penalties for inaccurate information might also encourage greater use of positive rather than negative campaigning and raise the level of political discussion.

Reducing the Influence of Organized Interests

A second institutional change to reduce the harm of direct marketing would be to place all political action committees on an equal footing with respect to payment of overhead costs such as rent and fund-raising expenses. This would decrease the advantages currently enjoyed by corporate, labor, and trade association PACs. Rather than allow the parent organizations to pay overhead expenses, every PAC would have to pay its own costs. This would reduce substantially the amount of money that nonideological PACs could contribute to congressional candidates. Because these economically oriented PACs give mainly to incumbents for the purpose of achieving special subsidies or tax breaks, reducing the funds available to these PACs could diminish the economic inefficiencies created by congressional logrolling and pork-barrel policies.

While economically oriented PACs typically support incumbents for special-interest purposes, ideological PACs spend relatively more to assist challengers and direct their efforts toward broader ideological issues. Placing all categories of PACs in the same financial position would decrease the current advantages of incumbents and increase the competition in the electoral process. And this change would improve the balance between the more narrow and more broadly based interests in society.

Although the curtailment of economic PACs would reduce the current imbalance between the organized and the unorganized in our society, it would not affect the current inequalities between the two major parties, an inequality that has led many Democratic officials to desert their party's traditional role of assistance to and protection of unorganized interests. The reduction of the advantages enjoyed by narrow organized interests requires substantial changes by both political parties and peak associations.[6]

The Republican party must utilize its direct-marketing resources to encourage its elected officials to vote for legislation that supports the party's platform rather than subsidizes narrow interests. The obvious difficulty with this proposal is that if Republican candidates do not solicit funds from corporate and trade association PACs, there will be that much more money available to Democratic candidates. If the current logrolling and pork barrel practices are to be curtailed, both parties must cooperate in the renunciation of these practices. And this is unlikely until the Democratic party becomes more successful in its direct-marketing program and the parties achieve greater parity in monetary resources.

An alternative method for reducing logrolling would be for ideological and broad-based economic interests such as the National Association of Manufacturers, the National Chamber of Commerce, and the AFL-CIO to base their campaign contributions on votes against logrolling measures as well as on votes in favor of their own interests. A few organizations, such as the Business and Industry Political Action Committee (BIPAC), could play a leading role in this effort. Each year, corporate PACs turn to BIPAC for recommendations concerning whom they should support. If BIPAC and other peak association PACs and lobbyists base their contributions and ratings on votes against special subsidies and tax advantages, the incentives to logrolling would be sharply reduced.

Are the above recommendations realistic? I believe they are. Members of Congress are aware that the logrolling and pork barrel policies of the past are leading the country into difficult economic times. And in the absence of a major tax increase, the only way that deficits can be reduced is through a reduction in spending. To a large degree, the cuts that can be inflicted on programs for the poor and unorganized in our society have already been made. This means that future cuts must come in areas such as student loans, veterans benefits, farm programs, social security, Medicare, federal pensions, and defense — programs that few members of Congress wish to reduce, and will not reduce unless the costs of *not* cutting them are greater than the costs of making the reductions. The Republican party, peak associations, and ideological PACs have the resources to make such a benefit-cost ratio possible. These organizations also have the incentives to encourage congresspersons to vote against special interest subsidies. In addition to patriotism and wanting the country to become more economically efficient, each organization represents a population of sufficient size that its total membership receives greater costs than benefits when Congress approves unjustified subsidies. And as the tax reform legislation of 1986 indicated, when costs are shared among congresspersons, reform is possible.

Notes

1. The largest differences occurred in two quite different studies. The first, by John Ellwood and Robert Spitzer, compared contributors to the Democratic telethon with other party contributors and found substantial differences between the two groups on support for aggressive behaviors. See "The Democratic National Telethons: Their Successes and Failures," *Journal of Politics* 41 (1979): 828-64. A second study found that individuals who had contributed to five or more political action committees with conservative or fundamentalist Christian ideologies showed significantly lower levels of tolerance than any other set of contributors. See James Guth and John Green, "Political Activists and Civil Liberties: The Case of Party and PAC Contributors" (paper presented at the annual meeting of the Midwest Political Science Association, 1984).

2. Thomas B. Edsall, *The New Politics of Inequality* (New York: Norton, 1984), 91-92.

3. Christopher Buchanan, "National GOP Pushing Hard to Capture State Legislatures," *Congressional Quarterly Weekly Report*, 25 October 1980, 3188.

4. For the sources of these data, see chapter 6, note 39.

5. To ensure that the offending institution would not simply dissolve itself and re-emerge under a new name, the penalties would need to include the requirement that any institution that had members of the penalized institution on its payroll would have to have the same statement concerning inaccurate information.

6. A *peak association* is an organization made up of other organizations. Examples are the AFL-CIO and the National Association of Manufacturers.

Appendix A
Environmental Action Survey*

Thank you very much for taking part in this survey. Only one thousand members of Environmental Action have been randomly selected to participate. Therefore, no matter what the extent of your involvement in EA has been, your opinions are of vital importance.

INSTRUCTIONS

1. The questionnaire should be filled out by the person to whom it is addressed if the membership is a joint one.

2. Please answer each question by *circling the number* which appears next to the response which best represents your view. If you wish to skip a question, please feel free to do so. DK will be used occasionally to indicate "don't know."

3. When you have finished, do not put your name on the questionnaire. Simply seal it in the enclosed, postage-paid envelope, and drop it in the mail. If at all possible, we would appreciate the return of the questionnaire *within the next five days*. This will save us the expense of sending you a reminder.

4. *If you wish to receive a report of the results, please put your name and address on the outside of the return envelope. We will send you a report by the end of the summer.*

1. How did you originally come to join Environmental Action? *(Circle one number)*
1 Through friends
2 Received a membership appeal in the mail
3 Someone gave me a membership as a gift
4 Saw the magazine and sent in for a membership
5 Other (please explain briefly)

2. How many years have you been a member of EA? _____ years

3. Do you pay for your current membership or does someone give it to you?
1 Pay for it   2 Receive it as a gift   3 Have a life membership

*Questionnaires sent to the Environmental Defense Fund, National Wildlife Federation, Sierra Club, and the Wilderness Society replaced "Environmental Action" with the appropriate group name.

4. During the past year, about how much money did you contribute to EA as a gift, over and above the basic membership fee? (Do not include money spent on the purchase of books or other merchandise.)
1 none   2 approximately $_____

5. How active do you consider yourself in the organization?
1 Very active   2 Active   3 Not very active   4 Not active at all
5 Not applicable

6. How active are you in its local branch or chapter?
1 Very active   2 Active   3 Not very active   4 Not active at all
5 There is no local branch or chapter as far as I know

7. Some groups have special mailing lists of people who agree to respond to issue alerts and write their Congresspeople. Are you on such a list for EA? If you are, how many times have you been able to respond to such an alert in the past year?
1 No, I am not on such a list
2 Yes, I do receive such a mailing and have written approximately _____ letters in the past year.
3 Don't know

8. How many of your friends are aware that you belong to EA?
1 Most   2 Some   3 Only one or two   4 None   5 I don't know

9. Groups in American society differ widely in the degree to which their members or contributors are given the opportunity to have a voice in the organization's affairs. How important is it to you that you have a voice in EA's affairs?
1 Very important 2 Important 3 Neither 4 Unimportant 5 Very unimportant

10. In your opinion how much opportunity is there for a member of EA to have a voice in its affairs?
1 Considerable   2 Fair amount   3 Some   4 Little   5 None   6 Don't know

11. How satisfied are you with the opportunities provided to you by EA to have a voice in its affairs?
1 Very satisfied   2 Satisfied   3 Neither   4 Dissatisfied   5 Very dissatisfied

12. If you are dissatisfied, in what way do you think the opportunity to have a voice should be changed?
1 Decreased   2 Increased   3 Other (please specify)

13. Please indicate your own personal use of the following methods to have a voice in the organization's affairs (when available) over the past five years:

In the past five years have you?	Often	At least once	Never	Inapplicable
Written letters to magazine or staff	1	2	3	4
Voted for members of the national board	1	2	3	4

In the past five years have you?	Often	At least once	Never	Inappli-cable
Participated in local or national level policy discussions	1	2	3	4
Voted for delegates to national and/or regional conventions and/or the council, etc.	1	2	3	4
Voted for officers at the local level	1	2	3	4

14. How appropriate or inappropriate would the following descriptions be if applied to you personally?

	Very appropriate	Appropriate	Neither	Inappropriate	Very inappropriate
Environmentalist	1	2	3	4	5
Conservationist	1	2	3	4	5
Into new life styles	1	2	3	4	5
Back packer	1	2	3	4	5
Rock climber	1	2	3	4	5
Hunter	1	2	3	4	5
Fisherman	1	2	3	4	5
Birder	1	2	3	4	5
Vegetarian	1	2	3	4	5

15. How often have you done the things listed below during the past year?

	Regularly	Frequently	Occasionally	Once	Never
Read an environmental/conservation magazine	1	2	3	4	5
Read a book on an environmental/conservation issue	1	2	3	4	5
Tried to persuade someone to join the organization	1	2	3	4	5
Demonstrated against polluters	1	2	3	4	5
Contacted a public official about an environmental matter	1	2	3	4	5
Collected paper and/or glass for recycling	1	2	3	4	5
Given money for environmental/conservation activities	1	2	3	4	5
Sacrificed to conserve energy	1	2	3	4	5
Avoided environmentally damaging products	1	2	3	4	5
Birding and nature study	1	2	3	4	5
Gone day hiking	1	2	3	4	5
Visited a national park	1	2	3	4	5
Visited a wilderness area	1	2	3	4	5
Worked in a garden	1	2	3	4	5

16. People have many different motivations for belonging to organizations like EA. We are very interested in *why* you belong to EA. Below are a number of possible factors which may or may not be important to you. Please rate the importance of *each* of them to you personally using this scale:

1 Very Important 2 Important 3 Neither 4 Unimportant 5 Very Unimportant

I belong to EA because . . .	VI	I	N	U	VU
1. I enjoy *Environmental Action* magazine and/or other benefits of membership like outings very much.	1	2	3	4	5
2. Some important aspects of my life are threatened by environmental/conservation problems.	1	2	3	4	5
3. Solving environmental problems is so important that I try to support any effort aimed at that goal.	1	2	3	4	5
4. My contribution to EA is helping to influence government action on conservation/environmental problems.	1	2	3	4	5
5. Of the encouragement of my friends.	1	2	3	4	5
6. I personally gain much from the information I receive from EA.	1	2	3	4	5
7. Many knowledgeable and influential people support EA.	1	2	3	4	5
8. Without contributions like mine, EA would be unable to work for improved environmental quality.	1	2	3	4	5
9. If EA achieves its goals, my life and children's lives will directly benefit.	1	2	3	4	5
10. If I dropped my membership in EA, I would find it difficult to live with myself.	1	2	3	4	5
11. Belonging to EA makes me feel really good about what I am doing with my life.	1	2	3	4	5
12. If we don't act now to preserve the environment, things will get much worse.	1	2	3	4	5
13. Someone gave me a membership.	1	2	3	4	5

Now please look back over this list. Of those items you circled "very important" or "important" which two or three are your *most important* motivations for belonging to EA? Please place the item numbers in the spaces provided.

_____Most important _____Next most important _____Third most important

Please give your opinion on the following questions about Environmental Action by circling one number opposite each statement using the following scale:

1 Strongly Agree (SA)   2 Agree (A)   3 Neither Agree nor Disagree (N)
4 Disagree (D)   5 Strongly Disagree (SD)   6 Don't Know (DK)

	SA	A	N	D	SD	DK
17. Many of my close friends are also members of EA.	1	2	3	4	5	6
18. My views on environmental/conservation issues were already developed before I joined EA.	1	2	3	4	5	6
19. EA is very effective in influencing national conservation/environmental policy.	1	2	3	4	5	6

	SA	A	N	D	SD	DK
20. I don't think of myself as a member of Environmental Action, I just send money because I think it is a worthy cause.	1	2	3	4	5	6
21. The *Environmental Action* magazine is the major reason why I belong to EA.	1	2	3	4	5	6
22. I think of EA as representing my views on environmental/conservation issues to the government.	1	2	3	4	5	6
23. I would be willing to give up my vacation to work for EA.	1	2	3	4	5	6
24. My parents were members of EA before I joined.	1	2	3	4	5	6
25. EA should actively involve itself in the environmental/conservation problems of such special groups as the urban poor and ethnic minorities.	1	2	3	4	5	6
26. I almost always agree with the policy stands taken by EA.	1	2	3	4	5	6
27. Belonging to EA is one of the most important things in my life.	1	2	3	4	5	6
28. Because sufficient progress is being made nationally in conservation and environmental matters, there will be less need for organizations like EA within a few years.	1	2	3	4	5	6
29. EA keeps me well informed about the policy stands it takes.	1	2	3	4	5	6

30. There are a large number of national voluntary organizations in the United States. Listed below are 31 of them which are concerned with environmental/conservation matters. Which of these groups have you heard of or do you belong to? *Please place the appropriate number from the list below in the space preceding each name:*

1 I *currently belong* and/or contribute to the organization.
2 I do not belong or contribute to the organization, but *I have heard of it.*
3 I *have never heard* of the organization

____American Forestry Association
____Common Cause
____Conservative Foundation
____Cousteau Society
____Defenders of Wildlife

____Mobilization for Survival
____National Audubon Society
____National Parks and Conservation
    Association
____National Wildlife Federation

____Environmental Action
____Environmental Defense Fund
____Environmental Policy Center
____Friends of Animals
____Friends of the Earth
____Funds for Animals, Inc.
____General Conservation Society
____Izaak Walton League
____League of Conservation Voters
____League of Women Voters
____Mobilization for Survival

____National Resources Defense Council
____Nature Conservancy
____New Directions
____Public Citizen
____Save the Redwoods League
____Science for the People
____Sierra Club
____Union of Concerned Scientists
____The Wilderness Society
____World Wildlife Fund
____Zero Population Growth

31. Besides the national environmental/conservation organizations listed above, what types of *state and local* environmental groups do you belong to? *(Circle the number opposite each that applies.)*

1 Outing, mountain or river club
2 Bird or garden club
3 Sportsmen's group
4 Anti-nuclear group
5 Ad-hoc group opposing some aspect of local development (such as a shopping center, highway, power transmission lines)
6 Ad-hoc or permanent group seeking to protect a particular natural area (mountain, wilderness area, river, etc.)
7 State or regional organization (e.g., Colorado Open Spaces Council, Carolina Action)
8 Community of people who seek to live in an ecologically sound manner utilizing alternative lifestyles
9 Other (please describe briefly)

32. Did you become actively concerned about conservation/environmental issues as a result of your involvement in a particular local or regional issue or battle?
1 Yes   2 No, other reasons   3 Not actively concerned

VIEWS ON ENVIRONMENTAL/CONSERVATION ISSUES

33. Below are a number of conservation/environmental issues and approaches. Please read them over. Then use the three columns provided to do the following:
Column

A Check each item which is *very important* to your personally.
B Check each item which you think should be a *high priority* for EA.
C Check each item which *you would be willing to spend time working on* if asked.

A B C
__ __ __ 1 Runaway technology
__ __ __ 2 Wilderness technology
__ __ __ 3 Alternative technology
__ __ __ 4 Self-sufficient communities based on ecological principles
__ __ __ 5 Population problems
__ __ __ 6 No-growth or conserver society

A B C
___ ___ ___ 7 Opposition to nuclear power
___ ___ ___ 8 Preserving natural areas that are not necessarily wilderness (parks, wetlands, open spaces, etc.)
___ ___ ___ 9 Animal protection
___ ___ ___ 10 Air pollution
___ ___ ___ 11 Water pollution
___ ___ ___ 12 Alternative energy sources, energy conservation
___ ___ ___ 13 Wildlife: animals and birds in their natural habitat
___ ___ ___ 14 Toxic substances in food and drinking water
___ ___ ___ 15 Wildlife management for improved hunting and fishing
___ ___ ___ 16 Controlling recombinant DNA research
___ ___ ___ 17 Food supply
___ ___ ___ 18 Rational planning for the use of our nation's land
___ ___ ___ 19 Urban environment
___ ___ ___ 20 International environment
___ ___ ___ 21 Noise pollution
___ ___ ___ 22 Shortage of mineral resources
___ ___ ___ 23 An issue other than those above (please specify on back of page)

Which issue, if any, is most important to you personally?
(place number here) ____
Which issue is next most important? ____   Third most important? ____

34. Overall, how serious are the nation's environmental problems today?
1 We are rapidly approaching disaster   5 They are not very serious
2 They are very serious   6 The nation has basically solved its
3 They are serious   environmental problems
4 They are somewhat serious   7 Don't know

35. How serious do you think *air* pollution is in *this state*?
1 Very   2 Fairly   3 Not too   4 Not serious   5 Don't know

36. How serious do you think *water* pollution is in *this state*?
1 Very   2 Fairly   3 Not too   4 Not serious   5 Don't know

37. What are the most important causes of environmental problems? Please rate each of the following potential causes as to their importance using the following scale:
1 Very important cause   2 Important cause   3 Unimportant cause
4 Very unimportant cause   5 Don't know

	Very Imp.	Imp.	Unimp.	Very Unimp.	Don't know
Government failure	1	2	3	4	5
Science and technology	1	2	3	4	5
Carelessness of people	1	2	3	4	5
Industry	1	2	3	4	5

	Very Imp.	Imp.	Unimp.	Very Unimp.	Don't know
Population growth	1	2	3	4	5
Economic growth	1	2	3	4	5
How many possessions people have	1	2	3	4	5

38. Currently there is much discussion in the media and among the scientific community about the regulation of research using recombinant DNA. This type of experimentation has been called "gene splitting" or "genetic engineering." How much do you know about this debate? *(Circle one number)*

1 A great deal   2 A fair amount   3 A little   4 Very little   5 Nothing

39. Below are some statements about recombinant DNA research. What is your opinion about each one?

1 Strongly agree   2 Agree   3 Disagree   4 Strongly disagree   5 DK

	SA	A	D	SD	DK
This type of research has the potential to yield important benefits for society.	1	2	3	4	5
It is important for environmental/conservation organizations to become involved in the debate about recombinant DNA.	1	2	3	4	5
There should be an immediate moratorium on all recombinant DNA research which would produce novel genetic combinations, pending further public discussion of the risks and benefits as well as the social and ethical implications.	1	2	3	4	5
It is not enough to have only the experts and politicians in on the policy making on this research; the general public *must* be directly included in the decision making at both the federal and local levels.	1	2	3	4	5

VIEWS ON ENERGY

40. How serious would you say the energy situation is in the U.S.?

1 Very   2 Fairly   3 Somewhat   4 Not serious   5 Don't know

41. Taking into account all you have heard or read, how do you feel toward nuclear power plants in general?

1 Very favorable   2 Fairly favorable   3 Fairly unfavorable
4 Very unfavorable   5 No opinion

42. How would you feel about having a nuclear power plant within 20 miles of where you live?

1 Very favorable   2 Fairly favorable   3 Fairly unfavorable
4 Very unfavorable   5 No opinion

43. Which of the following statements best express your present view on conventional nuclear power (not the breeder reactor):

1 No more nuclear power plants should be built and the present plants should be taken out of use whether or not the problem of the storage of nuclear wastes is solved and improved safety features are developed.

2 No more nuclear power plants should be built until the problem of the storage of nuclear wastes is solved and improved safety features are developed. Present plants should be allowed to operate.

3 More nuclear power plants should be built, but only as needed in the last resort to meet the nation's power requirements and if extensive efforts are made to solve the waste problem and improve the plant's safety features.

4 More nuclear power plants should be built as needed.

5 Don't know.

44. How much interest do you personally have in solar power?
1 None   2 Little   3 Some   4 Quite a bit   5 Great deal   6 Don't know

45. *If you have at least some interest in solar power:* How important a role have the following factors played in stimulating your interest?

	Very important		Very unimportant	
Need to find a nonpolluting substitute for conventional fuels	1	2	3	4
Need to find a substitute for nuclear fuels	1	2	3	4
Need to decentralize control of power away from large corporations	1	2	3	4
Need to find a renewable and inexhaustible source of power for future generations	1	2	3	4

VIEWS ON CONSERVATION ISSUES AND VALUES

46. Some people say that people ought to be allowed to make their own decision about whether they want to risk getting cancer by using saccharin, tobacco, or hair dyes. Others say that the only solution is for government to ban potentially dangerous products like these. Which approach do you favor?
1 Individual risk   2 Government ban   3 Don't know

47. Recently the government banned certain food dyes used in things like cherries and hot dogs because of studies showing that they might cause cancer. Do you generally approve or disapprove of what the government did?
1 Strongly approve   2 Approve   3 Disapprove
4 Strongly disapprove   5 Have not heard about it   5 Don't know

48. Here are two different viewpoints on the human use of natural resources. With which do you most agree? *Person A* believes that we have already gone too far in exploiting nature and that the balance should be restored in nature's favor. The future use of resources should never interfere with the integrity, stability, and beauty of natural systems.

Person B believes that it is an unavoidable necessity to interfere with some natural system. This is only permissable, however, when the interference is held to a minimum through careful and sensitive environmental planning.

1 Strongly agree with A   2 Agree with A   3 Agree with B
      4 Strongly agree with B   5 Don't know

Please give your personal opinion about each of the following statements by circling the number corresponding to the following range of answers.

1 Strongly agree   2 Agree   3 Disagree   4 Strongly disagree   5 Don't know

	SA	A	D	SD	DK
49. If the price of a beautiful and healthful environment is the cessation of further economic growth, it is a price worth paying.	1	2	3	4	5
50. An industry causing substantial pollution should not be forced to stop operations if this would put people out of work.	1	2	3	4	5
51. If I had to choose between a coal or nuclear power plant for my area, I would prefer nuclear.	1	2	3	4	5
52. The present is, all things considered, to be preferred to the way things were fifty or sixty years ago.	1	2	3	4	5
53. An endangered species must be protected, even at the expense of commercial activity.	1	2	3	4	5
54. Environmental/conservation issues seem much more complex today than they were a few years ago.	1	2	3	4	5
55. Nonreturnable beverage bottles should be prohibited.	1	2	3	4	5
56. All things considered, industrial society produces greater benefits than costs.	1	2	3	4	5
57. It is a good idea for environmental leaders to engage in dialogue with industry to try to break down the stereotypes and see if there is any common ground for the solution to specific conflicts.	1	2	3	4	5
58. Modern cities may have problems, but they are still the most exciting and interesting places to live.	1	2	3	4	5
59. Many people are taking notice and becoming worried by our social and environmental problems. As a result, over the next fifty years we shall see a cleaner, better world.	1	2	3	4	5
60. Nuclear power is a moral issue, not a practical question concerning our supply of electricity.	1	2	3	4	5
61. When there are plenty of deer, killing off the surplus is not much different from harvesting any other resource.	1	2	3	4	5
62. Society must be decentralized.	1	2	3	4	5

	SA	A	D	SD	DK
63. Further additions to the nation's protected wilderness should have a high priority for the federal government.	1	2	3	4	5
64. People would be better off if they lived a more simple life without so much technology.	1	2	3	4	5
65. I believe that plants and animals exist primarily for man's use.	1	2	3	4	5
66. These days I'm much more interested in environmental/conservation problems in my local community and area than I am at the national level.	1	2	3	4	5
67. The key to our problems is to develop "alternative" or "soft" technologies which are nonpolluting and low energy and resource consuming.	1	2	3	4	5
68. The future welfare of our society largely depends on the discoveries of science.	1	2	3	4	5
69. We have already let technology run away with us.	1	2	3	4	5
70. One person's right to a clean environment is not as important as another's right to gainful employment.	1	2	3	4	5

VIEWS ON VALUES AND GOALS

71. There is a lot of talk these days about what the aims of this country should be for the next ten years. Here are some of the goals to which different people would give top priority. Would you please indicate which of these you personally consider the most important? And which would be the next most important?

1 Maintaining a high level of economic growth

2 Making sure that this country has strong defense forces

Most important ＿＿＿

3 Seeing that people have more say about how things are done at their jobs and in their communities

Next most important ＿＿＿

4 Protect nature from being spoiled and polluted

72. If you had to choose, which one item in the following list would you say is most desirable? What would be your second choice?

1 Maintaining order in the nation

Most important ＿＿＿

2 Giving the people more say in important government decisions

Next most important ＿＿＿

3 Fighting rising prices

4 Protecting freedom of speech

73. In your opinion, which one of these is most important? Which is next most important?

1 A stable economy
2 Progress toward a less impersonal and more humane
society   Most important ____
3 Progress toward a society in which ideas count
more than money   Next most important ____
4 The fight against crime

74. Looking at all the goals considered in the previous three questions, please choose the one which you think is *most* desirable of all. Which is next most desirable? And which one of all the aims is *least important* from your point of view.

1 Economic growth   Most important ____
2 Strong defense
3 More say about jobs/communities
4 Protecting nature   Next most important ____
5 Maintaining order
6 More say in government   Least important ____
7 Fighting rising prices
8 Freedom of speech
9 Stable economy
10 Fighting crime
11 Humane society

VIEWS ON POLITICS AND CHANGE

75. How often do you do the following?

	Often	Some-times	Seldom	Never
Work with others to help solve community problems	1	2	3	4
Attempt to persuade friends to vote the same way as you	1	2	3	4
Read about politics in the newspapers	1	2	3	4
Contact public officials or politicians	1	2	3	4
Discuss politics with friends	1	2	3	4
Attend political rallies or meetings	1	2	3	4
Spend time working for a political party or candidate	1	2	3	4

76. Which *one* of the following views of American society and American life best reflects your own feelings?

1 The American way of life is superior to that of any other country.
2 There are serious flaws in our society today, but the system is flexible enough to solve them.
3 The American system is not flexible enough; radical change is needed.
4 The whole system ought to be replaced by an entirely new one. The existing structures are too rotten for repair.

77. Over the last twenty years a number of social movements have sought to change society. What was your personal feeling about the following movements?

	Very sympa-thetic	Sympa-thetic	Un-sympa-thetic	Very un-sympa-thetic	Don't know
1 Civil rights movement	1	2	3	4	5
2 Antiwar movement	1	2	3	4	5
3 Ecology movement (Earth Day)	1	2	3	4	5
4 Black power movement	1	2	3	4	5
5 Women's movement	1	2	3	4	5
6 Consumer movement	1	2	3	4	5
7 Right to life movement	1	2	3	4	5
8 Antinuclear movement	1	2	3	4	5

78. Which of these movements, if any, were (are) you active in? Please put the numbers of each movement here: _____   _____   _____   _____   _____

79. One hears more and more about groups of people going off to live off the land and settling in agricultural and rural areas. Is this something that would interest you for a year or more?
    1 A year or two   2 Permanently   3 No appeal   4 Not sure

80. Have you written a letter, sent a telegram, or called your congressperson on any environmental issues during the past year?
    1 Yes, approximately _____ times   2 No   3 Don't know

81. What is your assessment of the Carter administration's environmental record?
    1 Excellent   2 Good   3 Fair   4 Poor   5 Don't know

82. How do you feel about each of the following types of political action which people use to effect change?

	Strong approval	Approval	Dis-approval	Strong dis-approval
Blocking traffic with a demonstration	1	2	3	4
Joining in wildcat strikes	1	2	3	4
Destroying property	1	2	3	4
Attending lawful demonstrations	1	2	3	4
Signing a petition	1	2	3	4
Refusing to pay rent or taxes	1	2	3	4
Occupying buildings or factories, sit-ins	1	2	3	4

National polls frequently ask the following types of questions. What are your opinions?

83. Looking to the future, which would you say is the biggest threat to the well being of this country—big business, big labor, or big government?

1 Big business   2 Big labor   3 Big government
        4 Other (please specify)   5 Don't know

84. What do you think is the ideal number of children for a family to have?
_____ children

Please use this scale for these questions:
1 Strongly agree   2 Agree   3 Disagree   4 Strongly disagree   5 Don't know

	SA	A	D	SD	DK
85. I don't think public officials care much what people like me think.	1	2	3	4	5
86. You can just about always trust the federal government to do what is right.	1	2	3	4	5
87. Sometimes politics and government seem so complicated that a person like me can't really understand what's going on.	1	2	3	4	5
88. The federal government should pay for abortions for poor people.	1	2	3	4	5
89. In spite of what some people say, the lot (situation/condition) of the average man is getting worse, not better.	1	2	3	4	5
90. People like me don't have any say in what the government does.	1	2	3	4	5
91. The federal government is pretty much run for the benefit of a few big interests.	1	2	3	4	5
92. The disparity in income and living standards between the poor and the rich in American society is too great; we must develop ways to redistribute income.	1	2	3	4	5
93. Further economic growth is essential if we are to meet society's needs (e.g., better living standards, housing, jobs and health).	1	2	3	4	5

94. All in all, compared to 10 years ago, do you feel the quality of life in this country has:
    1 improved?   2 grown worse?   3 stayed the same?   4 not sure

95. In 1980, Carter ran for President on the Democratic ticket against Reagan for the Republicans. Do you remember whether or not you voted in that election?
    1 Voted   2 Did not vote   3 Ineligible to vote   4 Don't know/can't remember

96. *If you voted:* Did you vote for Carter or Reagan?
    1 Carter   2 Reagan   3 Other candidate

97. *If you did not vote or were ineligible:* Who would you have voted for, for President, if you had voted?
    1 Carter   2 Reagan   3 Other   4 Wouldn't vote   4 Don't Know/Can't remember

98. Generally speaking, do you usually think of yourself as a Republican, a Democrat, an Independent, or what?

1 Strong Democrat
2 Not very strong Democrat
3 Independent, closer to Democrat
4 Independent, closer to neither

5 Independent, closer to Republican
6 Not very strong Republican
7 Strong Republican
8 Other (specify) _____
9 Don't know

99. Regardless of your party identification, would you call yourself?

1 Strong conservative
2 A moderate conservative
3 Middle of the road

4 A moderate liberal
5 A strong liberal
6 A radical

PERSONAL BACKGROUND AND EXPERIENCE

100. When you were a child, how interested were you in each of the following:

	Very	Fairly	Not too	Not at all interested
Observing and identifying birds	1	2	3	4
Wild animals	1	2	3	4
Pets	1	2	3	4
Camping and hiking	1	2	3	4
Hunting and/or fishing	1	2	3	4

101. When you were young (in grade school and high school) were your parents:

	Definitely Yes	Yes	No	Definitely No	DK
Active in conservation/environmental groups	1	2	3	4	5
Interested in nature and wildlife	1	2	3	4	5
Interested in social problems and causes	1	2	3	4	5

102. In what type of a place (town or city) were you brought up? (If you were brought up in several types of places, pick the one where you spent the most time during your high school years.)

1 Very large city (1,000,000+)
2 Large city (250,000 to 999,000)
3 Suburb of a very large city
5 Medium-size city (50,000 - 249,000)

6 Small city or town (under 50,000)
7 On a farm or ranch
8 In open country but not on a farm or a ranch

Place number from scale above here:

103. In what type of place do you currently live? _____

104. If you had your choice, in what type of place would you most prefer to live? _____

105. Altogether, how many different addresses have you lived at over the last five years? _____ addresses

106. How many years have you lived in your present town, city or rural area? _____ years

107. Are your currently employed?*
1 Employed   2 Unemployed   3 Student   4 Homemaker   5 Retired

*Working for pay at a job; or running a business, profession, or farm; or working without pay in a family business or farm.

108. *If you are currently employed, is it?* 1 Full-time   2 Part-time

109. Which of the following do you (or your spouse if you are unemployed) work for?

1 Government (at all levels)
2 Nonprofit institution (including all schools)
3 Large corporation or business

4 Medium size corporation or business
5 Small corporation or business
6 Self-employed
7 Other

110. Which of the following categories best describes your occupation?
1 Professional, technical and kindred workers
2 Managers and administrators (except farm), sales workers
3 Clerical and kindred workers
4 Craftsmen and kindred workers (mechanics and repairmen, carpenters, etc.)
5 Machine operators (except transport machines)
6 Transport equipment operators; laborers (except farm)
7 Farmers, farm managers, farm laborers, and farm foremen
8 Service workers (including private household)
9 Other or uncertain (please describe your occupation briefly)

111. Are you or your spouse a member of a labor union? 1 Yes   2 No

112. In what year were you born? _____

113. What is your sex? 1 Male   2 Female

114. What is your main or ethnic inheritance?
1 White   2 Black   2 Mexican-American   4 Other

115. Are you now?   1 Married and living with spouse
2 Single, divorced, widowed, separated   3 Other

116. *If you are married and living with spouse:* Is your membership in the organization in both your names or just yours?
1 My name alone   2 Both our names   3 My spouse's name   4 Don't know

117. Do you have children?   1 Yes   2 No   *If yes:* How many? _____

118. How many brothers and sisters do (did) you have?
_____ brothers and sisters

119. Are you now attending or enrolled in school?
1 No   2 Yes, full-time student   3 Yes, part-time student

120. What is the highest grade you have finished and got credit for in regular school, college, or graduate school? *(circle one)*

Grade School		High School	College	Graduate School
1	5	9	13	17
2	6	10	14	18
3	7	11	15	19
4	8	12	16	20 +

121. What is the highest grade your mother, father, and spouse (if married) finished and got credit for? *(use numbers from question 120.)*
Mother _____   Father _____   Spouse _____

122. Thinking about the time when you were 16 years old, compared with American families in general then, would you say your family's income was far below average, below average, average, above average, or far above average?
1 Far below average   2 Below average   3 Average   4 Above average
5 Far above average   6 Don't know

123. Please circle the number on the list below which best represents your *total family income** before taxes.
1 Under $6,000   4 $10,000-11,999   7 $20,000-29,999
2 $6,000-7,999   5 $12,000-13,999   8 $30,000-39,999
3 $8,000-9,999   6 $14,000-19,999   9 $40,000-49,999
                                10 $50,000 and over

* Including wages and salaries, net income from business or farm, pensions, dividends, interest, rent, and any other money income received by all those people in the household who are related to you.*

124. How many wage earners contributed $4000 or more to your total family income last year?
1 One   2 Two   3 Three or more

125. If you were asked to use one of *these* names for your social class, which would you say you belong to?
1 Lower class   2 Working class   3 Lower-middle class
4 Middle-middle class   5 Upper-middle class   6 Upper class

126. In what religion were you raised? If you were raised in more than one religion, please indicate the one you are more likely to identify with.
1 Protestant   2 Catholic   3 Jewish
4 No organized religion   5 Other (specify)_____   6 None

127. What is your present religion, if any?
1 Protestant   2 Catholic   3 Jewish
4 No organized religion
5 Other (specify) _____   6 None

128. In the past year, about how often have you attended formal religious services?
1 More than once a week   2 About once a week   3 2 to 3 times a month
4 A few times a year or less   5 Not at all

129. Aside from attending religious services, how important would you say your religion is to your life?
1 Very important   2 Fairly important
3 Fairly unimportant   4 Not important at all

130. Do you own a summer or second home (alone or with one or two other people)?
1 Yes, house   2 Yes, condominium   3 No

131. *If yes:* What kind of area is the home located in?
1 Wilderness type area   2 Relatively unpopulated natural area
3 Rural area   4 Relatively built-up vacation area   5 Other

132. How often do you read a daily newspaper?
1 Every day   2 A few times a week   3 Once a week
4 Less than once a week   5 Never

133. On the average day, about how many hours do you personally watch television?

0 hours	6 hours
1 hours	7 hours
2 hours	8 hours
3 hours	9 hours
4 hours	10 hours
5 hours	11 hours or more

134. How much do you rely upon the following sources of information for your understanding of social problems and current news events?

	Almost exclusively	Quite a bit	Some-what	Very little	Not at all
Books	1	2	3	4	5
TV news	1	2	3	4	5
TV specials	1	2	3	4	5
Daily newspaper	1	2	3	4	5
Time, Newsweek, or *U.S. News & World Report*	1	2	3	4	5
Sunday newspaper	1	2	3	4	5
Other (specify)	1	2	3	4	5

135. Is there any book you have read which has had a major influence on your thinking about conservation/environmental issues?

    1 Yes, one book   2 Yes, several books   3 No

136. *If you answer yes*, please write the name and author of the book which has most influenced your thinking on these issues here:

_____

_____

137. Which state do you live in? *(Circle the number opposite the state.)*

1 AL	19 KS	37 ND
2 AK	20 KY	38 OH
3 AZ	21 LA	39 OK
4 AR	22 ME	40 OR
5 CA	23 MD	41 PA
6 CZ	24 MA	42 PR
7 CO	25 MI	23 RI
8 CT	26 MN	44 SC
9 DE	27 MS	45 SD
10 DC	28 MO	46 TN
11 FL	29 MT	47 TX
12 GA	30 NE	48 UT
13 GU	31 NV	49 VT
14 HI	32 NH	50 VA
15 ID	33 NJ	51 VI
16 IL	34 NM	52 WA
17 IN	35 NY	53 WV
18 IA	36 NC	54 WI
		55 WY

138. Which state(s), including your present state, would you *most* like to live in if you had your free choice? Place number from question 137 in the blanks.

    _____   _____   _____

139. Circle the number next to *each one* of the following magazines which is regularly read in your household.

1 *Co-evolution Quarterly*	7 *New Republic*
2 *Environment*	8 *Newsweek*
3 *Field and Stream*	9 *Ranger Rick*
4 *Mother Earth News*	10 *Science*
5 *National Geographic*	11 *Time*
6 *National Review*	12 *U.S. News & World Report*

Appendix B
Questionnaire for Citizen Action Group Leaders

Organization_____   Leader_____

    1. How did you happen to come to work for (group name)?

    2. How long have you worked for (group)?

    3. What did you do before coming here? Have you worked for any other public interest groups?

    4. What kind of career pattern do you see for yourself? Do you have any plans to leave your current job in the next year or so? How about within the next five years?

    5. Could you give me a brief description of what your typical day is like? For example, how much time do you spend contacting policymakers? How much time do you spend in committee hearings? How much time with members of Congress? Their staff?

    6. What proportion of your efforts is spent on grass-roots lobbying such as getting your members to write their congressperson?

    7. (same question as 5 except that the question concerns the movement as a whole rather than just the individual lobbyist)

    8. (same question as 6 except that the question concerns the group as a whole)

    9. Do you use telephone trees, mail alert programs, or other system for quickly contacting your activists?

    10. (If yes to 9) How are these lists constructed and who keeps them up to date? Are the lists organized by state, congressional district, region?

    11. How does (group) decide when to use these lists? How often do you try to mobilize your own activists? (Probe for types of issues and events that lead to mobilizations.)

    12. Do you personally keep lists of members who know their congressperson or senator personally? Does (group)? (Probe to determine how much effort is required of the lobbyist activating the mailing.)

    13. How responsive do you believe Congress is to grass-roots efforts? How efficient are grass-roots tactics compared to direct lobbying by staff? When do you think grass-roots lobbying is most effective?

    14. Many lobbies frequently join political coalitions with other groups in the same area. Does your group do this frequently?

    15. With which groups are you most likely to join in a coalition effort? How about your group as a whole?

16. What percentage of (group) resources goes into coalition lobbying? What percentage goes into grass-roots lobbying? Into direct lobbying?

17. In your opinion, what have been your most successful lobbying efforts? How about for your group as a whole?

18. What lobbying techniques work best for you personally?

19. When you are choosing which issues to lobby on, how important is it that the issue have media coverage? How about for (group) as a whole?

20. Does (group) have any formal procedures for getting member input on which issues the group will lobby on? Informal procedures?

21. How much influence do you think members have on the selection of lobbying issues?

22. How does (group) keep its members interested in what the organization is doing? Do you think this is important?

23. Does your group have any special incentives for highly active members or for large donors?

24. Look at the following card and mark the salary range that reflects your current salary. less than $15,000; $15,000-19,999; $20,000-24,999; $25,000-29,999; 30,000-34,999; more than $35,000.

The following questions were asked of the executive director or a person on the direct-mailing staff.

1. What proportion of (group)'s funds come from direct-mail solicitations? Does that include annual dues from members?

2. What is the size of your house or membership list? Your activist list? Your special donors list?

3. What is the average response rate to your prospect mailings? Your house mailings?

4. What is the average contribution to your prospect mailings? To house mailings?

5. What is the average cost of your mailings?

6. Do you have a special department or part of your organization that does the mailings? How large is it? How often do you mail for donations? For activist mobilizations?

7. When did your direct mail program begin? Has it ever been temporarily halted? Why?

8. Do you have any special feelings about direct mailings? Do you think it has helped or hurt your movement? Your group? The country?

Bibliography

Abramowitz, Alan. "Party and Individual Accountability in the 1978 Congressional Elections." In *Congressional Elections,* ed. Louis Maisel and Joseph Cooper. Beverly Hills, Calif.: Sage, 1981.

———. "National Issues, Strategic Politicians, and Voting Behavior in the 1980 and 1982 Congressional Elections." *American Journal of Political Science* 28 (1984): 710-21.

Adamany, David. "Political Parties in the 1980s." In *Money and Politics in the United States: Financing Elections in the 1980s,* edited by Michael Malbin. Chatham, N.J.: Chatham House, 1984.

Alexander, Herbert. *Financing the 1980 Election.* Lexington, Mass.: Lexington Books, 1983.

———. *Financing Politics: Money, Elections, and Political Reform.* 3d ed. Washington, D.C.: CQ Press, 1984.

Barber, Benjamin. *Strong Democracy: Participatory Politics for a New Age.* Berkeley: University of California Press, 1984.

———. "Voting Is Not Enough: How Modern Communications Can Enhance the Ideal of Citizenship." *Atlantic* 253 (June 1984): 45-53.

Becker, Ted. "Hawaii Televote: Measuring Public Opinion on Complex Policy Issues." *Political Science* 33 (July 1981): 52-65.

———, et al. *Report on 'New Zealand Televote.'* Wellington, New Zealand: Victoria University, 1981.

Bell, Daniel. "The End of American Exceptionalism." *Public Interest* 41 (1975): 193-224.

Berry, Jeffrey. *Lobbying for the People.* Princeton: Princeton University Press, 1977.

———. *Lobbying and the Interest Group Society.* Boston: Little, Brown, 1984.

Broder, David. "When Campaigns Get Mean." In *The Fear Brokers,* edited by Thomas J. McIntyre and John C. Obert. Boston: Beacon Press, 1979.

———. "When Washington Gets Mean." *Washington Post,* 31 October 1982, C7.

Brown, Kirk. "Campaign Contributions and Congressional Voting." Paper presented at the annual meeting of the American Political Science Association, 1983.

Buchanan, Christopher. "National GOP Pushing Hard to Capture State Legislatures." *Congressional Quarterly Weekly Report,* 25 October 1980, 3188.

Caro, Robert. *The Years of Lyndon Johnson.* New York: Vintage, 1981.

Chubb, John E. "Federalism and the Bias for Centralization." In *The New Direction in American Politics,* edited by John E. Chubb and Paul E. Peterson. Washington, D.C.: Brookings Institution, 1985.

Cigler, Allan, and J.M. Hansen. "Group Formation through Protest: The American Agricultural Movement." In *Interest Group Politics,* edited by Allan Cigler and Burdett Loomis. Washington, D.C.: CQ Press, 1983.

Cobb, Roger W., and Charles D. Elder. *The Political Uses of Symbols*. New York: Longman, 1983.

Common Cause. *People Against PACs: A Common Cause Guide to Winning the War Against Political Action Committees*. Washington, D.C.: Common Cause, 1983.

Conover, Pamela, and Virginia Gray. *Feminism and the New Right: Conflict over the American Family*. New York: Praeger, 1983.

Cook, Mary Etta, and Roger H. Davidson. "Deferral Politics: Congressional Decision Making on Environmental Issues." In *Public Policy and the Natural Environment*, edited by R. Kenneth Godwin and Helen M. Ingram. Greenwich, Conn.: JAI Press, 1985.

Costain, Anne. "The Struggle for a National Women's Lobby: Organizing a Diffuse Interest." *Western Political Quarterly* 33 (December 1980): 476-91.

———. "Representing Women: The Transition from Social Movement to Interest Group." *Western Political Quarterly* 34 (March 1981): 100-113.

Cotgrove, Stephen, and Andrew Duff. "Environmentalism, Middle Class Radicalism, and Politics." *Sociological Review* 28 (May 1980): 333-51.

Cover, Albert, and Bruce Blumberg. "Baby Books and Ballots: The Impact of Congressional Mail on Constituent Opinion." *American Political Science Review* 76 (June 1982): 347-59.

Deckard, Barbara. *The Women's Movement*. New York: Harper & Row, 1979.

Dieter-Opp, Karl. "Soft Incentives and Collective Action." *British Journal of Political Science* 15 (1985): 269-94.

Drew, Elizabeth. *Politics and Money: The New Road to Corruption*. New York: Macmillan, 1983.

Edsall, Thomas B. *The New Politics of Inequality*. New York: Norton, 1984.

Ellwood, John W., and Robert J. Spitzer. "The Democratic National Telethons: Their Successes and Failures." *Journal of Politics* 41 (1979): 828-64.

Etzioni, Amitai. *An Immodest Agenda: Rebuilding America Before the 21st Century*. New York: McGraw-Hill, 1983.

Feigert, Frank B., and M. Margaret Conway. *Parties and Politics in America*. Boston: Allyn and Bacon, 1976.

Fenno, Richard. *Home Style: House Members in Their Districts*. Boston: Little, Brown, 1978.

Freeman, Jo. *The Politics of Women's Liberation*. New York: McKay, 1975.

———. *Social Movements of the Sixties and Seventies*. New York: Longman, 1983.

Frendreis, John, and Richard Waterman. "PAC Contributions and Legislative Behavior: Senate Voting on Trucking Deregulation." *Social Science Quarterly* 66 (June 1985): 410-12.

Gelb, Joyce, and Marian Leif Palley. *Women and Public Policies*. Princeton: Princeton University Press, 1982.

Gibson, James, Cornelius Cotter, John Bibby, and Robert Huckshorn. "Whither the Local Parties? A Cross-Sectional Analysis of the Strength of Party Organizations." *American Journal of Political Science* 29 (February 1985): 139-60.

Godwin, R. Kenneth, and R. C. Mitchell. "Rational Models, Collective Goods, and Nonelectoral Political Behavior." *Western Political Quarterly* 35 (June 1982): 161-80.

———. "The Impact of Direct Mail on Political Organizations." *Social Science Quarterly* 65 (Fall 1984): 829-39.

Goldenberg, Edie, and Michael Traugott. *Campaigning for Congress.* Washington, D.C.: CQ Press, 1984.

Gopoian, David. "What Makes PACs Tick? An Analysis of Allocation Patterns of Economic Interest Groups." *American Journal of Political Science* 28 (May 1984): 259-81.

Guth, James L. "The New Christian Right." In *The New Christian Right,* edited by Robert Liebman and Robert Wuthnow. Hawthorne, N.Y.: Aldine, 1983.

Guth, James L., and John C. Green. "Political Activists and Civil Liberties: The Case of Party and PAC Contributors." Paper presented at the annual meeting of the Midwest Political Science Association, 1984.

Hall, Donald R. *Cooperative Lobbying.* Tucson: University of Arizona Press, 1968.

Hansen, John M. "The Political Economy of Group Membership." *American Political Science Review* 79 (1985): 79-96.

Hayes, Michael T. "Interest Groups: Pluralism or Mass Society?" In *Interest Group Politics,* edited by Allan Cigler and Burdett Loomis. Washington, D.C.: CQ Press, 1983.

Heclo, Hugh. "Issue Networks and the Executive Establishment." In *The New American Political System,* edited by Anthony King. Washington, D.C.: American Enterprise Institute, 1978.

Hershey, Marjorie Randon. *Running for Office: The Political Education of Campaigners.* Chatham, N.J.: Chatham House, 1984.

Hershey, Marjorie Randon, and Darrell M. West. "Single-Issue Politics: Prolife Groups and the 1980 Senate Campaign." In *Interest Group Politics,* edited by Allan Cigler and Burdett Loomis. Washington, D.C.: CQ Press, 1983.

Hinckley, Barbara. "House Reelections and Senate Defeats: The Role of the Challenger." In *Congressional Elections,* edited by Louis Maisel and Joseph Cooper. Beverly Hills, Calif.: Sage, 1981.

Hodgson, Richard S. *Direct Mail and Mail Order Handbook.* 2d ed. Chicago: Dartnell, 1977.

Hyman, Herbert, and C.R. Wright. "Trends in Voluntary Association Memberships of American Adults: Replication Based on Secondary Analysis of National Sample Surveys." *American Sociological Review* 36 (April 1971): 191-206.

Jones, Ruth, and Warren Miller. "Financing Campaigns: Macro Level Innovation and Micro Level Response." *Western Political Quarterly* 38 (June 1985): 187-210.

Jacobson, Gary. *The Politics of Congressional Elections.* Boston: Little, Brown, 1983.

————. "Money in the 1980 Elections." In *Money and Politics in the United States: Financing Elections in the 1980s,* edited by Michael Malbin. Chatham, N.J.: Chatham House, 1984.

————. "The Republican Advantage in Campaign Finance." In *The New Direction in American Politics,* edited by John Chubb and Paul Peterson. Washington, D.C.: Brookings Institution, 1985.

Kayden, Xandra. "The Nationalizing of the Party System." In *Parties, Interest Groups, and the Campaign Finance Laws,* edited by Michael Malbin. Washington, D.C.: American Enterprise Institute, 1980.

————. "Parties and the 1980 Election." In Campaign Finance Study Group, *Financing Presidential Campaigns.* Cambridge, Mass.: John F. Kennedy School of Government, Institute of Politics, Harvard University, 1982.

Kenski, Henry C. "The President, Congress, and Interest Groups." In *Public Policy and the Natural Environment,* edited by R. Kenneth Godwin and Helen Ingram. Greenwich, Conn.: JAI Press, 1985.

Knoke, David, and James R. Wood. *Organized for Action: Commitment in Voluntary Associations.* New Brunswick: Rutgers University Press, 1981.

Kornhauser, William. *The Politics of Mass Society.* New York: Free Press, 1959.

Kriesberg, Louis, ed. *Research in Social Movements, Conflicts, and Change.* Vol. 2. Greenwich, Conn.: JAI Press, 1978.

Latus, Margaret. "Ideological PACs and Political Action." In *The New Christian Right,* edited by Robert Liebman and Robert Wuthnow. Hawthorne, N.Y.: Aldine, 1983.

_____. "Assessing Ideological PACs: From Outrage to Understanding." In *Money and Politics in the United States,* edited by Michael Malbin. Chatham, N.J.: Chatham House, 1984.

Liebman, R.C. "Mobilizing the Moral Majority." In *The New Christian Right,* edited by Robert Liebman and Robert Wuthnow. Hawthorne, N.Y.: Aldine, 1983.

Lockwood, Maren Carden. *Feminism in the Mid-1970s.* New York: Ford Foundation, 1977.

Longley, Charles. "Party Nationalization in America." In *Paths to Political Reform,* edited by William Crotty. Lexington, Mass.: Lexington Books, 1980.

Loomis, Burdett. "A New Era: Groups and the Grass Roots." In *Interest Group Politics,* edited by Allan Cigler and Burdett Loomis. Washington, D.C.: CQ Press, 1983.

Lowi, Theodore. *The End of Liberalism.* 2d ed. New York: Norton, 1979.

McCarthy, John. "Social Infrastructure Deficits and New Technologies: Mobilizing Unstructured Sentiment Pools." Paper presented at the annual meeting of the American Sociological Association, 1982.

McCarthy, John, and Mayer Zald. "Resource Mobilization and Social Movements: A Partial Theory." *American Journal of Sociology* 82 (May 1977): 1212-41.

McConnell, Grant. *Private Power and American Democracy.* New York: Knopf, 1966.

McFarland, Andrew. *Public Interest Group Lobbies.* Washington, D.C.: American Enterprise Institute, 1976.

_____. *Common Cause: Lobbying in the Public Interest.* Chatham, N.J.: Chatham House, 1984.

MacPherson, Myra. "The New Right Brigade." *Washington Post,* 10 August 1980, F1.

Maisel, Louis, and Joseph Cooper, eds. *Congressional Elections.* Beverly Hills, Calif.: Sage, 1981.

Malbin, Michael. "Teledemocracy and Its Discontents." *Public Opinion,* June/July 1982, 58-59.

Mitchell, Robert C. "National Environmental Lobbies and the Apparent Illogic of Collective Action." In *Collective Decision Making,* edited by Clifford Russell. Baltimore: Johns Hopkins University Press, 1979.

Moe, Terry M. *The Organization of Interests: Incentives and the Internal Dynamics of Interest Groups.* Chicago: University of Chicago Press, 1980.

Muller, Edward N. "An Explanatory Model for Differing Types of Participation." *European Journal of Political Research* 10 (1982): 1-16.

Muller, Edward N., and Karl Dieter-Opp. "Rational Choice and Rebellious Collective Action." *American Political Science Review* 80 (June 1986): 471-88.

Muller, Edward N., and R. Kenneth Godwin. "Aggressive and Democratic Participation." *Political Behavior,* Fall 1984, 129-46.

Nash, Edward L. *Direct Marketing: Strategy, Planning, and Execution.* New York: McGraw-Hill, 1982.

Olson, Mancur, Jr. *The Logic of Collective Action.* Cambridge, Mass.: Harvard University Press, 1965.

_____. *The Rise and Decline of Nations.* New Haven: Yale University Press, 1980.

Pratt, Henry J. *The Gray Lobby.* Chicago: University of Chicago Press, 1976.

Reichley, A. James. "The Rise of National Parties." In *The New Direction in American Politics,* edited by John Chubb and Paul Peterson. Washington, D.C.: Brookings Institution, 1985.

Riker, William, and Peter Ordeshook. "A Theory of the Calculus of Voting." *American Political Science Review* 62 (March 1968): 25-42.

Sabato, Larry J. *The Rise of Political Consultants.* New York: Basic Books, 1981.

_____. *PAC Power: Inside the World of Political Action Committees.* New York: Norton, 1984.

Salisbury, Robert. "Interest Representation: The Dominance of Institutions." *American Political Science Review* 78 (March 1984): 64-76.

Schattschneider, E.E. *The Semisovereign People.* New York: Holt, Rinehart and Winston, 1960.

Schlozman, Kay Lehman, and John Tierney. *Organized Interests and American Democracy.* New York: Harper & Row, 1986.

Smith, Kerry. "A Theoretical Analysis of the Green Lobby." *American Political Science Review* 79 (1985): 132-37.

Sorauf, Frank. *Money in Congressional Elections.* Glenview, Ill.: Scott, Foresman, 1988.

_____. "Who's In Charge? Accountability in Political Action Committees." *Political Science Quarterly* 99 (Winter 1984-85): 590-93.

Stallings, Robert A. "Patterns of Belief in Social Movements: Clarification from an Analysis of Environmental Groups." *Sociological Quarterly* 14 (Autumn 1973): 465-80.

Sullivan, John L., James Pierson, and George E. Marcus. *Political Tolerance and American Democracy.* Chicago: University of Chicago Press, 1982.

Tesh, Sylvia. "In Support of Single-Issue Politics." *Political Science Quarterly* 99 (Spring 1984): 27-44.

Thomas, Martin. "Election Proximity and Senatorial Roll Call Voting." *American Journal of Political Science* 29 (February 1985): 96-111.

Tillock, Harriet, and Denton Morrison. "Group Size and Contributions to Collective Action: An Examinaton of Mancur Olson's Theory Using Data from Zero Population Growth." In *Research in Social Movements: Conflicts and Change,* edited by Louis Kriesberg. Vol. 2. Greenwich, Conn.: JAI Press, 1978.

Topolsky, Mary. "Common Cause?" *Worldview* 17 (1974): 35-39.

Truman, David. *The Governmental Process.* New York: Knopf, 1958.

Tufte, Edward R. "Determinants of the Outcome of Midterm Congressional Elections." *American Political Science Review* 68 (1975): 812-26.

Tversky, Amos, and Daniel Kahneman. "The Framing of Decisions and the Psychology of Choice." *Science* 211 (January 1981): 453-58.

Verba, Sidney, and Norman Nie. *Participation in America: Social Equality and Political Democracy.* New York: Harper & Row, 1972.

Viguerie, Richard. *The New Right: We're Ready to Lead.* Falls Church, Va.: Viguerie Company, 1981.

Walker, Jack. "The Origins and Maintenance of Interest Groups in America." *American Political Science Review* 77 (June 1983): 390-406.

Welch, W.P. "Campaign Contributions and Legislative Voting: Milk Money and Dairy Price Supports." *Western Political Quarterly* 35 (1982): 478-95.

Wilson, James Q. *Political Organizations.* New York: Basic Books, 1973.

Wolin, Sheldon. *Politics and Vision.* Boston: Little, Brown, 1965.

Wootton, Graham. *Interest Groups: Policy and Politics in America.* Englewood Cliffs, N.J.: Prentice-Hall, 1985.

Index

About the Author

R. KENNETH GODWIN is associate professor of political science at the University of Arizona where he teaches courses concerning pressure groups and public policy. His Ph.D. is from the University of North Carolina at Chapel Hill.

Dr. Godwin previously taught and was chairman of the department at Oregon State University. He was a Rockefeller Environmental Fellow at Resources for the Future in Washington, D.C., and was a Research Scientist at the Battelle Human Affairs Research Center in Seattle, Washington.

He is the author of *Attitudes and Values Related to Modernization*, and co-author of *Psyche and Demos* and *Evaluating Land Use Control: Evaluation of Economic and Political Effects*. His articles have appeared in the *American Political Science Review*, the *Journal of Politics*, *Public Opinion Quarterly*, *Polity*, *Social Science Quarterly*, and the *Western Political Quarterly*.